TIPPETT ON MUSIC

Tippett on Music

EDITED BY

MEIRION BOWEN

CLARENDON PRESS · OXFORD

1995

Oxford University Press, Walton Street, Oxford OX2 6DP

Oxford New York

Athens Auckland Bangkok Bombay
Calcutta Cape Town Dar es Salaam Delhi
Florence Hong Kong Istanbul Karachi
Kuala Lumpur Madras Madrid Melbourne
Mexico City Nairobi Paris Singapore
Taipei Tokyo Toronto
and associated companies in
Berlin Ibadan

Oxford is a trade mark of Oxford University Press

Published in the United States
by Oxford University Press Inc., New York

British Library Cataloguing in Publication Data
Data available

Library of Congress Cataloging in Publication Data
Tippett, Michael, 1905–
Tippett on music / edited by Meirion Bowen.
Includes bibliographical references and index.
1. Music—History and criticism.
I. Bowen, Meirion.   II. Title.
ML60.T5533   1995   780—dc20   94-34148
ISBN 0–19–816541–2
ISBN 0–19–816542–0 (pbk.)

Set by Hope Services (Abingdon) Ltd.
Printed in Great Britain
on acid-free paper by
Bookcraft Ltd.
Midsomer Norton, Avon

TO ROBERT PONSONBY

with gratitude, affection, and esteem

Preface

Tippett on Music draws upon material from my previous collections of essays, *Moving into Aquarius*[1] and *Music of the Angels*,[2] both of which have been out of print for some time. The conception of this volume, however, is different: hence the reordering, re-editing, and updating of essays on related topics and the inclusion of a substantial amount that is new. The outer parts of the book (I and V) provide a framework of general statements. But the core of the book concerns music, starting with composers other than myself and compositions other than my own, in Part II; and although there is some non-musical material in Part III, it is intended as a context for an understanding of my own works; Part IV continues by dealing with questions of interpretation and performance.

This focusing on music—from its genesis and notation to its realization as actual sound—will, I trust, be found useful. Parts III and IV are, indeed, an attempt to help those studying my own somewhat variegated musical *œuvre*. Over some years, performers and conductors have sought guidance from me as to how to interpret my scores. Opera directors, too, have tried to obtain a sense of my own vision of how my five operas might appear on stage. At my age, I am far less capable of active participation in performances, recordings, and productions than I once was. These two sections of the book may in part fill the gap.

It goes almost without saying that the sixty years or so in which I have been active as a mature composer have seen tremendous changes in the character of music making and its dissemination. The ubiquity of recordings and their influence, the cross-fertilization of musical cultures—these are but two major aspects. Performance itself seems to start from different premisses, thereby arousing different expectations. Sometimes unconsciously, sometimes deliberately, I have sought stimulation from my vastly expanded experience of the musical (as well as spoken) vernacular. This will be apparent from the discussion of my later stage works and vocal compositions. Finally, I was impelled to imagine what it must be like to be a composer starting now, living and creating afresh, with a new millennium just around the corner.

[1] London: Routledge and Kegan Paul, 1959; rev. edn. with additional material, London: Paladin Books, 1974.
[2] London: Eulenberg Books, 1980.

Some of the material in this volume dates back fifty years or more, originating as radio talks for the BBC World Service or Third Programme. Where it would appear to have dated, I have made adjustments. But wherever possible, I have preserved the character and syntax of the original. By such a method, I indicate, on the one hand, changes of outlook; on the other, an integrity of temperament and stance. In any case, the sources of the essays are given in the Appendix; and where necessary, the footnotes have been amplified or corrected.

Music has always, for me, been inseparable from other creative and intellectual pursuits. Thus, much of the material in the more general parts of the book is concerned in one way or another with the question of what sort of world we live in and how we may behave in it. The 'we' changes from the human race in general to the various divisions that are appropriate. 'We'—at the time of my first volume of essays, *Moving into Aquarius*—used to mean the West, Europe, England. Now it means something rather wider. It also becomes the practitioners of the imagined world—poets, painters, composers, and so forth—as against engineers and technologists. Finally, 'we' disappears altogether into 'I'.

The 'I' that emerges is near to what Jung has named the *persona*. It is myself in my public function as a composer. At one level, what I am often committing to paper is a series of dramatizations of processes within myself, relating to my creative work. Such a relationship, I realized early on, is analogous to that of Shaw's prefaces to his plays. I can remember the excitement when *Back to Methuselah* was first published. Literary critics found themselves wrestling not only with five plays but with a lengthy essay on evolution. An ardent Shavian told me that this essay had already become a biology textbook in a Welsh university. It is clear enough now that if this is true, then the biology students were ill-advised. You will not get very far by reading the preface to *Back to Methuselah* as a scientific treatise. Shaw makes play with great scientific names like Darwin and Lamarck, but the more relevant names in the preface are Samuel Butler and Goethe. Butler had tilted against Darwin, as Goethe had tilted against Newton. Both were creative artists accepting the challenge of a divided world, trying to move over from the world of art into that of science, without denying their imaginative sensibilities. Neither of them, nor Shaw, was a scientist as Newton or Darwin was.

The energy which Goethe could spare for his scientific interests is something we can only wonder at. Yet we cannot complain that he failed to supply us with enough imaginative work. With Butler, on the other hand, we can fairly say that his quasi-scientific books are disproportionate to his imaginative work, much as though Shaw had written five prefaces to every one play. To some extent, my own acceptance of a world divided unnaturally between technology and imagination has been limited and desultory. This has been so, partly because the scientific world has become quite incomprehensible to the layman in its specialization—though television is doing an incredible amount to change all that; partly also because the dazzling achievements of modern technology have implications that are socially equivocal—thus we artists are thrown back into the imaginative world as into a fortress.

Shaw's prefaces are a true, though subsidiary, part of his work as a writer. But a composer rarely produces polished prose or verse which can stand on its own as literature. He uses words as discourses, and reserves the expression of artistic emotion for tones. To do so in this book has entailed blurring the distinction between the autobiographical and the musical.

A major acknowledgement is due, at this point, to Jung, who, in his Ascona meetings and the published Eranos Yearbooks initiated a tremendous activity of comprehension, even where his own contribution was small. Early on, I took this to be, as it were, a movement from the other side. The distinguished specialists meeting yearly at Ascona and contributing papers were for the most part practitioners of certain scientific disciplines who wanted to move towards the world of the spirit without abandoning their scientific intelligence. They were aware of the challenge of our unnaturally divided world, as any creative artist has been. A hopeful sign. Our society as a whole has put value upon scientific technology. It only puts value upon imaginative art piecemeal. I, as a composer, who attributes value to imaginative art equal to that which society places upon scientific technology, cannot alter the general situation. Nor is that situation really altered by the fact that science students may be assiduous concert-goers and buyers of recordings. This distinction between the *social* value and the *personal* value has to be borne in mind; for often in the course of argument, I set out from the acceptance of the social value *as a fact* to the refusal of the value *as an ideal.*

MICHAEL TIPPETT

1994

Acknowledgements

First, I have to thank Oxford University Press for taking on the publication of this volume at short notice, after an earlier arrangement had failed to reach fruition. In particular, I am grateful to Bruce Phillips and Helen Foster for editorial assistance.

I am much indebted to Meirion Bowen for helping me select and edit the previously published essays in this volume. He also assisted in doing research and preparing drafts of new material.

Amongst others to whom thanks are due are Nigel Fortune, Tim Lissimore, and Francesc Canals.

I am grateful to the following publishers for permission to reproduce excerpts as itemized below:

Schott & Co. Ltd.: musical examples from my own compositions.

Messrs Collins & Co.: excerpts from Boris Pasternak's *Dr Zhivago* and Alexander Solzhenitsyn's *The First Circle*.

CBS Records: excerpts from the sleeve note to a recording of Charles Ives's *Three Places in New England*.

Faber & Faber Ltd.: excerpts from T. S. Eliot's *The Family Reunion, Selected Essays, Poetry and Drama*, and 'East Coker'; excerpts from Edgar Wind's *Art and Anarchy*.

Friends of Covent Garden: excerpts from David Rudkin's translation of Schoenberg's *Moses and Aaron*.

Rupert Hart-Davis: excerpts from Loren Eiseley's *The Invisible Pyramid*.

BBC Publications: excerpts from Jacob Bronowski's *The Ascent of Man*.

A. P. Watt Ltd. on behalf of Ann Yeats: excerpts from the *Collected Poems of W. B. Yeats*.

Contents

PART I THE COMPOSER IN CONTEXT

1	A Composer's Point of View	3
2	Towards the Condition of Music	7
3	Art and Anarchy	16

PART II COMPOSERS PAST AND PRESENT

4	Schoenberg	25
5	Stravinsky and *Les Noces*	47
6	Purcell	57
7	Britten	66
8	Holst	73
9	Hindemith and *Ludus tonalis*	76
10	Shostakovich	79
11	Charles Ives	83

PART III TRADITIONS AND TEXTS

12	Archetypes of Concert Music	89
13	T. S. Eliot and *A Child of Our Time*	109
14	Sketch for a Modern Oratorio	117
15	The Nameless Hero: Reflections on *A Child of Our Time*	178
16	*The Midsummer Marriage*	185
17	The Resonance of Troy: Essays and Commentaries on *King Priam*	209
18	Dreams of Power, Dreams of Love	220
19	St Augustine and his Visions	228
20	Aspects of Belief	237
21	*The Mask of Time*	245

PART IV THE ART OF PERFORMANCE

22	The Score	259
23	The Stage	269

PART V AFTERWORDS

24	A Composer and his Public	277

25   The Composer and Pacificism   282
26   The Artist's Mandate   287
27   Too Many Choices   294
28   'Dreaming on Things to Come . . .'   307

Appendix   310

Index   313

Part I

THE COMPOSER IN CONTEXT

Chapter 1

A COMPOSER'S POINT OF VIEW

As a musician my sharpest sense is that of sound. I cannot help listening to things. Living as I do in the country, I notice every year when the nightingales have begun to sing again in the wood down the road. They sing, of course, in the daytime but I am more often indoors playing the piano. So it is at night, when other birds are silent, that I hear them with startling clearness, especially when the night is still. The peculiar, liquid tone of their song can sound like someone sobbing from heart-break, which makes us respond deep down inside. It may only be for a moment, when some quality in the night and the sound of the bird-song combine to make a specially intense image. At such time we respond. It is as though another world had spoken by some trick of correspondence between the outside and the inside. For the 'thing' inside only works if the proper image is offered from the outside.

Of course, it is not only nature and not only music which can provide the image. I am obviously much more susceptible to sound, being a musician. But I can remember on one occasion walking through a gallery, and unexpectedly seeing a statue; and something in the angle of vision from which I first saw it made the moment of impact so sharp that it took my breath away. In this case the trick seems more mysterious, for there was no living nightingale, only the cold stone. Pygmalion carved a statue so perfectly that it came to life to disconcert him; but it is not really mere life-likeness in carved stone which takes the breath away. It is what we usually call beauty, and we can't define it. We simply enjoy it, or reject it, certain only that it has a much longer life than any one of us. It remains like the majesty of great cathedrals, for centuries. Partly it is this touch of eternity which impresses us. Beautifully shaped dishes from thousands of years ago appear as fresh as when they left the hand of the potter, and certain music can sound as though it must always have been there.

Michelangelo spoke as though, for him, the beautiful forms of his statues were already there beforehand in the stone, embedded in the untouched lump of marble; as if he merely uncovered them, by chipping away the stone surrounding the image inside. I think that was really a descriptive picture of his own imagination, which saw the work as finished before it had been begun. It is very much what Mozart wrote in a letter about composition. He said that his best works of music appeared to him all at once, as though the time taken to have sounded them were reduced to a single moment. Then all he did was write it down: his greatest gift, according to him, was the phenomenal memory which enabled him to hold the music he had imagined for days in his head.

From my own experience, as one whose habit is to create things, this process of imagination is outside our control. It lives us, rather than we live it. It is continuous. It may go to sleep for a time—or the pressure of everyday things may keep it out of mind, but not for long. In fact if the everyday life becomes too insistent, the imaginative life inside can behave like a disease. It will offer a growing resistance to the outside engagements. This may begin as lethargy, inertia, or melancholy. But it can well end in a real illness. Also— and this has always been known—the imaginative life can play tricks on the artist, by making its own life appear the normal and the everyday.

Perhaps, this invasion of the everyday life by the imaginative life is not so absurd as it sounds. Poetry is made of the same words as we use for quite ordinary communication. It is the sea change the words suffer inside the poet which gives them the accent of poetry.

> Golden lads and girls all must
> As chimney-sweepers come to dust

That Shakespearean couplet is so well known and so accepted, that we forget the magic which has made poetry of a phrase so unpromising as chimney-sweepers.

It was easier for everyone to think in this way when magic was still part of the real world; but soon after Shakespeare's day the temper of the West gradually changed. People became increasingly drawn to the world of discovery, of inventions, of technics. Emotional energy, which before had been somehow divided between the real world and the inner world, tended to become centred in the one world of technics. Consequently, poetic imagination suffered an increasingly severe deprivation. In order to live, it became romantic and eccentric.

Today, the world of machines asks less and less for whole men, more for mass men with mechanical habits. The virtue of this world is precision; the vice, repetition. The true picture of the modern worker is no longer the craftsman potter at the wheel, or even the surgeon at the operating table, but the young woman at the conveyor belt, with the loudspeaker playing 'Music While You Work'. The music helps the rate of production.

Just how far this wave of mechanization is to carry us no one can guess. The agricultural countries of Eastern Europe are only just now starting to turn the peasant into the agricultural labourer, supplied with tractors from the factory. It probably seems very new and revolutionary and exciting, and releases energies which had got stuck in an old system. But we in England are becoming much more aware of the price. Industrialization is nothing new to us. Something else will be new, but our own preoccupation with social effi-

ciency may well resist it. For if we want a man's work to have again some relation to his imaginative life, we shall have to relax the mechanical precision of
the conveyor belt. But then how are we to fill our homes with all the gadgets
we feel we need unless we make them for ourselves in the factories?

The creative artist, who must transmute the everyday for the sake of poetry,
is unfitted, by his imaginative gift, for work requiring constant attention to
mechanical precision. But so are lunatics, and all neurotics in whom the fantasy world is compulsive. The man at the conveyor belt, on the other hand,
must have his fantasy life in control. The machine demands control and
induces depreciation. This, I think, is the explanation of the repulsion and yet
fascination which thousands, probably millions, of people feel nowadays for
neurotic psychology and the occult. It is a primitive attempt by nature to
restore the balance. And the more we seek salvation in yet further technics, the
greater this fascination will grow—and the more dangerous. What we need is
some experience of release: something which can bring the outer and inner
together again. In a primitive way this happens to us when we go to see the
Marx Brothers, where the everyday world is once more both real and unreal.
Harpo Marx and the seventh dwarf, Dopey, who cannot speak and act from
intuition, are true and exact pictures of our own imaginative life. It has not yet
grown up, it can only communicate by signs; but it is by no means merely negative. When Dopey locks up the treasure-house and then leaves the key hanging by the door, his act is clean contrary to our matter-of-fact world of
burglary and insurance, but it's a true world all the same. In any case it is spiritual treasure. The more we give away, the more is left behind. And if any
merely matter-of-fact person got as far as the treasure-house, he would be
quite certain there was nothing of value in it, just because it was not locked up.

That is one of our troubles. We find it difficult to locate our spiritual treasure, because it does not come to us labelled 'Treasure'. Or because it is not
precise and factual like our world of machines. But just because we have
starved our imaginative life of energy, we have forced it to be childish and
dubious. Yet it is in this underworld that the new pictures are being made.
And I for my part believe we shall see the way out more like a picture, a
dream, than a blueprint. Then, one day, we shall put our passion behind our
picture of a new world, and bring the picture to life. There will still be
machines in the picture, but in a different place. At present, I think we are still
more in love with the latest radio machine for the power it gives us to twid-
dle the knobs and get anything and anywhere, rather than for the tremendous
possibilities it offers to enrich our everyday lives. And yet I, who spend a lot
of my time in the world of imagination, can speak through the machine of just
this other life. And this other life has a point of view. It sees a portion of the
truth—but a truth, which has meaning only for persons, not masses. Indeed,
all enrichment, all renewal of our spiritual life will come first from persons.
What matters at this moment is that I as a person speak truth to others as persons who sit in homes I shall never enter.

Truth is some sort of an absolute. If we begin to tell lies for any cause, however good, we hurt ourselves, whether we know it or not. Beauty is another absolute. When we let the common level of our social life sink away too far from the beautiful and the comely, we suffer as sharply as if we took the children's milk to make whipped cream for the wealthy. Part of the poet's, the painter's or the musician's job is just that of renewing our sense of the comely and the beautiful. If, in the music I write, I can create a world of sound wherein some, at least, of my generation can find refreshment for the inner life, then I am doing my work properly. It is a great responsibility: to try to transfigure the everyday by a touch of the everlasting, born as that always has been, and will be again, from our desire.

Chapter 2

TOWARDS THE CONDITION
OF MUSIC

There is a knowledge concerning art, and this knowledge is something quite different from the immediate apprehension of works of art, even from whatever insight we feel we have gained by perceiving and responding to works of art. A simple statement such as 'Art must be *about* something' is innocent enough till we want to give a name to this something. Then invariably we delude ourselves with words, because with our discursive or descriptive words we cross over into the field of writing or talking *about* art. We have reversed ourselves.

This fundamental difficulty has made all discussion of art, as indeed all discussion of quality, a kind of elaborate metaphor. And since all metaphor is imprecise, the verbal misunderstandings in aesthetics have always been legion. It is only when we remain deliberately in the field of enquiry concerning the facts *surrounding* art that we amass knowledge of the kind we expect to obtain through such intellectual disciplines as history, anthropology, psychology, or philosophy. We can confidently say that we have vastly increased our knowledge concerning art during the last hundred years, chiefly of course the history of art. Anthropology has added further dimensions to our sense of history as a whole, and so to the history of art. Psychology, in my opinion, will eventually make much more precise the terms with which we discuss the processes of artistic creation and enjoyment. Philosophy, in the sense in which we speak of Platonic or Christian philosophy, has often assigned limits or directions to art considered as a social function. At the present time, when the pretensions of Islam or Christianity to do this are everywhere receding, only Marxist philosophy and the Communist states make the attempt. The most disturbing feature of Stalinist aesthetic dogma was (in China *is*) the apparent fear of the spontaneous (including the ineffable) element in art, which is gravely endangered by extreme social systematization. Plato, for all his systematizing tendency, accepted this. Socrates says in the *Phaedrus*:

There is a third form of possession or madness, of which the Muses are the source. This seizes a tender, virgin soul and stimulates it to rapt passionate expression, especially in lyric poetry. But if any man comes to the gates of poetry without the madness of the Muses, persuaded that skill alone will make him a good poet, then shall he and his works of sanity with him be brought to nought by the poetry of madness and see their place is nowhere to be found.[1]

Plato names three other forms of divine madness besides the artistic: namely, the prophetic, the expiatory, and that of the lover. To understand Plato's term 'madness', we must recall the argument of the *Phaedrus* in more detail. Socrates considers first whether what we call madness might not really be of two kinds. One kind is clearly a disease—the rational mind being disordered and unamenable to the will—and even if we picture it as though the sufferer's personality has been possessed by some other and alien personality, yet this possession is unhealthy and often markedly antisocial. But the other kind might be a madness where the invading personality, though unaccountable and irrational, is yet beneficent and creative: possession not by a devil, but by a god.[2] It is this 'divine madness' of Plato's which I call the spontaneous (including the ineffable) element in art, and I think that the intuitions of Plato concerning this spontaneous element are upheld by the findings of psychology, especially depth psychology. From such psychology we have obtained a concept of apparently spontaneous psychic generation; of unconscious psychic drives and inhibitions; of, possibly, an inner psychic collectivity which is boundless and non-discrete. Yet to use the word 'concept' for such notions is, surely, a paradox. In the same way, at the point now at which this discursive essay needs to consider the immediate experience of, and the insight (if that is the right word) obtained from works of art *in themselves*, then, as has been pointed out above, this paradox reappears.

We must begin with the fact of works of art existing objectively and created to be appreciated. And we must accept that even if a state of mind, or an artefact rising from a state of mind, is spontaneously generated and only to be experienced immediately, or even ineffably, it is none the less a natural phenomenon, a fact of human existence. In rare experiences of this sort, such as the states of mysticism, the number of human beings to whom the experiences spontaneously come (or who have desires and techniques to induce them) is, at least in the West, small. Yet the tradition is so constant and the phenomenon so well established that we all have reasonable grounds for accepting them as factual and natural even when we can never ourselves have known them. They can clearly be spiritually refreshing, and may yet turn out to be one of man's hitherto undeveloped social qualities. For if psycho-social survival depends, as it well may do, on correctives to the present overwhelming social valuation given to material welfare, then evolutionary necessities may begin to operate, in an admittedly as yet unimaginable way, on seemingly socially valueless meditative disciplines.

[1] Plato, *Phaedrus*, trans. with introduction and commentary by R. Hackforth (London, 1952), 57.

[2] See Ch. 26 below for a further discussion of this whole problem.

While it would appear that the mystic can only render to society the refreshment received personally from mystic experiences through the quality of his conduct, the creative artist, from whatever source or in whatever medium he receives the spontaneous element, must, by the nature of his mandate, create objective works of art. These works then subsist in society independently of their creator, and many thousands of human beings receive enjoyment, refreshment, and enrichment from them. This is a commonplace fact. Perhaps indeed every human being alive has experienced immediately something of this kind. Because the experience is so common and yet capable of being heightened to embody our profoundest apprehensions, it has in every age demanded intellectual understanding of itself. Modern psychology has provided new counters with which to play this age-old game.

If I now proceed to play this game in an up-to-date mode, it must be remembered that all discussion of what art *is*, or what it is *about*, is semantically imprecise. (We are probably on safer ground when we discuss what art *does*.) So it is hardly possible to proceed without the danger of misunderstanding, although our modern counters for discussion are, in my opinion, an improvement on some of those of the past—that is, are probably semantically less equivocal.

Works of art are images. These images are based on apprehensions of the inner world of feelings.[3] Feelings in this sense contain emotions, intuitions, judgements, and values. These feelings are therefore generally supposed to be excluded from scientific enquiry. I make this statement, in so far as it is true, not as an implied judgement, but solely as a fact, in order to emphasize the semantic problems of aesthetic discussion. It is not an easy matter to pass over from language used in the observation of natural objects extended outside us in space and time to language used to discuss or describe the inner world of feelings, where space and time (at least in certain states of mind) are differently perceived altogether. Even where we succeed in such an attempt, the description is always at one remove. The images which are works of art are our sole means of expressing the inner world of feelings objectively and immediately. If art is a language, it is a language concerned with this inner world alone.

As 'inner' and 'outer' remain philosophically extremely difficult terms, so the dichotomy I have (at least verbally) established between space and time considered outside us and space and time perceived within is certainly not rigid. Hence it often appears as though the raw material of artistic creation was obtained from observation of nature outside us, and that the creative activity resided in the organization and construction which the artist applies to this raw material. The danger of this way of considering the matter is that very quickly we come to talk of works of art as *derived from* nature, which is much too simple. It loses sight of the one absolute idiosyncrasy of art, that

[3] Cf. Suzanne K. Langer, *Feeling and Form* (London, 1953).

works of art are images of *inner* experience, however apparently representational the mode of expression may be.

This difficult matter is best set out by considering first the extreme case of space in painting (I use the word 'extreme' because the matter is not quite the same in architecture) and secondly the opposite extreme of time in music.

The vital fact of all pictorial works of art is that the space in the picture is always virtual, not real. The space in the room and of the wall on which the picture hangs is real. Part of the means by which a picture becomes an image of the inner world of feelings is the contrast between the real space of the wall or the room and the virtual space in the picture. Hence it is not of vital concern to the art of painting whether the virtual space is constructed by representational methods or the reverse. We accept this if we are gifted or trained to do so, without demur. We find it difficult if we consciously or unconsciously believe that art *derives* from experiences of outer nature and not, as is the basic fact, from the inner world of feelings. The representations of outer nature, if present, are always images of the inner experience, which the artist has organized.

At the other pole to paining, music offers images of the inner world of feelings perceived as a flow. As our concept of external time is itself an equivocal one,[4] it is perhaps less easy even than with space in painting to realize that the time we apprehend in the work of musical art has only a virtual existence by contrast with the time marked by the clock-hands when the work is performed. Works appear short or long from other considerations besides that of performance time, and our sense of performance time will be markedly modified by them.[5]

Because music is concerned not with space but with time, this method of artistic creation seems to bypass the problems of representationalism, present in some degree in all the other arts. Hence the dictum 'All art constantly aspires towards the condition of music'. This aphorism, wrenched from its original context in an essay of Pater,[6] has nowadays been commonly used in this much looser and wider sense, precisely, in my opinion, to draw attention to this real tendency. For if the matter-of-factness of the outer world gets too much into the foreground of art, then expression of the inner world of feeling is probably correspondingly more difficult. By dispensing *a priori* with all the problems arising from expressing inner feelings through representations of the outer world, music can seem a very favoured art. This is not always a merit. Music's easiness quickly degenerates into escapism; escapism not only

---

[4] Cf. Henri Bergson, *Durée et Simultanéité*, (2nd edn., Paris, 1923); also C. G. Jung, *Synchronicity: An Acausal Connecting Principle*, in *The Structure and Dynamics of the Psyche*, in *Collected Works*, viii, trans. R. F. C. Hull (London, 1960).

[5] Cf. Igor Stravinsky, *Poétique musicale: Sons forme de six leçons*. The Charles Eliot Norton Lectures for 1939–40 (Cambridge, Mass., 1942). Trans. Arthur Knodel and Ingolf Dahl as *Poetics of Music* (Cambridge, Mass., and London, 1947).

[6] Walter Pater, 'Giorgione', in *The Renaissance* (London, 1873), 106.

because music seems absolutely abstracted from real objects, but also because the emotional content of music is both obvious and permitted.

To a certain degree, all appreciation of art is escapism—to leave behind the world of matter of fact. The important question is always: escape into what? Escape into the true inner world of feelings is one of the most rewarding experiences known to man. When entry into this world is prevented, and still more when it is unsought, a man is certainly to some degree unfulfilled. Yet even escape into the simpler states of appreciation is often self-denied. Darwin wrote in his *Autobiography*:

now for many years I cannot endure to read a line of poetry . . . I have also lost my taste for pictures and music . . . My mind seems to have become a kind of machine for grinding general laws out of large collections of facts . . . The loss of these tastes is a loss of happiness and may possibly be injurious to the intellect, and more probably to the normal character, by enfeebling the emotional part of our nature.[7]

Darwin puts his finger unerringly on the danger. He uses the word 'machine'. In the vast social apparatus which modern science and technology demand, the person often becomes lost in a 'machine'. Eventually there arises the danger of too great mechanization of the social life in every field.[8] At this point creative artists are sometimes driven to use the shock tactics of a genius like D. H. Lawrence—or in another field, Kokoschka.

As I have already pointed out, within the dazzling achievements of the modern knowledge explosion we must include the lesser portion of a greatly increased knowledge about art. But the contemporary explosion in the means and methods of art itself over the last hundred years is not of the same kind. The new art is not related to problems of the outer world at all, but to apprehensions of the inner world. What can certainly be deduced from the contemporaneity of the two explosions is that the psycho-social change and consequent adaptation demanded of modern man is without precedent in its totality.

It may in fact be misleading to speak of art as primarily or always responsive to social change—though in many obvious senses this is true. For art is unavoidably and primarily responsive to the inner world of feelings. And this inner world may be spontaneously generative (in the sense I attempted to define the term earlier) independently of, for example, the social consequences of scientific technology. Or it may be attempting to restore some sort of psycho-social balance. I would say that it is all these things. Yet clearly changes (and these are constantly happening) in our ideas of human personality will be reflected in certain arts, if not necessarily in music. Music may always appear to bypass such considerations, but literature and drama in all their forms certainly cannot. It may be that changes in our ideas of human

[7] Cf. Francis Darwin, *The Life & Letters of Charles Darwin* (London, 1887), i, ch. 2 ('Autobiography'), 100–2.

[8] Cf. n. 2 above.

personality reflect changes in the inner world of feelings, and not vice versa. We are not yet able to judge properly what happens in this complex and inter-related field; we cannot yet be certain what is cause and what is effect.

At the present time, for example, we can only see that the knowledge explo-sion in all the sciences is a challenge to psycho-social adaptation, while the violent changes in methods in all the arts are symptomatic of deep-seated changes in man's inner world of feelings.

Modern psychology is indeed beginning to produce a kind of relativity of personality, especially in personal relations. This is sufficiently far advanced in the West (it may be nothing new for the East) for it to be satirized by a car-toonist like Feiffer. Here is a caricatured conversation between a young cou-ple suffering from this relativity of personality—that is, valid uncertainty as to what is real in their notions of one another and what is projection.

SHE. You're arguing with me.
HE. I'm *not* arguing with you. I'm *trying* to make a point.
SHE. There is a difference between making a point and embarking on a sadistic attack.
HE. If sadism is your equivalent to impartial judgement then I admit to being a sadist.
SHE. How *easy* to be flip when one precludes responsibility.
HE. How irresponsible of one so irresponsible to speak of responsibility.
SHE. Since you *must* project your own inadequacies into a discussion of the facts I see no point in carrying this further.
HE. How like you to use attack as a disguise for retreat.
SHE. Ah, but if we were not arguing as you so heatedly claim, what is it that I am retreating from?
  (*silence*)
HE. I'm getting a stomach-ache.
SHE. Me too.
HE. Let's knock off and go to a movie.

Behind this caricature is something real, to which art cannot be indifferent. This denouement is also quite serious. We knock off to go to a movie. This is not merely an escape from the currently insoluble problems, it is a therapeu-tic necessity. We project our problems, whether of dual or multiple relation-ship, momentarily on to the movie—that is, on to an objective work of art. Movies are generally works of popular art; and they are socially immensely valuable. For most of us there can be no objective examination of the con-stant and developing situation such as that caricatured by Feiffer, except by recourse to the movie or its equivalent: the splendid value of this recourse being that it is mostly unselfconscious and indeed an enjoyment.

The enjoyment of popular art, in my opinion, is much more often of the same kind as the enjoyment of more serious art (though not of the same qual-ity) than snob circles like to think. There is of course a vast mass of sentimen-tal popular music (to take my own art) which is poor and dispiriting. But there is a great deal indeed of jazz and rock where the dissonances and distortions of the voice or the instruments, and the energy and passion and often brilliant timing of the performance combine to produce an enjoyment which is of better quality, and is also expressive of the tensions produced in man by the inner and outer changes of his life. Carried on the pulse of this music, we really do renew in a limited degree our sense of the flow of life, just because this music gives hints of deeper apprehensions through its qualities of style and even form.

As the purely emotional element recedes and the formal element comes forward, the music ceases to appeal to vast masses: this is always happening in the world of jazz and rock. When the limitations of popular musical harmonies, rhythms, melodies, and forms are left entirely behind, as in music for the concert-hall, then the public further diminishes. Yet symphonic music in the hands of great masters truly and fully embodies the otherwise unperceived, unsavoured inner flow of life. In listening to such music, we are as though entire again, despite all the insecurity, incoherence, incompleteness, and relativity of our everyday life. The miracle is achieved by submitting to the power of its organized flow; a submission which gives us a special pleasure and ultimately enriches us. The pleasure and the enrichment arise from the fact that the flow is not merely the flow of the music itself, but a significant image of the inner flow of life. Artifice of all kinds is necessary to the musical composition in order that it shall become such an image. Yet when the perfect performance and occasion allow us a truly immediate apprehension of the inner flow 'behind' the music, the artifice is momentarily of no consequence; we are no longer aware of it.

Music of course has a tremendous range of images, from the gay (and, if perhaps rarely, the comic) to the serious and tragic. On the serious side music has always been associated with religious rituals and been a favoured art for expressing certain intuitions of transcendence. That is to say, certain music, to be appreciated as it is, expects a desire and willingness on our part to see reflected in it transcendent elements, unprovable and maybe unknowable analytically, but which infuse the whole work of art. This quality in music has permitted such works as the *St Matthew Passion*, the Ninth Symphony of Beethoven, or *The Ring*.

According to the excellence of the artist—that is, to his ability to give formal clarity to these analytically unknowable transcendent intuitions—these works of art endure to enrich later minds when the whole social life from which they sprang has disappeared. Hence the enduring quality of a work such as the Parthenon, even when maimed and uncoloured. And it is these formal considerations alone which enable us to set perhaps the *St Matthew Passion* and the Ninth Symphony above *The Ring*. Apparent from all this is the fact that art does not supersede itself in the way science does. Methods and modes may change, and of course, in music, instruments and occasions for making music. These are the things which can make it difficult for us to

appreciate, for example, Pérotin (Perotinus Magnus) now as the great composer his period considered him to be. We may have superseded Pérotin's
methods, but we have scarcely superseded his imaginative intuitions. And yet,
in another sense, we have. Because the material from the inner world is never
quite the same. The extreme changes in the art of the present time are, I am
sure, due to more than changes in techniques.

The techniques of music have always changed from time to time with the
development of new instruments—for example, the pianoforte—and even
more through the changes of social occasion and means of dissemination—
for example, the invention of the concert-hall or of radio. At the present time
there are new electronic methods of producing every imaginable sound
known or as yet unknown, and these methods, though they cannot supersede
the older ways altogether, will certainly be added to them.

The techniques of musical composition change also. There is a widespread
preoccupation at present with the methods of serial composition. Changes in
composition technique are more the concern of the composer than of the listener, who is usually disconcerted during the period of experimentation, as
with serial technique now. The deeper reasons for this constant renewal of
artistic techniques are still somewhat mysterious.[9]

The most striking novelty in music was the gradual invention of polyphony
in the late Middle Ages. All known music up to that time, and right up to our
own time in all cultural traditions outside the European and its derivatives,
had been, or is still, monodic. This means that in general the melodic line,
endlessly decorated and varied, is the essential (as in India and Asia and until
the invention of polyphony in Europe). Or combinations of dynamic or subtle rhythms have been used to build as unending a stream of rhythmical variation as the unending line of monodic invention (Africa, Indonesia). In both
these kinds of music, harmony is incidental and secondary. But European
polyphony produced the combination of many disparate lines of melody, and
such a combination immediately posed problems of harmony new to music.
Over the centuries these problems have been resolved in one way or another,
and there have been periods of European music when the harmonic element,
initially derived from the practice of polyphony, has become primary, and
what polyphony the music contains secondary. We are at present in a time
when European-derived music has experimented to an unprecedented degree
with harmony. This has been pure invention. At the same time discs, tapes,
and printed collections of folk-songs and dances, and discs and tapes of
African, Indonesian, Indian, and Chinese music, have stimulated, or been
used as basis for, a considerable experimentation in rhythm. The melodic element on the other hand (and the formal element in my opinion) has been secondary.

Now European polyphony has proved so powerful an expressive medium

⁹ Cf. Anton Ehrenzweig, *The Psycho-Analysis of Artistic Vision and Hearing* (London, 1953).

that it is mostly sweeping over the whole world and carrying away much of the indigenous traditional music with it. In this way Europe and America appear still as musical initiators for the globe. But this will not last. When the time is ripe, the values of the non-European musical traditions, where they have been temporarily lost, will be rediscovered. The speed at which we are having to become industrially and politically one world would seem to be such that the problems of forging a unified expressive medium may be coming upon us faster than the European composers are as yet aware. This question may well, in my opinion, solve itself first through popular music, just because popular music is by definition and purpose music of the people. Popular music is an open music. In order to entertain, it will take everything offered, from Bali to New Orleans, and whatever is successful will be amplified round the world. Popular music will become increasingly global rather than local.

In all the manifestations of music the enduring portion is the sense of flow, of the kind I have described above, organized and expressed formally. A wide-ranging humanism, whether secular or religious, will always seek to extend to more and more people, through education and opportunity, the enrichment of the personality which music gives. In our technological society we should be warned by Darwin:

The loss of these tastes (for one or more of the arts according to our predilections) is a loss of happiness and may possibly be injurious to the intellect and more probably to the moral character, by enfeebling the emotional part of our nature.

These are wise and serious words. We are morally and emotionally enfeebled if we live our lives without artistic nourishment. Our sense of life is diminished. In music we sense most directly the inner flow which sustains the psyche, or the soul.

Chapter 3

ART AND ANARCHY

When listening to the 1960 Reith Lectures on BBC Radio (before I read any of them) I felt I was continually stimulated by new bits of knowledge—that is, new to me. Thus almost a whole lecture centred on the technique of ascription in cases of unsigned or debatable paintings, and round the extreme forms of connoisseurship to which this problem, or passion, of ascription might lead. This was all so new and interesting to me, as a musician and not a painter, I probably paid more attention to it than to the argument deduced from it: which was that we are in danger of being persuaded by this connoisseurship to overvalue the fragmentary and immediate sketch above the finished and studied painting; and that, as a consequence, we tend to ask only for the fragmentary and immediate in contemporary art: thus reinforcing, as by a kind of concealed patronage, the general marginal condition of art in our time.

When I came later to read this lecture, the information about Morelli's methods of ascription was no longer new to me. So it fell into the background and I paid much more attention to the general argument: that art in our time is marginal, and that connoisseurship is one of the factors that help to make it so. But this special question of connoisseurship now worried me concerning the first of Professor Wind's terms in his general title *Art and Anarchy*: because 'art' is used in English in two rather confusing ways; and Professor Wind's English is so idiomatic that he uses the word 'art' in this double way as often as the rest of us.

The point about the word is simple. We traditionally use 'art' to mean specifically the art of painting. We have a Royal College of Art (meaning painting) as we have a Royal College of Music. But we have also come to use 'art' as a direct translation of the German word *Kunst*. Thus we distinguish art from science, and then we mean all the arts and all the sciences.

It is fatally easy to use this double-meaning word with both meanings in the same sentence. I have just done it myself. I spoke of fragmentary and immediate painting, then of the fragmentary in contemporary art (implying the art of painting), then of the marginal condition of art in our time (implying all the arts). But this disguises the important fact that connoisseurship, in Professor Wind's use of the term for the purpose of his lecture, does not exist in music. There is really no problem of ascription. We do not value the immediate sketch before the finished work (if indeed such sketches exist). So that we are not thereby induced to ask for the immediate and fragmentary in contemporary music. There is a danger nowadays that in the spate of our words about movements of contemporary art in general, and about the place of art in modern society, we are talking without properly defining our terms. In the *Times Literary Supplement* (to give an instance ready to hand), a correspondent writes about the 'cult of dumbness' in the theatre, which, it has been suggested, might lead to drama not in words but in mime. He writes: 'When this new mime is perfected it will be tantamount to the arrival of abstraction in art, or atonalism in music.'[1] Such misleading and misconceived analogies appal me. But they are widespread. It seems to me that if we want to discuss imaginative art in general, or the place of art in society, then we can only make statements of comparable width and generality. There *are* things to be said in this huge field, and many of them were said in the Reith Lectures. But the moment we come to consider each art separately, we are involved in their differences. And if we gloss over the differences for the sake of any general argument, we are as likely as not falsifying something.

We think of Picasso as one of the great innovators of modern painting. We observe his almost chameleon-like ability to change his style at will. We go to see his film in which he makes and unmakes the immediate and fragmentary pictures before our eyes. If we now try to argue from the particular of this aspect of Picasso to the general—that is, to include the other arts—we find ourselves in difficulties. It is just possible to find something of Picasso's change of styles in Stravinsky. But the composer's name more often used to match that of Picasso is Schoenberg. Schoenberg has never practised the immediate or spontaneous or fragmentary. Exactly to the contrary—the whole movement of serialism was to produce the greatest possible degree of intellectual coherence. Every single note of the piece of music is to be ordained by its relations within the series.

So that if we want to make out a case that imaginative art in our scientific age is marginal, we must eschew any arguments which seem to uphold the case, but only in respect of one of the arts. For it is reasonably certain that its contrary will be found in another art.

We must also be wary of large, plausible statements, which may be less precise than we imagine. Professor Wind said in his first lecture:

Diffusion brings with it a loss of density . . . If a man has the time and the means he can see a comprehensive Picasso show in London one day and the next a comprehensive Poussin exhibition in Paris, and . . . finds himself exhilarated by both. When such large displays of incompatible artists are received with equal interest and appreciation, it is clear that those who visit these exhibitions have acquired a strong immunity to them.[2]

---

[1] Charles Marowitz, letter to the *Times Literary Supplement*, 6 Jan. 1961, p. 9.
[2] Edgar Wind, *Art and Anarchy* (London, 1963), 9.

This argumentation worried me. If Poussin and Picasso are indeed incompatible, then presumably many other historically separated painters are also incompatible. So that a walk round the Louvre or the National Gallery must be a constant temptation to indifference if we seek to appreciate too many of their varied exhibits. I doubt it. Nor do I think Professor Wind really meant this. I think his argumentation is unclear because his first term, 'diffusion', has not been tested out sufficiently. It needs breaking down statistically. A sentence like 'More music is offered and heard today than in any age in history',[3] may be much less important than it seems when we have divided 'more' by the vastly increased population.

Summing up the points I have made so far, they are two. First, that in speaking of art generally we must stick firmly to the basic and general, and beware of intellectually attractive analogies between the various arts which are false. For, to make a basic statement myself, art, in the works of the various creative geniuses alive at any one time, is endlessly varied. This is a fact of European history, and is a fact today. It may be an annoying fact when we are trying to uncover the *Zeitgeist*, the general spirit of a time, or of our time. But it is also salutary. It reminds us that though time, or shall we say the climate of opinion, is a reality, the spirit 'moveth where it listeth'. I cannot help remembering in this respect that the Gnostics, who believed the heart of the matter lay in knowledge, held that time, to the creative spirit, is discontinuous. This is a very difficult notion for us to grasp. But it may contain some portion of hidden intuitive truth.

My second point was that even our general terms, like Professor Wind's 'diffusion' or his 'disruption',[4] are dangerously imprecise. We should be much less confused by our own language if some Confucius would truly 'rectify the names' for us. But, failing a Confucius, we must try our own hand at rectification as we go along. Professor Wind also uses the term 'disruption'. He says:

If we think, for example, of Manet, Mallarmé, Joyce, or Schoenberg, almost all the artistic triumphs in the last century were triumphs of disruption: the greatness of an artist became manifest in his power to break up our perceptual habits and disclose new ranges of sensibility.[5]

Once again I find myself believing I understand what Wind is really saying, and that what he is saying contains a valuable perception. But all sorts of things worry me in his manner of saying it. Thus, Manet, Mallarmé, Joyce, Schoenberg; but suppose I say Cézanne, Tolstoy, Yeats, Wagner—have I said any lesser names? Have I moved out of the last century? Do we really think the artistic triumphs of these men, even Wagner, to be triumphs of disruption? Yet Cézanne and Wagner without question had 'power to break up our perceptual habits and disclose new ranges of sensibility'.

---

[3] Edgar Wind, *Art and Anarchy* (London, 1963), 8.   [4] See p. 282–5 below.
[5] Wind, *Art and Anarchy*, 18; in the revised version, Stravinsky is substituted for Schoenberg.

I wish Professor Wind had gone much more deeply than he did into the meaning of his term 'anarchy'. He begins by giving it a tremendous sweep, from Plato by way of the Italian Renaissance to Goethe and Baudelaire. He then includes in it the terms 'imagination and disruption'. He says in the first minute of his first lecture:

Art is . . . an uncomfortable business, and particularly uncomfortable for the artist himself. The forces of the imagination, from which he draws his strength, can be very disruptive.[6]

And, as the final words of his last lecture, he quotes this passage from William James with approval:

Man's chief difference from the brutes lies in the exuberant excess of his subjective propensities . . . Had his whole life not been a quest for the superfluous, he would never have established himself . . . as he has done in the necessary.[7]

So that when Professor Wind says: 'Almost all the artistic triumphs of the last century were triumphs of disruption'[8] he is really putting the accent on triumph. But at the same time he contrives to make us feel that these nineteenth-century triumphs are in some way slightly perverse, or at least off-centre:

Art has been displaced from the centre of our life not just by applied science, but above all by its own centrifugal impulse. For more than a century most of Western art has been produced and enjoyed on the assumption that the experience of art will be more intense if it pulls the spectator away from his ordinary habits and preoccupations.[9]

With Sophocles and Euripides dead, I can imagine that sentence spoken by a Greek, 100 years or so after *Oedipus Rex*, the *Bacchae*, and *Hippolytus*. Perhaps I am distorting Professor Wind's thought. But I do it solely to drive home the fact that in all times, where an artist has experienced the forces of the imagination disruptively, and especially when he has needed to use directly anarchic images, the quality of artistic triumph lies in the power of formal creation. No material is more anarchic than *Oedipus Rex*. No stage play has greater formal clarity and power.

There is, in my opinion, no necessary relationship between the appearance of such an extraordinary masterpiece and the social life around its creator, because the acts of the creative spirit may be truly anarchic, spontaneous, discontinuous. And yet that is only one side of the coin. We recognize *Oedipus Rex* to be of its time, the more we come to know through classical scholarship what the special quality of the time was. We do not need classical scholarship

---

[6] Ibid. 2; in the revised version, the second sentence becomes: 'The forces of the imagination, from which he draws his strength, have a disruptive and capricious power which he must manage with economy.'

[7] Ibid. 101–2.

[8] Ibid. 18; in the revised version, 'the last century' becomes 'the last hundred years'.

[9] Ibid. 18.

to make us aware of the special quality of our own time. We feel we know that immediately, because we live in it. We certainly rationalize our experience of it in various ways: and in general we believe our time to be particularly prey to disruptive forces. We certainly, if naïvely, expect art to be responsive to such social disruption. As Professor Wind said: 'Art just happens to be the most sensitive place in which acute disturbances make themselves felt.'[10] That being so, we fancy we enjoy barbaric, primitive art more than our forefathers; that we are more attuned than they to the extreme forms of Greek tragedy; even perhaps to the more gruesome of Shakespeare's plays. So that expressionist art can be accounted for, we think, by the general chaos of the time. Yet is our aesthetic pleasure in such art really a reflection of our concern with the disruptive social forces?

Professor Wind puts an apt pin through this fallacious bubble in his account of his own first youthful experience of German expressionist painting. He says:

In the midst of these pleasures I was struck with a thought which troubled me greatly . . . It occurred to me that if all these intense pictures, one after the other, had been experienced by me with the intensity they demanded, I ought to be out of my mind.[11]

Here we see where our naïvety may get us. To be 'out of one's mind' is to be insane. One is insane because one cannot face up to the terrors of real life. If these expressionist paintings had turned Professor Wind insane, they would not be triumphs at all, but failures. Indeed, I would turn Professor Wind's sentence round and say: 'If all these intense pictures . . . had been experienced by me with the intensity they demanded, I ought to be particularly sane.' One

[10] The original paragraph (*Listener*, 22 Dec. 1960) reads: 'Today the knights of the razor are not a sect, they are the majority; and they are not—in any sense of the word—*raseurs sympathiques*. To them art is a nuisance because it resists automatism. The various forces that have been discussed in these talks can be related to this overriding impulse: for when things look odd in the artistic life of an age, it is certain that the oddity is not confined to art, but pervades the entire mode of living. Art just happens to be the most sensitive place in which acute disturbances make themselves felt. The fear of knowledge, the mechanization of art, the fallacy of pure form, the cult of the fragment for the sake of freshness, are simplifications which spare us the trouble of getting upset, transformed, and Platonically endangered by a passionate participation in art, and every device of modern scholarship, from the connoisseur's list to the iconographer's label, can be misused, to make art look more manageable than it is.'

Cf. the revised version, *Art and Anarchy*, 99–100: 'Today the knights of the (i.e. Occam's) razor are not a sect, they are the majority; and they are not—in any sense of the word—*raseurs sympathiques*. They prefer not to wrestle with the angel: it takes too long; it is uneconomical; and one is likely to get one's thigh out of joint. The avoidance of risk has become a ruling passion, and many of the forces that have been discussed in these lectures can be related to this overriding impulse: a desire to spread all manner of art so widely that its effects cancel each other out. Nietzsche saw modern man in his aesthetic Eden "surrounded with the styles and arts of all times so that, like Adam with the beasts, he might give them a name". Classification has indeed proved a trouble of participation; and above all, it eliminates the will.'

[11] Wind, *Art and Anarchy*, 27.

suspects that the problem of how therapeutic we want certain kinds of contemporary art to be (for that is the problem lying behind this argument) is
bedevilled in this instance by the general fact that expressionist art is weakest
in its formal power. Few of its manifestations, even of a genius like Strindberg,
can be equated to *Oedipus Rex*.

Perhaps, after all, it is not the disruptive forces of our time which we hope,
or fear, to see reflected in modern art, but the scientific interests, the passions
of order and precision. Abstract painting and functional architecture seem to
be excellent examples of such a tendency. Abstract painting at its purest (as
with Mondrian or Nicholson) seems to turn its back finally on all the inner
and outer disruption, chiefly by a process of exclusion. Contemporary architecture, as Professor Wind rightly points out, at its creative best, accepts the
mechanically prefabricated materials as effectively as at another period it
used a greater preponderance of craftsmen-shaped stones or beams.

If we do naïvely equate formal and functional elements in modern art with
a specifically scientific outlook, then it is time, I think, we took a look at the
ambiguities of science itself. This is a point that Professor Wind did not raise
in his lectures, though he spoke often of science. It is simply that there has
been a knowledge explosion in all the fields of science, with such consequential technological advances, that the social life of the entire world is undergo-
ing continual transformation and adjustment. Viewed from this angle,
science, not art, would seem to be the really disruptive force.

But equally, we might suppose from the general concern with psychiatric
maladjustment that the psyche was the true source of disruption. It is obvious
enough that whichever way we look at it, our social life is being changed and
disrupted by tremendous forces. Is it as obvious that modern art is directly
responsive to these forces; whether to express them, tame them, or reject
them? I do not think so: I believe, because as a reactive artist I feel it, that the
inner world of man's psyche is in ferment. And that this ferment is forcing up
new, and often unwanted, images. But I am not certain at all that the outer
ferment or the inner ferment is a cause or effect of the other. It seems to me
equally possible that the simultaneity of these two processes is accidental,
although the effects on us of having such a double transformation to accomplish are frightening. I am certainly haunted by the feeling that creative time
may really be spontaneous and discontinuous. I cannot easily see how the
truly spontaneous can be merely the effect of some cause which we can rationalize.

It is not only that creation forms apparently eternal works of art out of the
disruptive, anarchic images from without and within. It is that creative *genius*
responds immediately to the spontaneous, timeless spirit. This spirit cannot,
I believe, be finally circumscribed by history. So that a crop of geniuses
vouchsafed to us in our time would knock all our theories of the marginal
nature of modern art out of the ring.

Part II

COMPOSERS PAST AND
PRESENT

Chapter 4

SCHOENBERG

MOVING INTO AQUARIUS

The astrological heading is, of course, deliberate—and Schoenberg, I am sure, would have approved; it is designed to draw attention to the idea of seasonal change. In astrological jargon, our present world month, which began its 2,000-year life round about the birth of Christ, and is called after the zodiacal sign of the Fish, is coming to its end. A new world month will soon begin, when the sun finally enters the house of Aquarius, the Water-carrier. Very many people in the Roman Empire beside the early Christians had a sense of the portentous, the catastrophic, as that great period of revolution set in. Like ourselves now, they were aware of being in such a period, and like ourselves, they could not of course see very far forward but only backward. Some of the very early Christians do seem even to have expected an actual end of the world in historical fact at that time. To us now, looking back at them, we are less excited by the world that was ending than by what was beginning. 'A culture never falls to pieces; it gives birth.'

My plan is certainly not to defend astrology; nor to suggest that great changes of world feeling move only with the Zodiac. So far as I know anything at all about the movement of the stars, I do not think any zodiacal change really corresponds to the tremendous climacteric that came between: that is, to the transformation of Christian medievalism into Reformation, Enlightenment, and scientific materialism. But I do think that our present prolonged catastrophe (moving into Aquarius) has more analogies to the changes before and after the year One (moving into Pisces) than to the birth pangs of the Renaissance. And I hazard a guess that we have more medieval hangover to contend with even now than our emancipated selves would care to believe possible. Certainly that, I think, is what Victorianism was (something not confined to England—but to all Europe). The fight against Darwin was the last reverberation of the war on Giordano Bruno. A refusal of something, a pressing something down—a something which no one *seems* to be upset about now. But of course other things were pressed down too. Victorian morals, Victorian piety, Victorian charity; even the last named wanted to press something down. And so movements that allied themselves with what would not be pressed down had the force of an eventual explosion. Wickedness, wickedness! But so it was.

We might pause for a moment at Victorian morals, because I am sure they were the root of the matter, and at the real disturber, Freud. Freud was a scientist, an idealist. He went to the battle with the purity of David against Goliath. He looked at a typical Victorian moral picture—the infant at the loving mother's breast—he tore aside the sentimental covering and exposed a truth, which he proved by monotonous iteration of accumulated data, that the pleasure of suckling was really infantile sexuality. We can hardly realize now the violence of the affront to Victorian self-esteem. But Freud was so driven by his daemon that he had no time to consider the storm he was creating. He went on to the Victorian father and Victorian money fetish—which he likened to certain subconscious desires; ;and these things have still power to wound. Then the strangest things happened. Faced with all these unpleasant instinctual truths, what was the good Victorian bourgeois to do? Freud told him: he should sublimate. But again, before anyone had the time to point out that sublimation might be only another word for the old morality, his disciples drove him yet further back along the road, forcing him to assume a God-the-father cloak himself and to declare his theories to be dogma. We seem to have come full circle. Perhaps, after all, no one can really leap out of his time. For, even if he was hounded as a figure of scandal, Freud seems to come out in the end on the side of convention and morality, as though Victorian pressing down could go on after all, in a disguised form. But if people really hoped it could go on after all, they were grievously mistaken. The real scandal, the *real* catastrophe of the Great War, came and went. What happened to Victorian culture is brilliantly and bitterly described in the preface to *Heartbreak House*.[1]

Now the consternation that Freud caused was only possible because, despite his ineradicable Victorianism (as I see it), he was in revolt and standing for something to come. There were similar figures in every walk of life. Music was certainly not excluded. My account of Freud, schematized nearly to caricature, may already have appeared as oddly similar to what we know of Schoenberg. Here certainly was another Victorian figure in revolt. In the very early works, of course, there was little or no sign of it, but rather of emotionalism, monumentality, and prolixity. That was not the real Schoenberg. Like Freud, he had a further destiny—to revolt, to attack, to destroy, to root out precisely all those attitudes which he had accepted before. 'A culture never falls to pieces; it gives birth.' It is hard to believe that when all we can see at first glance is the pulling down, the clearing out of the way. Like the good people of Vienna, we can easily think of Schoenberg as a kind of monster. In reality the matter is more objective than we realize. The violence of

---

[1] G. B. Shaw, *Heartbreak House* (London, 1920); in this connection it should be noted, I think, that a positive pre-1914 avant-gardism can, half a century or more later, seem like a debilitating evasion of a real response to the situation.

the artistic revolt against Victorian sentiment was (and is) in exact relation to the amount of hidden sentimentality masquerading behind the façade of fine feeling. The revolt took two forms: the one, expressionism—which was to try to be truthful, however unpleasant that might be (similar to Freudian unmasking of the subconscious); the other, cubism—to take sentiment out of the artistic means (that is, in music, out of the notes) and to produce an art of apparent abstraction. No important artistic figure of this century has really escaped this dilemma—that the two ways forward out of Victorianism seem to be equally dispiriting to the general public.

For Schoenberg, at least (as for Freud) there was never any doubt. The bitterness of the struggle around his name is witness to his entire lack of compromise. Like Freud, he was an idealist driven by a daemon. As with Freud, his daemon drove him down a road of over-simplification, towards a dogma—the law of the twelve-tone system. Like Freud, I think, it was just the consequent sense of estrangement from fellow professionals and the public that caused him to draw the bonds of his pupil circle so tight. That he exercised a tyrannic fascination over them all is not in doubt. That they induced in him a God-the-father attitude is equally apparent. He paid a heavy price to his daemon for his gifts. But it is not the prices they pay but the work they do which determines the scientists', the artists' permanent value. If we keep our eyes firmly fixed on what these controversial figures were being driven to do and refuse to be side-tracked by prejudice or gossip, I think we can begin to see certain constants. The sequence runs something like this: a revolt against Victorian (or, if you prefer, bourgeois) complacency and sham; a passionate search for truth, however distasteful; a dogmatic attitude to the truth uncovered; a need for an inner esoteric brotherhood of initiates.

Now the closed circle round a controversial artist is usually so small that the big public outside easily sees it as an object of ridicule. But so far, in our turbulent period, the big public has never seen itself as ridiculous when it is all inside some ambivalent experience, such as the German public under the Nazis. Like the artist and his circle against a hostile philistia, the bigger congregations draw together positively on the basis of a shared experience and a shared value; negatively, to arm in self-defence against a congregation outside that is perforce ignorant of the experience and which denies the value. The ensuing catastrophes have been so great, beginning with the First World War, that reality makes mock of aesthetic esotericism. For example, because of his distasteful circle, which seems now like a parody of the collective mania that ensued, many people find it difficult to realize that the poet Stefan George was not bought over by the Nazis.

So universal in our time seems this experience of collectivities, parties, groups, that the really strange figures are those who do the dedicated, difficult work, who face the crisis, alone. Bartók, for example. He had as tough a struggle in Budapest as Schoenberg in Vienna. What gave him the strength to stand alone? And is that strength a value of his music? Personally I believe so. But I shall deliberately turn from Bartók (great figure though he is), because I want to follow my central theme (the new breaking out of the old) into other arts than music. I must turn instead to James Joyce. He, like Bartók but unlike Schoenberg, never needed the experience of beloved master, adoring circle, and dogma, but discharged all his life energy into the experience of artistic truth. During the years of the Great War he was withdrawn, writing *Ulysses*. *Ulysses* is the artistic truth into which he discharged himself. A truth so factual, so everyday, so commonplace, so accumulative, so boring, that any of us who try to read *Ulysses* with any remaining shred of Victorian taste, find ourselves excessively irritated, baffled, resentful. Not finding what we expected of art—that is, not finding motive and choice and theme and sense—we project our resentment first upon the book, then upon the author. But suppose the virtue of the art is precisely in the absence of these things? Then the matter is even worse. A sense of inferiority is awakened, and our resentment deepens. How many times have not all of us had this experience with modern art? For instance with Schoenberg? And is there then no mercy? As though to add insult to injury, our accustomed, deepest values suddenly appear horribly travestied. In *Ulysses* they are spoken to us like this—in a brothel.

Boys do it now. God's time is 12.25. Tell mother you'll be there. Rush your order and you play a slick ace. Join on right here. Book through to eternity junction, the nonstop run—just one word more. Are you a good or doggone clod? If the second advent came to Coney Island, are we ready? Florry Christ, Stephen Christ, Bloom Christ, Zoe Christ, it's up to you to sense that cosmic force. Have we cold feet about the cosmos? No, be on the side of the angels. Be a prism. You have that something within the higher self. You can rub shoulders with a Jesus, a Gautama, an Ingersoll. Are you all in this vibration? I say you are. You once knobble that, congregation, and a buck joy ride to heaven becomes a back number. You get me? It's a life brightener, sure; the hottest stuff ever was. It's the whole pie with jam in. It's the cutest, shappiest line out. It is immense, super-sumptuous. It restores.[2]

Why does Joyce take the trouble to do all that? I think he himself gives the answer. As the speaker of the words I have quoted says: 'Be a prism.' That is: be something that breaks up the sweet sunlight into its scientifically real components. Be an absolutely impersonal eye. So, for the greatest modern painter, it has been an equally merciless pilgrimage. Picasso may begin with a blue period of natural objects. Do not be deceived! The blue is not that of the summer sky; but of night, of moonshine—of cold water. And before long the thin, syphilitic prostitute appears, the white acrobat, the tragically dislocated harlequin. Objects fall apart, to be reconstituted as cubism. An abstraction in which for the sake of purity everything that could engage our natural sympathy is deliberately refused: that is the point, deliberately refused. Natural objects here are quite neutral and equal. A half nose has as much

² James Joyce, *Ulysses*, Bodley Head edn. (London, 1960), 625.

value as a whole nose. This is what upsets us; but this is the nature of the art. The poet, the painter, the composer seem to exercise themselves only to baffle and rebut the recipient of their message. For their message, such as they have one, lies in just this attitude of truth and abstraction. So in Joyce's *Finnegan's Wake*, as if to make quite sure we shall understand nothing, the very words are dismantled and reassembled. The immense book goes round in a huge circle. We end where we began. It would probably be quite as proper to read it backwards. In the *Lyric Suite* of Alban Berg, one of the fast movements is written in mirror form. Would it do the same for us in this piece if it were played backwards—or upside down? Probably. Take it or leave it. An apparently valueless, heartless art of truth or abstraction, that tells us so ungraciously to take it or leave it, is in continual danger of misunderstanding. Certainly the big public imagines it leaves it.

But does it? Perhaps, in the transparent sense that it prefers the classics— or the romantics. But just as modern art is an art of the naked fact, and of the necessary and voluntary acceptance of fact, so it is itself a fact, not a conspiracy: one of the objective resultants of a total situation in which the public is involved as much as the artist. *Fin de siècle* attitudes were not confined to the handful of names that I have mentioned. The lyrically sensuous Victorian dance music of Vienna, even that went down before something much more primitive from an outcast race in America.

I remember when I was a little boy before the Great War, hearing the new popular music for the first time, to words something like these:

> Everybody's doing it, doing it, doing it,
> See that ragtime couple over there,
> Watch them throw their shoulders in the air,
> Everybody's doing it now.

In actual fact, at that time, everybody was not doing it. It is difficult to realize that the now universal jazz was once itself new and severely frowned upon. It would be interesting to discuss jazz properly, as another seismograph of the crisis. It too is full of schools and initiates and abstractions. But it would take us too far afield. Because jazz is a musical vernacular, it has attracted many serious composers, thinking to find in it a way through to the big public—or just a means to refresh serious music by the primitive. Stravinsky leaps to my mind. His *Rag time* for eleven players was finished at Morges at 11 a.m. on 11 November 1918 (and his *L'Histoire du soldat* not long before). He had begun his pilgrimage from the enchanted garden of the *Firebird*, through the primitive puppet world of *Petrushka* and the orgiastic *Rite of Spring*, to end on the sublimated summit of neo-classicism and the absolute objectivity of the artwork. In the terms I used earlier, he went out of the Victorian garden first by the road of expressionism, then by the road of cubism. So, of course, he is a controversial figure too.

One of our anonymous music critics has assessed Stravinsky as a man who was a composer once, while Schoenberg he (or she) considers never to have been a composer at all. Clearly this critic has not taken it, but left it. But the fact that a critic is puzzled does not impinge upon the problem of creative artists in relation to a crisis at all.

You may leave it, and you may leave yourself out—not of course out of everything, but out of certain things that will go on whether we like them or not. We cannot turn back the clock to Victorianism through the two world wars. The sun will enter the house of Aquarius. Keenly serious and sensitive people will enter with a complete dedication upon the task of helping to birth what is to be; a midwifery, as I have suggested, disconcertingly and ungraciously factual. At the same time we see as little of what is to be as those who passed into Pisces just under 2,000 years ago. Some very unpleasant people faced the future, some very pleasant people faced the past. And vice versa.

The present separation of creative artist from the public is really a reflection of this: that we have no clear idea of Man, with a capital M, to whom we shall confidently speak. A bishop, I remember, once asked me if I could write new Anglican responses, clean and strong and simple like Tallis's, but modern. I replied: 'Give me a Christian congregation with a taste for clear, strong, modern music and I will provide it.' That, written large, is the nature of the wider problem. Positive art can only be addressed to a public whose ideal conception of Man is generally understood and assented to. There is no such agreed ideal conception now. All is relativity of conception. There was lately Nazi man, with no soul. There is Communist man, whom many suspect of having no soul. There is Catholic man with perhaps a medieval soul. Each a value and an offence. Is there a whole man with a non-medieval soul? Or is the soul so ageless that there is no sense in relating her to anything so short as a world month? Do the purgative qualities of modern art deny us a soul? Or would modern art be warmer if modern man had found his soul?

That I (and my betters) belong body and soul to the artistic midwifery which I have described is our pride. That few of us will ever have the purity of purpose of Schoenberg is certain. That modern man can find his soul is true. That art will speak again entire is as sure as the Zodiac.

FROM VIENNA TO LOS ANGELES

The text of Arnold Schoenberg's oratorio *Die Jakobsleiter* (Jacob's Ladder) lies before me. It is an important document for the understanding of Schoenberg's artistic philosophy—and he wrote it himself. It opens with the words spoken by the archangel Gabriel.

GABRIEL. Ob rechts, ob links, vorwärts oder rückwärts, bergauf oder bergab—man hat weiterzugehen, ohne zu fragen, was vor oder hinter einem liegt.

   Es soll verborgen sein: ihr dürftet, müsstet es vergessen, um die Aufgabe zu erfüllen.

(Whether to the right, or to the left, forwards or backwards, uphill or down—you must go on, never asking what lies in front or behind. That will be hidden from you: you should, you must forget it. So that the Task can be fulfilled.)

That last sentence is decisive for Schoenberg's artistic intentions. He set himself a certain task: to make himself first of all a medium of what he felt to be new ideas in music (his Vienna period, before the First World War). Having uncovered these latent ideas, he set himself to systematize them—and show, by actual musical examples, that every traditional form of music could be renewed by them (roughly his Berlin period, before dismissal by the Nazis). Finally he wanted to turn his back on such exemplifications and write freely and freshly with the new techniques thus mastered (his American period, till his death).

I speak of periods, because, to discuss his life and times, I have divided the span of fifty years or so of his maturity into four. First, Vienna 1900–14, when he had to fight like Mahler, Karl Kraus, Adolf Loos, and the others, tooth and nail, against the innate if not insensate conservatism of that town. Second, the period of the Great War itself, when Schoenberg was fallow, and there is opportunity to discuss his need for a school, his most famous pupils, and other new composers: that means Berg, Stravinsky, Bartók, and Hindemith. Third, Berlin after the war, when Schoenberg, at Busoni's death, was appointed to the master class for composition at the State Academy for Music. This was the period of his greatest material and public success, ending with his flight to Paris and his return to the Jewish faith of his fathers in a ceremony before the Chief Rabbi. Fourth, the life in America in the strange world of the continental emigration to California. *My* task, in the Schoenbergian sense, is to show a picture, tell a story, give a guide to fifty years of artistic history, as mirrored in this man.

I must return to Gabriel's words—'Whether to the right or to the left, forwards or backwards, uphill or down.' The four directions to which the artist must give himself, might equally refer to the four permitted aspects of the tone-row. Schoenberg once described what he meant by a tone-row in terms of a hat. One can see a hat from below, above, in front, behind—yet it still remains a hat. The trouble with this metaphor is obvious. A hat is a physical object, to which these spatial terms, above, below, behind, in front, properly belong. A musical tone-row is a succession in time—and the spatial terms, especially that of backwards, are in matters of time fundamentally improper. And that brings me to the element of the apparently arbitrary in Schoenberg's ideas, which is not really to be argued away by inaccurate metaphors. I think I can give you the *feel* of what it really was in Schoenberg (as opposed to its objective value) by another quotation: 'Seine Geburt war unordentlich, darum liebte er leidenschaftlich Ordnung, das Unverbrüchliche, Gebot und Verbot.' In English, roughly: 'His birth was disorderly, therefore he loved, and with passion, order, the inviolable, commandment and prohibition.'

That is not a quotation from Schoenberg, but is the opening sentence of Thomas Mann's story of Moses, called *Das Gesetz* (The Law). The story is a joy to read, for its mixture of perception, sympathy, and urbane irony. Mann's account, for example, of Moses' defence before Aaron and Miriam of his dark-skinned concubine, to which Jehovah gave assent by an earthquake, is at the other end of the world to Schoenberg's excessive emotionality controlled by extreme formality—by the *law*, of the twelve-tone system. And Schoenberg had plenty of serious reasons to give, if you asked, why the law of Jehovah had ten commandments while the law of the new music had twelve tones. We can see that Mann and Schoenberg were already opposite psychological types before they came to such tragic disagreement in America, ending up in a *law* suit. The Mann–Schoenberg controversy over Mann's novel *Dr Faustus* is more than journalism. It ties up with Schoenberg's Jewishness, his Swedenborgian mysticism, his attempt to supersede his oratorio *Jacob's Ladder* by the opera with the significant title *Moses and Aaron*. For *Jacob's Ladder* was never finished. Schoenberg's first wife, Alexander von Zemlinsky's sister, who entered with feminine susceptibility into his Swedenborgian world, told him one day prophetically that as soon as he completed the score of *Jacob's Ladder* he would die. Schoenberg at once stopped the composition of the oratorio, which one might say was reborn as the opera *Moses and Aaron*.

This is not the time or place to enter on a discussion of the relation of Schoenberg's personal life to his compositions, even if I had the knowledge. Schoenberg's first wife died, and later the eldest daughter of the marriage died. Schoenberg married again, and his widow, the sister of Kolisch (leader of the famous string quartet), lives in Los Angeles. There are children of this marriage, so all these matters must wait. What should be said, I think, is that Schoenberg's imaginative life was unusually rich and powerful. Portions of the psyche, not immediately related to musical composition, were constantly being stirred by what Jung would call 'meaningful coincidences'. But Schoenberg was of an older generation than Jung. He inhabited the Vienna of Freud. The connection of Schoenberg's artistic processes with depth psychology is real, but difficult to make precise. It is an as yet uncharted sea.

Recently one of Schoenberg's pupils came to visit me in my home, a man of great charm and most extensive knowledge, whose eyes were still clear, straight-looking, and untroubled despite the tortures of the Nazis—a Jew of Alban Berg's generation, a Viennese. We walked up the hill together, talking, talking. Being Viennese (for I almost became Viennese myself during his visit) we talked and talked and talked—so that it might have been the Café Griensteidl in pre-pre-war Vienna, where Schoenberg talked with his great friends Kraus and Loos and Peter Altenberg. Half-way up the hill my visitor stopped. Like every Schoenberg pupil, he had submitted to the *Zauberei*, the magical fascination of the master. (That is the most striking thing about any Schoenberg pupil.) But now he said unexpectedly and rhetorically: Did I know Schoenberg's real weakness? Of course I did not. Then he said simply:

'Ping-pong.' For Schoenberg was madly keen on table tennis. So keen indeed that he played for hours on end, stopping for a meal, only to begin playing ping-pong again—and smoking innumerable cigarettes. But he was an acute sufferer from asthma, so that one must think of his voice as rather hoarse and throaty. But hours on end of ping-pong and boxes of cigarettes are no diet for an asthmatic. His health was therefore never as good as it should have been.

When he was first in America, he played ping-pong with Gershwin, who, like Schoenberg himself, was not only a passionate table-tennis player, but an amateur painter. Gershwin when he died appears to have left behind him an oil portrait of Schoenberg; while Schoenberg has left behind some self-portraits, particularly one as seen from the back. But the curious thing about Schoenberg's painting activities is that while in *music* he demanded incessant technical studies before composition, in *painting* he would take no lessons at all. He came to painting through his friendship with Kokoschka and later Kandinsky; so that he once found himself publishing music, prose, and painting in *Der Blaue Reiter*, which was an avant-garde magazine of all the arts, published in Munich. The prose piece he published in the magazine is a discussion on the relations of words to music, a problem with which he was then extensively occupied. The poetry that chiefly fascinated him was that of Stefan George. George had spent his youth in Paris and sat at the feet of Mallarmé and Baudelaire. When he returned to Germany, he began to use French symbolist methods in his own German poetry—and curious as it may sound, it was in searching for the melodic line to match this poetry that Schoenberg found himself driven towards atonality. The decisive moment is the setting of Stefan George's *Das Buch der hängenden Gärten* (The Book of the Hanging Gardens).

Did Schoenberg complete his task? That is, was he able in America to forget the arguments and the techniques and write fresh new music? It is a difficult question. There are young composers in Paris now who say that he failed to go where he might have gone, just because he felt he had to show that the traditional forms *could* be composed with the new techniques. They hold that a waltz, for example, in twelve-tone technique, is an equivocation, a confusion; that the real and next step is to find new forms, especially new rhythms, to match properly the new methods. Good luck to them! As they used to say in my country childhood—it will all come out in the wash. One day. There is too much future in it for our present purposes. Schoenberg's early music was not written in Messiaeniste Paris of 1950, but in Vienna (or near it) in the first decade of the century. The two giants Brahms and Wagner were then only lately dead. Their more petty followers were still fighting; but greater figures like Strauss and Mahler were producing music stemming from them both. Mahler was at the Hofoper, hanging on precariously. At one of the scandalous scenes at a Schoenberg première, when a member of the audience, in the expressive phrase, 'blew upon a latch-key', Mahler came to Schoenberg's defence by boxing a young man's ears. I may have mixed up two stories, but the point is that in reactionary Vienna the tiny clique of people who were really to make artistic history had to cling together or go under. Schoenberg's first official job came through the recommendation of Strauss. It is well to remember this when we match the splendours of *Rosenkavalier*, produced in 1911, against the emotional intensities, the miseries of Schoenberg's early music.

'AIR FROM ANOTHER PLANET'

Through the kindness of Mrs Schoenberg, Arnold Schoenberg's widow, I was able to read the complete text of Schoenberg's own libretto for his unfinished opera *Moses and Aaron*. All along I had a hunch that it would be interesting— not only because I knew that Schoenberg himself gave it a lot of attention, but also because when anyone takes traditional material for his artistic purposes, whatever he does to this material will be critically significant.

Schoenberg left no commentary, so far as I know, to his text for *Moses and Aaron*, so it is with a sense of obvious inadequacy that I try to give some critical background to his text, and I shall only do it in the slenderest way, hoping that someone more authoritative may fill it all in later. And I consider my attempt only possible at all, just because the material is traditional. There is something 'given', which is the story as we have it in the Bible. For the words of the Bible have not changed for centuries. They are the words our forefathers read. If they seem different to us, or do different things to us, then it is we who differ in our tastes and manners from our forefathers, not that the Vulgate or the Authorized Version has changed, even if Moffat is relatively new.

Schoenberg made his selection from the biblical material with an eye to showing Moses and Aaron in their relations to each other as joint servants of their God. The biblical verses which would seem to have been closest to Schoenberg's hand are one or two in the scene of the burning bush, that scene where Jehovah first speaks to Moses directly, calling him to his task, and making little of his hesitancies. It may be that Schoenberg was drawn to this scene because he felt himself to have been called to the task of speaking a new message in tones which few have wished to hear. But the possibility has little importance. Or rather, the problems of religious or even artistic calling and dedication and expression can never be truly contained within any one personal biography. If I thought the sum of *Moses and Aaron* were only the sum of its author's own problems, I would not pursue the matter an inch further. Do not imagine that I have case-book material up my sleeve on Schoenberg's psychology—for I have none. I have merely been reading Schoenberg's libretto and reading the Bible. And it is the biblical verses in which Jehovah states the problem that are, I think, significant. For Moses pleads with

Jehovah that he has no liking for the task of calling the people to be chosen of God, or power to move them, because he, Moses, has not the gift of words. In the Bible story Moses says: 'O my Lord, I am not eloquent, neither heretofore, nor since thou hast spoken unto thy servant: but I am slow of speech, and of a slow tongue.' Jehovah is angered with Moses, and replies in these significant verses:

Is not Aaron the Levite thy brother? I know that he can speak well. And also, behold, he cometh forth to meet thee: and when he seeth thee, he will be glad in his heart.

And thou shalt speak unto him, and put words in his mouth: and I will be with thy mouth, and with his mouth, and will teach you what ye shall do.

And he shall be thy spokesman unto the people: and he shall be, even he shall be to thee instead of a mouth, and thou shalt be to him instead of God.

So Jehovah is to speak directly to Moses, who is to speak directly to Aaron, who is to speak directly to the people. In the first act of Schoenberg's opera this is exactly what happens. Jehovah does speak direct to Moses, who (in the next scene) speaks direct to Aaron. But they *both* try to speak direct to the people; which does not work at all. Very soon Moses withdraws to the back of the stage and gives up, to the significant words: 'Mein Gedanke ist machtlos in Arons Wort', (My thought is powerless in Aaron's word). And that is really the basis of such drama as the opera displays. To use platonic language: the Idea can only be expressed by the Image. But the Image may begin to exercise the power properly due only to the Idea. If, for the purposes of drama, we personalize the Idea and the Image, then the theatrical situations will develop themselves out of the play between (in this case) Moses's divine Idea, Aaron's gift of Imagery, and the people's need for both. To complete the scene I was describing, and thereby the first act of the opera, Aaron gives visible ground for Moses' fear that the power of his thought is usurped by Aaron's word, for he says to Moses: 'Silence! I am the Word and the Act.'

And if we recall the beginning of St John's Gospel ('In the beginning was the Word'), we realize how clearly Aaron's phrase contains the hint of usurpation. But the people, despite Aaron's miracles—the serpent, the leprous hand, the Nile water becoming blood—still apprehended the hierarchy of power as running clearly God—Moses—Aaron. The Idea still controls the Image. And there the act ends.

In the second act Moses is away on the mount of revelation—the Idea has withdrawn to itself. So the Image takes on a life of its own. Consequently there follows (in the opera) the scene of the golden calf. There is no thought or argument in this long scene, just display, on quite a Hollywood scale, and much more detailed than the story as told in the Bible. When Moses returns from the mountain (in the last scene of Act II) the opera text returns to its normal argumentative course. The two protagonists discuss at length the epistemological problem. At the end Aaron seems to be having the best of it, and

Moses is once more in despair. The Image now means more to the people than the Idea.

Such are the first two acts of the opera, and I believe the music of these acts was already completed before Schoenberg left Europe for America. The text of the third act had already been written, too, but not all the music. This was never finished even in America. Perhaps Schoenberg was dissatisfied with this third act text. It is a bit strange. It is much shorter than the other acts, only one scene. Moses leads Aaron on to the stage chained to two guards. The argument begins all over again: Picture against Thought, Image against Idea. After two pages of typescript text Aaron gives up, and Moses begins the longest metaphysical and philosophical lecture I have ever read in any libretto, a lecture which is rather disconcertingly interrupted at last by the two guards who say: 'Shall we kill him?'

But Moses disdains an answer, and continues for another half-page, during which he asserts that every time the people leave the desert of aspiration, purity, and righteousness for the lesser values of competition and various other false pleasures, they will be forced back eventually into the desert again. Then he turns to the guards and orders Aaron to be set free—to live if he is able. The stage direction runs: 'Aaron, free, stands up and falls dead.'

So Moses (the Idea) is alone, for Aaron (the Image) is dead. Moses speaks: 'But in the wilderness the people are unconquerable and will reach their destination: to be at one with God.'

Now, one might say that just because this last act contained an unmediated, undigested discussion of Schoenberg's artistic problems, it was bound to differ as it does so markedly from the Bible story. For the traditional, biblical relation between Moses and Aaron never takes this Schoenbergian ending. In the Bible Jehovah gives Moses minute measures and exact materials for the wonderful 'breastplate of judgement', the 'ephod', and all the lovely garments which Aaron, the high priest, is to wear; and it is a long time after the solemn investiture of Aaron and his sons when Aaron dies on the top of Mount Hor and is mourned by the people for thirty days, 'even all the house of Israel'. By the very substitution of an epistemological discussion for the traditional story, Schoenberg (in the final act of his opera) clearly takes energy from the Image and gives it to the Idea. The destination is 'to be at one with God'—but God as Idea and Thought. What is rejected as impure is God as Image. 'Thou shalt not make unto thee any graven image, or any likeness of any thing that is in heaven above, or in the earth beneath.' Such is the second commandment. Naturally, if this commandment is kept literally, then art ceases. Where an artist gets fascinated by this commandment, then the psychological struggle is terrible. Such, I believe, to have been Schoenberg's. And when I have clarified things to this temporary abruptness, I feel myself a Greek to Schoenberg's Jew. Damned by Jehovah though I may be, rejected even by Plato, on more occasions than I propose to tell you, the Image has been for me divine. Not of course, I hasten to add, an Image of God himself, but often of his breath.

But the second commandment has never been kept literally. If I think of the burning bush, what springs to my mind at once is a *picture*—a self-made still from the film of *The Green Pastures*.[3] Nor is the image only visual. I can at any time recall the crackle made on the film sound-track as the bush burnt. *The Green Pastures* dressed the Bible story in a manner which I must skate over by calling it nineteenth-century conventional; with local colouring. For we see the film through the dream-laden eyes of a piccaninny hearing the voice of an old Negro reading to her at a village Sunday school in the deep South. I believe the artistic quality of the film was sufficient to lift the conventional and local out of time and place. If I am right, it will live.

But of course many things were operating against that nineteenth-century conventional picture. For instance, historians and anthropologists began to care less for what was written on the tables of the law, more for the fact that Moses was able to write at all. With what alphabet? That was the real question. The question as to what kind of clothes Moses could have worn was subsidiary. But it was also asked and answered. So in another climate of taste the biblical story could look different again: as it did for Thomas Mann in his account of Moses and Aaron: *Das Gesetz*. Like Schoenberg, Mann also juggles with the Bible story for his own purposes, which is always with a slant towards the civilized. Pharaoh's daughter seducing Moses' handsome young father (a scene, I may say, not in the Bible) might be anyone from the Victorian upper classes. And the alphabet? That is there too. Can we wonder that in America when Mann gave his not too pleasant hero in *Dr Faustus* some of the musical characteristics of Schoenberg, Schoenberg took offence. It would be only too easy, given their so different natures, and despite their friendship. Behind the quarrel lies a dichotomy of taste. Once such vast impersonal problems of taste and attitude are involved, personal intercourse ceases. The camps drew up to battle. I can state it thus dispassionately only because I am not in *that* fight. With regard to *that*, I remain by *The Green Pastures*.

Yet there is still another way of treating the traditional Bible material which I need to mention. It arises from the growing interest in comparative religion and mythology. Here the question is not what was written on the tablets, nor with what alphabet, but how in fact did Moses apprehend the numinous on the mountain-top? And the significant Bible verses would be those describing how Moses' face shone after he had been in contact with Jehovah, so that in speaking to the people he had to veil it.

But when Moses went in before the Lord to speak with him, he took the veil off, until he came out. And he came out, and spake unto the children of Israel that which he was commanded.
And the children of Israel saw the face of Moses, that the skin of Moses' face shone: and Moses put the veil upon his face again, until he went in to speak with him.

[3] See pp. 112 and 132 below.

Neither Schoenberg's opera nor Mann's novel is concerned with these verses, partly I think because this mythological approach to such material is of a later date. Yet, curiously enough, not many hours after I had read and pondered over these verses from the Bible, I found myself reading them again, because they come in that strange novel of Balzac's, *Séraphita*,[4] by which Schoenberg was so fascinated. The verses appear in the long account of Swedenborg's life and ideas which is given to the reader soon after the novel's remarkable beginning. For the plot of the book, such as it is, is based on the triangular relations between a pure young girl, a middle-aged, much experienced man, and a Swedenborgian being, who appears as Séraphitus, a god-like young man, to the girl and as Séraphita, the perfection of young womanhood, to the man. Truly not for nothing did Schoenberg set to music George's line 'Ich fühle Luft von anderem Planeten' (I feel an air from another planet).

It is the key to his being. One is not surprised that he picked this one novel out of all Balzac. Nor is the book merely a curiosity. The Swedenborgian parts are very eighteenth-century—a kind of source-book for Blake. Sometimes the effect is very odd. For instance, Swedenborg's account of how he was called to the spiritual life after a good dinner at a London lodging-house in 1745: 'un brouillard épais se répandit dans sa chambre. Quand les ténèbres se dissipèrent, une créature qui avait pris la forme humaine se leva du coin de sa chambre, et lui dit d'une voix terrible: "Ne mange pas tant!" Il fit une diète absolue' (a dense fog spread around his room. When the gloom dissipated, a creature that had assumed a human form rose in a corner of the room, and said to him in an awful voice: 'Do not eat so much!' He was on a strict diet).

I doubt if anyone is called like that now. But the story part of the novel has a more romantic flavour, and, allowing for the different kind of supernaturalism, has for me a touch of E. T. A. Hoffmann. At the end of the novel the wonderful being, Séraphitus–Séraphita, is assumed into heaven in words and imagery of quite Dantesque grandeur. 'To be at one with God.' The girl and the man, after the grace of divine vision, return to ordinary life with a sense of exile. How deeply Schoenberg understood what that feeling was! Not merely because of his political exile in America. For as Kolisch, his brother-in-law, said so wisely, he was no more of an exile in America than he always had been in Europe.

In Los Angeles he lived an outwardly gracious life: a beloved wife, adored children, many good friends. But the exile was in his inward being. 'My thought is powerless in Aaron's word!' Every time his creative gift moved with joy to its work, his obsessive distrust of the image laid a cold finger on his heart. Thomas Mann's dramatic illness in America was not heart trouble, but Schoenberg's was. The stroke practically killed him. He was only brought

[4] See also p. 243 below.

back to life by, I think, a direct injection into the cardiac muscles. When he had regained consciousness, he called for music paper, and wrote at speed the sketches for the String Trio. He had in fact a few years yet to live, but the end was near. It has already been published in America how in 1951 an old Viennese friend of his wrote to Schoenberg pointing out that he was 76 years old. The year was most dangerous for him, because 7 and 6 make 13. This American information seems to have been false, or at best inaccurate. However that may be, on the thirteenth day of each month Schoenberg fell into ever-increasing premonitory fears. On 13 July (he had been born on 13 September) he kept to his bed, and did not wish the nurse, and maybe the doctor too, to leave the place. He had the tennis courts rung up to get the immensely cheering news for him that his son had become champion. He slept and wakened and slept again. He woke the last time shortly before midnight. He asked the date, he asked the time. So few minutes to go. He seemed hopeful. But then he called his wife, looked into her eyes and murmured to her, 'Harmonie! Harmonie!' and died.

MOSES AND AARON

Schoenberg's *Moses and Aaron* is neo-romanticism, just as Stravinsky's *The Rake's Progress* is neo-classicism. That is a melodramatic way of stating their difference, but often these over-sharp contrasts help us to find our way around and to know what we are looking at. Romanticism and classicism are enduring attitudes as well as ways of depicting periods of history. They have never absolutely excluded each other. This is why I think neo-romanticism and neo-classicism have appeared in modern music simultaneously. Neo-romanticism tends towards expressionism, while neo-classicism tends towards abstraction.

There is a third modernistic tendency in opposition to both, which is anti-art or Dada, but both Schoenberg and Stravinsky have been too positive in their traditional allegiances ever to dabble with Dada. Both these tremendous figures were revolutionaries once, but are known now to be part of the unbroken continuity we call a tradition. T. S. Eliot, writing of tradition, said:

The existing monuments [of art] form an ideal order among themselves, which is modified by the introduction of the new, the really new work of art among them. The existing order is complete before the new work arrives. For order to persist out of the supervention of novelty, the whole existing order must be, if ever so slightly, altered.[5]

Eliot's point is that the new and the old, the revolutionary and the traditional, is a two-way traffic. The old affects the new; that is obvious. But Eliot believed that what he calls the really new affects the old. If this is so, and leaving

---

[5] T. S. Eliot, *Tradition and the Individual Talent* (London, 1917); see *Selected Essays*, 3rd edn. (London, 1951), 15.

anti-art and Dada aside, then the really new works of art are only those by which our view of the whole pre-existing order of works of art is ever so slightly altered. The greatest works of Schoenberg and Stravinsky are in this category.

Traditions within which these composers have worked can still be different in locality and temper. Schoenberg was rootedly Germanic in his music. Stravinsky begins by writing music out of the Russian tradition, and it is only after what has been called the 'Sacrifice to Apollo' that his music entered into his neo-classic period. Once his neo-classicism becomes a confirmed temper of mind, it is hardly surprising when his one full-length opera, *The Rake's Progress*, reaches back to the techniques of the eighteenth century: recitatives, arias, set ensembles. In the same way, operatic neo-romanticism as in *Moses and Aaron* reaches back to the techniques of nineteenth-century German leit-motivs, transpositions of unchanging themes. Finally, Stravinsky and all his librettists are Catholic Christians, so behind Tom Rakewell stands Don Giovanni. Schoenberg's own librettist was a Jew, and his opera is deeply Judaic. There stands no direct Judaic hero behind Moses, but there seems to me to be the Nordic, non-Christian figure of Wotan. Tom Rakewell and Don Giovanni are utterly human; transcendents or gods act on them as it were from the outside. Moses and Wotan are non-human, and the problems of transcendence are inside them. Most of the theatrical time of *The Rake's Progress* and *Don Giovanni* is a presentation of their hero's escapades, and only the final scene hints at or exemplifies a divine retribution. All the theatrical time of *Moses and Aaron* or *The Ring* is about transcendence of the Divine in contradiction with itself. Wotan's withdrawal into burning Valhalla at the end of *Götterdämmerung* is curiously similar in feeling to Moses' abdication for Aaron at the end of Act II. Perhaps that is a hint as to one of the many reasons why Act III of *Moses and Aaron* was never composed.

I think, therefore, it is worthwhile when considering the story of the opera to examine why Schoenberg turned, for Judaic, not Christian, reasons, to the Bible.

Schoenberg was born a Jew racially. His family did not practise the cult: they were agnostic, humanist, even perhaps vaguely Christian; but anti-Semitism, especially after the Great War in Germany, affected Schoenberg deeply. He wrote to Kandinsky in April 1923:

I have at last learnt the lesson that has been forced upon me during this year, and I shall not ever forget it. It is that I am not a German, not a European, indeed perhaps scarcely even a human being (at least, the Europeans prefer the worst of their race to me), but I am a Jew.[6]

In 1933 he was forced to leave Germany, and as a kind of protest he formally rejoined the Jewish community which he had left as a young man. He wrote to Alban Berg about this ceremony, which took place in Paris:

[6] Arnold Schoenberg, *Letters*, ed. E. Stein (London, 1964), 88 (letter 63).

As you have doubtless realised, my return to the Jewish religion took place long ago and is indeed demonstrated in some of my published work . . . and in *Moses and Aaron*, of which you have known since 1928, but which dates from at least five years earlier; but especially in my drama [*The Biblical Way*], which was also conceived in 1922 or '23.[7]

Schoenberg does not bother to mention the unfinished oratorio *Jacob's Ladder*, which Berg knew all about; the point for us is that *Moses and Aaron* had two forerunners, and is the artistic culmination of Schoenberg's Jewishness but not at all of Jewish racialism: solely of the Judaic sense of God and of the impossibility of communication with the utterly transcendent. As the psalmist expressed it: 'Even the heavens are not clean in Thy sight.'[8]

In another letter of 1933, to the author Walter Eidlitz, who had sent him his book written also about Moses,[8] Schoenberg wrote:

The elements in this tremendous subject that I myself have placed in the foreground are: the idea of the inconceivable God, of the Chosen People, and of the leader of the people. My Aaron rather more resembles your Moses, although I have not portrayed him in so many aspects or shown him in terms of his human limitations, as you have. My Moses more resembles—of course only in outward aspects—Michelangelo's. He is not human at all.[9]

If Schoenberg says his hero is not human, then what is he? There is no clear answer. I think this contradiction in the character is why Moses is both remote and fascinating.

Wotan is a god, reaching out through the moral contradictions of omnipotence towards the richer world of humanity. Moses, despite Schoenberg's statement, is a man reaching out towards the purity of the inconceivably omnipotent Godhead. Both fail tragically. But a work of art, as in all true tragedy, in the demonstration of their struggle enhances us.

Of Schoenberg's three elements which he placed in the foreground—the inconceivable God, the chosen people, and the people's leader—the first is the most difficult. If God is inconceivable, it is virtually impossible to represent him. In fact, as we all know from the second commandment, representations of God in any form are Judaically taboo. Schoenberg solves this problem just as the Bible did, by allowing God to speak. In the opera this Voice is represented by a six-voice invisible choir. The chosen people are the easiest. They are represented in the traditional way by the visible operatic chorus. The people's leader is difficult again, but for a different reason, and this difficulty is the essence of the drama. For Moses and Aaron are both leaders of the people, but they have different views on what the nature and quality of this leadership is. This difference is set out for us in the first scene.

---

[7] Ibid. 184 (letter 156).

[8] Walter Eidlitz, *Der Berg in der Wüste* (The Mountain in the Wilderness) (Leipzig, 1923).

[9] Schoenberg, *Letters*, 172 (letter 151).

When the curtain rises, on Moses beside the burning bush, he is praying aloud to the

> Only God infinite, dwelling in every thing
> Whom none can see, no mind imagine: oh God![10]

This God, then, is Judaic, not Christian. There is here no Trinity of Three in One, no Virgin Mary, Mother of God's Son. This inconceivable God speaks to Moses out of the burning bush, calling to him to be a prophet. Moses wrestles with his God in his unwillingness, springing from his humility, to take up the burden of prophecy. He agrees only because God assigns Aaron, his brother, to be Moses' voice. A hierarchy is proposed. God speaks to Moses, who speaks to Aaron, who speaks to the people. This hierarchy contains all the metaphysical problems concerning communication between the incommensurable Transcendence and the finite creature. For the purpose of poetry, a parable; for operatic representation, a bush burns which is unconsumed, and a Voice speaks from the bush. But Moses, I am sure, was really like Blake, who could perceive the infinite despite all appearances, however common, including bushes which do not burn and are silent. And Aaron also half intuits Moses' thoughts by a kind of spiritual telepathy. All this is made clear by the Voice from the burning bush:

> Just as from this thornbush,
> sombre, till the light of
> truth shone, burning through,
> so you'll hear My voice speak to you,
> through anything.[11]

With this covenant agreed, Moses accepts his calling.

In the second scene of Act I, Moses and Aaron meet and argue. Already from what I have said, you can see why Schoenberg makes Moses use only speech-song, while Aaron alone sings. It is an operatic symbol of the Moses and Aaron part of the covenant; also, why their conversation goes on simultaneously. For this simultaneity is a musical symbol of the telepathy which unites their minds directly. But their argument is both about the problem of the covenant with God and about the problem of the chosen people: it is Aaron singing alone who eventually states this new matter unequivocally. Only an Almighty God could choose out so weak and downtrodden a people, to show His might and His miracles to them, to teach them to believe only in Him. But while Aaron delights in such miracles to convince the impious masses of God's power, Moses in his inner soul abhors them, so the leader of the people is fatally split in two.

Schoenberg now presents us with his third character: the chosen people. Their disputes and arguments fill out the third scene, which then leads directly to the fourth, in which the chosen people meet their leader, fatally

---

[10] Libretto, trans. David Rudkin (London, 1965), 11.   [11] Ibid. 12.

split as we have seen into two, and this leader brings them a covenant with a new God. This new God is, according to Moses, inconceivable, invisible, a God of pure spirit. This new God, according to Aaron, is omnipotent, even a God of wrath and vengeance, and will show forth His power before His chosen people by a miracle. This is just what the people want. And the new God in Aaron's view prevails. As Moses describes it, in prayer to the God of his vision:

> Almighty God, all my power has gone from me
> and my vision is helpless in Aaron's word.[12]

For within the hierarchy of the covenant, Moses' thought can only be expressed by Aaron's intuition of it.

The libretto's consequent stage direction makes the dramatic meaning clear. It reads: 'Aaron begins to dominate the scene.'[13] So, with Moses more and more in the background, Aaron snatches Moses' staff, much as Siegfried takes Wotan's spear, and himself performs the biblical miracles of a staff turned into a snake, Moses' hand made leprous, the Nile water turned into blood. This completes Act I. It makes a splendid procession of scenes, from the calling of Moses to the co-option of Aaron to the decision of the chosen people to flee from Pharaoh and take to the desert, with no more tangible goal than a promised land, far in the future.

Before Act II is a choral interlude. Once in the desert Aaron is even more in the foreground and Moses withdrawn even more into the background, until he once more reaches his own solitary vision of God. The chosen people sense this withdrawal as a loss, 'Where is Moses?', they whisper. 'Where is this Almighty God?'[14] So that when Act II begins, the stage is set for open revolt against a leader who had vanished for forty days already to the mountain-top, and against a God whose transcendence is too remote from human conditions to be communicated with. And this leads in the second scene to the idolatrous worship of the golden calf, an act of total and horrible impiety from Moses' point of view, of natural religious abandon from Aaron's. Certainly Schoenberg was not all on Moses' side. In the letter to Walter Eidlitz from which I have already quoted, he says:

what is interesting is that we come fairly close to each other in the introduction, formal presentation, and even in the evaluation of the scene with the golden calf. For me too this signifies a sacrifice made by the masses, trying to break loose from a 'soulless' belief. In the treatment of this scene, which actually represents the very core of my thought, I went pretty much to the limit, and this too is probably where my piece is most *operatic*.[15]

What Schoenberg means by 'most operatic' and 'pretty much to the limit' is operatic stage spectacle. Speaking entirely for myself, I find this stage spectacle old-fashioned, even though it deals with what Schoenberg calls the very

---

[12] Ibid. 19.   [13] Ibid.   [14] Ibid. 25.   [15] Schoenberg, *Letters*, 172.

core of his thought. I would have welcomed something more abstract, but I do not suppose this fantastic scene, the dances round the golden calf, strikes anyone else that way. The dances move from religious exaltation to bestiality, human sacrifice. Exhaustion follows satiety, then Moses returns from the mountain, with the tablets of the Ten Commandments. To the golden calf he cries: 'Away! Vile Image of impotence that would bind the Boundless on a bounded image.'[16] And so the calf vanishes. The chosen people cry:

> The gleam of the gold is no more.
> Now our god is out of sight again
> All our joy, all our rapture, all we'd hoped for
> . . . is gone
> All again is dark and lightless.
> We must run away from this Power.[17]

This final scene of the act is a tremendous dispute between the brothers. The quick-tongued Aaron wins the day. He argues that even the tables of the law are some kind of graven image. In despair, Moses breaks them. Aaron then shows Moses how through him, Aaron, the chosen people are led by the pillar of fire at night and the pillar of smoke by day. To Moses this is still idolatry. So, left alone, he sinks in despair to the ground:

> So I am defeated.
> That was all delusion, then, I
> Believed before,
> None can, none may give Him utterance.
> Oh Word, Word, Word, that I lack![18]

Schoenberg finished the music to the end of Act II, but he never wrote the music to Act III. The libretto which he did write has one long scene of further dispute between the brothers. Aaron is somehow in chains, and Moses in the ascendant. Nothing in the finished two earlier acts hints at how or why this reversal is obtained. Moses finally releases Aaron for him to live as he can, but Aaron at once falls dead. There is no biblical authority for this scene; Aaron in fact outlived Moses, and there is no dramatic inevitability. I am certain Schoenberg sensed this. I am even more certain that Covent Garden was right to produce the opera in two acts, and not to have the libretto of the third act either read or spoken over a repetition of some music in the first act. This second attempted solution, which was used in the Berlin performance which I saw, is particularly unpleasant and stupid. If *Moses and Aaron* is a torso, it is a torso of immense satisfaction and significance. Fate somehow intervened for it to be left to posterity in this form. It must be accepted as it is, and rejoiced in.

When we come to consider the music, there are problems: but not of the music itself; in my opinion, only, of the intellectual and emotional attitudes

---

[16] Libretto, 32.   [17] Ibid.   [18] Ibid. 35.

that bedevil us all from the outside. These attitudes—pros and cons—are so embedded that they will not be changed by anything I say here. So I am going to cut through the crust of this attitudinizing to the music itself. For the music is indeed intellectually and emotionally ordered, and this order can be tolerably discussed pragmatically without descent into mere grammatical parsing.

I have said that *Moses and Aaron* is in the tradition of neo-romanticism. Its forebears are the operas of Wagner, not Verdi. Essential to this tradition is the notion of the opera being musically through-composed; it is all in one piece: not so much by the proportion of the individual numbers, as all Verdi is, but by the endless variation of a limited set of procedures—particularly chosen for the opera in mind. These procedures can be of many kinds, but their signal character is to be germinatory.

The simplest example is that of the musical procedure which opens *Tristan and Isolde*, because we all now accept the extraordinary fact that the whole of that enormous opera proceeds somehow from the opening harmonic and melodic sequence. I put harmonic before melodic deliberately; without the underpinning harmony, the melodic movement is merely banal. I believe Schoenberg to be in this respect—that is, in regard to the contrast between melody as a self-generating totality of line and melody as conditioned by the underpinning harmony—entirely German. This is the tradition in which *Moses and Aaron* has been composed, and if you can appreciate it in Wagner, you will appreciate it in Schoenberg. *Moses and Aaron* begins, like *Tristan*, with just such a German harmonic procedure.

Just as the *Tristan* motto carries us immediately to the heart of the matter, the romantic love, so the *Moses and Aaron* motto carries us immediately into the heart of Schoenberg's matter: the representation, the symbolization, of pure spirit, of the single, eternal omnipresent, invisible, and inconceivable God. The sound that we hear is a six-voice choir. There are no words to this, true to the music of the angels, only a single vowel, 'O'.

The musical procedure is simply a set of four three-part chords which resolve or move in such a way that they form a kind of internal symmetry—intellectually and emotionally complete. They never return in this pristine purity, but they return in variations, endlessly and inexhaustibly. Their first appearance occupies three bars; at bar 12 comes a six-note theme which also returns in variations endlessly and inexhaustibly. As much as *Tristan* is derived from the initial bars, so the whole of *Moses and Aaron* can be shown to derive from these chords and this theme. This is of no intrinsic importance, but we should be conscious of it. I speak of it because this is to help place the opera for us in the unbroken history. I must dramatize this point all over again. Stravinsky's *The Rake's Progress* lies within the tradition of neo-classicism. It was preceded in the composer's *The Poetics of Music* by an acclamation to Bellini and the power of line.[19] *Moses and Aaron* lies within the tradition of

19 Stravinsky, *Poetics of Music*, lecture 2.

neo-romanticism, or, if you prefer, expressionism. *Moses and Aaron* therefore is musically extremely close-knit; it is a pattern of sound symbols and reaches back to many such tremendous patterns of sound symbols. The final disposition of these musical symbols, when Moses falls in his despair to the ground at the very end, has a mastery that is deeply, tragically moving, a frightening but glorious moment of the theatre.

Chapter 5

STRAVINSKY AND *LES NOCES*

Stravinsky's life span covered a quite unprecedented period of change and upheaval. So our first duty, always, is to try to imagine what it was like to grow up in Czarist Russia before 1900—or rather, because that is more important here, what it meant to be thirty years old, a composer in Paris, in 1912.

Secondly, when we come to consider a work like *Les Noces*, we must first remember that it is dedicated to Diaghilev: and it simply isn't possible to understand how *Les Noces* came to be written at all without some account of that extraordinary man: how he revolutionized ballet and the musical theatre, and how he set the young Stravinsky on a royal road.

Thirdly, Stravinsky wrote the words of *Les Noces* himself. They are based on his long study of Russian folk poetry. *Les Noces* is simply, in English, 'The Wedding'. In Germany it is known as 'Russian Peasant's Wedding', and the published score has a subtitle, *Russian Choreographic Scenes*. Stravinsky cannot be critically understood unless we attempt to evaluate the struggle between his innate Russian-ness, and his lifelong intellectual fascination for West European classical forms. After *Les Noces* the Russian element weakens.

Fourthly, *Lex Noces* is scored for four pianos and percussion, as an accompaniment to singing that is absolutely continuous. This unusual orchestration is anything but an accident. It sums up many of the most decisive musical interests and influences in Stravinsky's life at that time—and indeed later. There is a lot to be said about it.

These four aspects—Stravinsky in relation to his, and our, time; Stravinsky in relation to Diaghilev and the musical theatre; in relation to Russia and the countries of his exile; in relation to a certain kind of verbal and musical sound—these are essential preliminaries to any account of the scenario of *Les Noces*.

Stravinsky was born in 1882. From about that date to the end of the century the temper of all the arts in Europe became tinged with a kind of malaise, engendered by an irrational self-consciousness concerning the approaching new century. The term *fin de siècle* was coined to describe this malaise. The weaker characters gave way to pessimism and decadence. The stronger and more flamboyant were revolutionary and shocking. They set out quite deliberately to shock, because they could see no other way of shaking the complacent respectability of the bourgeois society whose values were still unquestioned, and whose art seemed, to the younger men, so tame and stuffy, so sentimental and idealistic—and never at all tough and realistic, or even experimental. There is no better example of the new shocking, vigorous realism than the plays of Bernard Shaw. Shocking in a different way, but equally typical of the time, was Oscar Wilde's *Salome*—which he wrote in French. Later, Shaw's musical hero—not his friend, Elgar, but his other hero, Richard Strauss—made *Salome* into a truly extreme and gruesome opera.

Now, seeing we live in a scientific age, it is natural enough that we take scientific innovations in our stride. All the vast mass of experiment and invention, which dates back to the turn of the century, and which has issued eventually in nuclear fission, was accepted and gloried in—until latterly, when a dreadful question mark seems to hang over all humanity. Already, however, innovation in a scientific discipline like psychotherapy caused a violent shock. Freud, by his birth date, is also a *fin de siècle* figure, and the shock of his discoveries is still reverberating round the world. But the uproar caused by the *fin de siècle* poets, painters, and musicians was far more immediate and violent, totally out of proportion to the small and restricted occasions of their display. The artists themselves did of course set out to shock; but the responsible ones certainly felt they were also renewing the language of their respective arts—as indeed they were. The art establishments and the public, however, were offended and embittered. The new art became at once the expression of, and the scapegoat for, the underlying and general malaise. Although the subsequent horrors and catastrophes of our own period have shaken bourgeois complacency, one would have thought, to its foundations, the art establishments and the public and the new state bureaucracies still prefer a mediocre, sentimental or idealistic art, and, if no longer so bitterly hostile to great figures like Picasso and Stravinsky, still commission the conventional and the second rate where they can.

Born into this *fin de siècle* period, Stravinsky, as a student in Moscow, caused no such scandal as, say, the young Kokoschka in Vienna. He belonged indeed to those circles in Russia that were interested in new music: but his sudden, wonderful maturity and development came only from his meeting with Diaghilev. Diaghilev was a unique and quite extraordinary figure. His enormous value, I think, lay in his power to stimulate the general condition of the arts as a whole. He first picked out Stravinsky through his music at a new music concert. He had hoped to become a composer himself. Failing in that, he organized a remarkable Moscow exhibition of new painting. But, naturally enough, he turned eventually and finally to the theatre, where many arts could be combined. And his outstanding and incredible artistic success with his first seasons of Russian ballet in Paris before the First World War, was due not only to the quality of the dancers he assembled, but equally to his inflexible determination to have the same quality in all the arts involved. Diaghilev never made the movements of the dancers an end in themselves. It was not dancing to music; but it was music danced. In the same way the scenery was not just painted wings and backcloths, it was an imagined stage space, wherein the dancers could move, and by which they were also conditioned within the scope of the collaborate enterprise. For what came out of all this was the clear necessity of early conference and collaboration between choreographer, designer, and musician. (This notion is not quite the same as Wagner's, though it might appear so, if for the simple reason that Wagner did not, or could not, collaborate with anybody.) It was the genius of Diaghlev to bring extraordinary, ever fresh individual talents into collaboration. The kind of work which resulted was summed up in an aphorism of Cocteau: 'a work of art must be inspired by all nine Muses.'

Stravinsky entered absolutely into this exciting Diaghilevian world. We must always remember that artists like Stravinsky can never be fettered in one art alone, even when the one art is their craft and profession. They inhabit naturally a whole world of sensibility that has as many intellectual and aesthetic forms as there are human tastes and characteristics. I find myself in immediate sympathy with this attitude. Judging by all that Stravinsky has written about his artistic life and his aesthetic views, I am certain I am nearer to him in presenting his work within the widest cultural context rather than just as important modern music. For despite the fact that *Les Noces* was not, in fact, a product of Diaghilevian collaboration (it was all Stravinsky's), yet it conforms to the general aesthetic attitude that Diaghilev stood for and that Cocteau expressed with his dictum that a work of art should be inspired by all nine Muses.

Now Diaghilev was too shrewd a showman not to see the publicity value of shocking the bourgeois art world and the conservative public. As I have pointed out, the general malaise at the time made it extremely easy to do so. We simply cannot imagine happening nowadays the sort of riot that accompanied the first performance of *Le Sacre du printemps*. Although Stravinsky's name (as a wild revolutionary, of course) became overnight a world name from this event, it is certain that Stravinsky did not intend it that way. He had merely, but unswervingly, gone the way he had to go in order to do his part in the collaboration that eventually produced the stage performance. But the general inclination of the period to be shocked and scandalized by artistic novelties could hardly be gainsaid. Whatever Stravinsky thought about himself, the public put him in the same boat as Picasso, or James Joyce. In his Harvard lectures of 1939, *Poétique Musicale*, Stravinsky denies that he was ever a revolutionary—even in *Le Sacre*. He says:

In truth, I should be hard pressed to cite for you a single fact in the history of art that might be qualified as revolutionary. Art is by essence constructive. Revolution implies a disruption of equilibrium. To speak of revolution is to speak of a temporary chaos.

Now art is the contrary of chaos. It never gives itself up to chaos without immediately finding its living works, its very existence, threatened.[1]

In order to understand how Stravinsky, the composer of *Le Sacre du printemps*, can yet present himself, as he tries to do, as a traditionalist, we must bear in mind that he, like the rest of us in this time, is a double man. His great quality lies in the strength of passion of the two sides of his nature. He had on the one hand the gift of immediately arresting and dynamic invention—on the other he had an equally extreme intellectual passion for order. When he writes about aesthetics, he tends to write solely from the intellectual, ordering side of his nature. Yet in the Harvard lectures he does say that 'we shall always find at the origin of invention an irrational element on which the spirit of submission has no hold and that escapes all constraint'.[2] Nevertheless, he concludes by saying: 'what is important for the lucid ordering of the work—for its crystallization—is that all the Dionysian elements which set the imagination of the artist in motion and make the life-sap rise must be properly subjugated before they intoxicate us, and must finally be made to submit to the law: Apollo demands it.'[3]

In the series of theatrical works *Petrushka*, *Le Sacre du printemps*, and *Les Noces*, Stravinsky's Dionysian tendencies were at their apogee. After *Lex Noces* Stravinsky made an apparently final and quite voluntary sacrifice to Apollo. The Dionysian elements never return in the same force. Instead we get the fullest possible development of Stravinsky's passion for classical order, clarity of texture, and precision of technique. That is why *Les Noces* is both a summation and a turning-point.

After the production of *Le Sacre du printemps* in 1913, Stravinsky settled with his family in Switzerland. In June 1914 he made his first visit to England, in order to attend performances of *Le Rossignol*.[4] In London he had the first embryonic conception of the work which nine years later would be completed as *Les Noces*. He imagined, so he writes in *Chronicle of My Life*, 'a grand divertissement, or rather a cantata, depicting peasant nuptials'.[5] After this visit to London he made a short trip to Russia—partly in order to secure material for the new composition. To quote from Eric Walter White's *Stravinsky*:

At Kiev he picked up a copy of the volume in Peter Kirjeievsky's *Collection of Popular Poems* devoted to marriage songs; and he arranged for various books, including Sukharov's *Collection* and Dal's *Dictionary of Russian Phrases*, to be sent to him from his father's library. A fortnight after his return to Switzerland via Warsaw, Berlin and Basle, war broke out. Thenceforward, he and his family were to live in exile, completely cut off from their native country.[6]

---

[1] Stravinsky, *Poetics of Music*, 12–13.   [2] Ibid., ch. 4.   [3] Ibid.

[4] Given at the Drury Lane Theatre, with Emile Cooper conducting, in June 1914.

[5] Igor Stravinsky, *Chroniques de ma vie* (Paris, 1935). Trans. as *Chronicle of My Life* (London, 1936), 90.

[6] Eric Walter White, *Stravinsky: A Critical Survey* (London, 1947), 54.

It is ironical that, having mentioned exile, I now discuss Stravinsky's Russian-ness. It is usual to equate the Dionysian element in Stravinsky's early music with his Russian birth, and the Apollonian element of his later music with Western influences. In a rough and tumble way this is probably correct. The point I want to make is that Stravinsky had a natural sympathy for both the religious mysticism of the Russian soul and the sceptical pessimism. In *Petrushka* the pessimism is at its strongest. *Le Sacre du printemps*, on the other hand, is a drama of renewal. But it is a renewal only at the cost of sacrificing a virgin girl. Life is renewed only by death. Yet life is renewed—if only by an ecstatic religious rite. *Les Noces* is also a drama of renewal, through marriage and the begetting of children; but where *Le Sacre du printemps* is deadly serious, *Les Noces* is fundamentally comic (in the high sense), though the same ingredients of religious feeling and sceptical pessimism are in the theatrical mixture. The more primitive pagan men and women of *Le Sacre* have changed, in *Les Noces*, to hard-headed, warm-hearted, naïvely religious Russian peasants. And though in a sense peasants are the same the world over, these peasants are, I should have thought, unmistakably Russian. He says:

According to my idea, the spectacle should have been a divertissement, and that is what I want to call it. It was not my intention to reproduce the ritual of peasant weddings; and I paid little heed to ethnographic considerations. My idea was to compose a sort of scenic ceremony, using as I liked those ritualistic elements so abundantly provided by village customs which had been established for centuries in the celebration of Russian marriages. I took my inspiration from those customs, but reserved to myself the right to use them with absolute freedom.[7]

This was written to explain his disagreements with Diaghilev over the eventual choreography to the first performance in 1923. I think Stravinsky had to pay the price that time for not having had earlier conference and consultation with the choreographer. The real point is, I think, that already in *Les Noces* we have that scaling down of orchestral apparatus, which is so colossal in *Le Sacre*, and which he seemed to need then to express the violence of the ritualistic dynamism, towards the tiny scale of *L'Histoire du soldat*, the Wind Octet, and later works. It was all part of the sacrifice to Apollo. And what was sacrificed (and perhaps had to be sacrificed because of exile) was inspiration from Russian customs and the divisions of the Russian soul. One should think, for a moment, of the nostalgia of another and contemporary Russian composer, Rachmaninov. Stravinsky can give expression to a fundamental pessimism, but not to nostalgia. This sceptical pessimism (and the religious element) is still there in a later stage work like *The Rake's Progress*, quite translated from Russian peasants into English eighteenth-century dandyism. But I doubt if the essentials have really changed.

During the First World War years Stravinsky lived in Switzerland and worked slowly on the vocal–piano score of *Les Noces*, along with some lesser

---

[7] Stravinsky, *Chronicle of My Life*, 174–5.

works. He became great friends with the Swiss writer Ramuz. Ramuz has described in his *Souvenirs sur Igor Stravinsky* what an intriguing figure Stravinsky was to the village women of Morges, during the composition of *Les Noces*. How the women sat knitting in the little square on to which Stravinsky's upper apartment window looked, and how, when a particularly violent sound of the piano issued from the work room in the ground floor they would look up and say: 'C'est le Monsieur Russe.'[8]

Ramuz agreed to do the translations of Stravinsky's Russian texts into French. He gives a fascinating account of how they tackled the problem. Stravinsky explained first of all that his verbal accents in Russian sometimes did and sometimes did not coincide with the musical accents, because he felt that there would be monotony if either coincidence or non-coincidence were made a rule. But, in general the accents do in fact coincide; and Stravinsky demanded from Ramuz that the French text had as exact a correspondence. Stravinsky gave Ramuz a word-for-word translation of the Russian and made him write down into a notebook the number of syllables in each word, the verbal accents, and then a metrical scheme of each voice part. Ramuz tells how he went home each evening on the last train his head full of 3/8s and 5/8s and every kind of 4 × 8. Because *Les Noces* has as one of its main musical features the uninterrupted flow of additive rhythm—that is, a never ending series of longs and shorts, 2/8 or 3/8 (counted 1, 2 or 1, 2, 3) combined into various larger groups, but always variable and free. During the morning Ramuz found, if he could, the best French text that would do what the composer demanded, and in the evening, in Stravinsky's home, it went on again. Slowly enough the whole work was translated. When I quote the words to *Les Noces*, I shall use Ramuz's text, because it is in essentials also Stravinsky's.

Stravinsky sometimes repeats monosyllabic words arbitrarily to fit the music—or even syllables within a word. Thus the whole work opens with a sentence about combing Nastasia's hair, which runs grammatically: 'Ma tresse à moi, elle l'avait peignée avec un peigne d'argent.' The line of the music has to give an effect of bells—marriage bells presumably—and to fit the music the sentence actually runs:

> Tresse, Tresse, ma tresse à moi, ma tresse à moi,
> Tresse, elle l'avait peignée etc.

Now although the music to *Les Noces* was finished by 1918, Stravinsky could not find the right orchestration. He began first of all with a few pages of scoring for the kind of orchestra one might have expected from the composer of *Le Sacre*. It needed perhaps 150 players, and was therefore abandoned. Besides, Stravinsky began to see that his continuously singing voices were the real instrumentalists, so to speak; that they did what in *Le Sacre* the strings and winds did. So he decided to accompany the voices by only instruments of percussion. And he naturally thought of those that were most novel to him at the

[8] C. F. Ramuz, *Souvenirs sur Igor Stravinsky* (Lausanne, 1929), *76*.

time. The first of these was the mechanical piano, the pianola. He was fascinated by this novelty of that time, and so his new scoring began with an electrically driven pianola.

Next, he was exceedingly taken with the Hungarian gypsy instrument, the cimbalom: and partly because, in playing it, the strings are struck by the player, with his two mallets, openly, for all to see. He was captivated by the virtuosity of the Hungarian player Aladar Rácz, who was in Switzerland at that time. (I myself had the good fortune to hear Rácz as an older man play privately at Budapest, in 1948. It was extremely exciting.) Anyhow, Stravinsky had managed to acquire a cimbalom, and had even taught himself to play it. So the new scoring had two cimbaloms—to which, with the pianola, he added a harmonium and normal percussion. He scored two tableaux in this second version, before he decided that the problem of synchronizing the electronic pianola with the rest was insoluble. Five years later he found what he really wanted. He chose an orchestra of four (non-mechanical) pianos, xylophone, timpani, two crotales, and a bell (which are all instruments of percussion with a definite pitch), and added to that two side-drums (with and without snares), two larger drums (with and without snares), tambourine, bass drum, and triangle. (These instruments have of course no definite pitch.)

Stravinsky has always liked the piano. He likes its percussive possibilities and the feel of his own hands playing. I'd even say that Stravinsky's music is often curiously tactile. He composes at the piano partly because he believes the fingers themselves can invent sometimes directly from some inner source. This is similar to some kinds of modern painting. But the chief thing about the final orchestration to *Les Noces* is the great step forward in clarity, mechanical precision, and hardness. The hardness is very hard indeed, but perfectly suits the unwavering linear counterpoint of the voices. There the lines are in themselves relatively simple and occasionally even soft, but they are made to overlap in ways that produce violent clashes. And these clashes the percussive orchestra deliberately makes absolutely certain and unmistakable.

Then the never ending additive rhythms have in themselves something quite mechanical. And again the orchestration aids and abets this mechanical effect, until it becomes in fact the chief effect. So that although *Les Noces* took Stravinsky longer to finish than any other piece of comparable length, it has an extraordinary unity. The notion of unity is one of the key notions in Stravinskian aesthetics.

The scenario of *Les Noces*, and the musical sequences that derive from the scenario, are basically very simple. There are four tableaux. In the first we see the bride being got ready by the act of combing her hair. In the second it is the bridegroom's hair that is being brushed. In the third the bride leaves her parents' house for that of the bridegroom. In the fourth the whole village partakes of a feast, and the bride and bridegroom are then put to bed, and the four parents settle down to wait outside the bedroom door.

Each tableau is stuffed out to the requisite length by small details of possible action and by the endless repetition of small sections of text. Thus the first tableau, at the bride's house, begins immediately with the combing of the hair. There is a kind of dialogue set up between the bride's complaints about the combing and her girl-friends' comments. Thus the bride says: 'Pauvre, pauvre d'moi, encore une fois!', and the other girls reply in chorus: 'Console toi, console toi, petit oiseau.' (It needs to be realized that the chorus who sing are not the dancers who are on stage. The singers are not always even of the same sex as the appropriate stage figures, and they have to be imagined in the orchestral pit.) The theme of the tress of hair goes on a longish time and as a kind of rondo.

Then the bride's parents begin to sing of the nightingale in the bride-groom's garden, how it sings really for the bride:

> C'est pour toi Nastasie Timofeevna,
> C'est pour toi qu'il chante, qu'il chantera.

Finally we come to the religious note, the simple request to the Mother of God to come into the cottage and help arrange the hair:

> Daigne, daigne très aimable mère
> Entrer dans notre chaumière,

always with the burden of the girls' chorus, which comes over and over again.

In the second tableau all is male, except for the bridegroom's mother. The music quite suddenly switches to the men's voices—and yet by using the same words and the same sentiments, Stravinsky underlines the unity in multiplicity. For the groom's men friends ask the Mother of God to *his* cottage to help with his hair.

> Daigne aimable mère, daigne entrer dans la chaumière,
> daigne nous aider les boucles à defaire, les boucles du marié.

It is very masculine and compelling.

In the men's tableau, Stravinsky gets an effect of mundane simplicity by embedding in the ever running music bits of text that are quite concrete—for example, where to buy the hair oil for the groom.

> Vite, amis, jetons nous dans les trois marchés de la ville;
> Et là-bas, là-bas une bouteille d'huile on aura.

and always, as with the girls', the men's chorus repeats afterwards their motto theme.

The parents of the groom now sing in turn of how their son's hair, and his person, belong now to the bride. The section begins quite gently, on a kind of variation of the bride's opening bell theme. We eventually reach perhaps the highest point of the whole work: the family blessing. First the parents are asked to bless:

> Et vous père et mère bénissez votre enfant.

then all outcasts and good-for-nothings:

> Rodeurs de route, traineurs de pieds et vous tous les pas grand chose,
>   frères, arrivez,
> Bénissez tous le jeune prince qui va se marier.

Then God himself and the saints.

> Seigneur Dieu, bénis nous tous du plus grand au plus petit

and

> Viens avec nous! Saint Luc également.

—altogether a wonderful build-up of ritual.

In the third tableau we return to the bride, and to the lamentation of the parents at losing their daughter. Stravinsky uses a bit of text from a fairy story: the princess happy in the parental palace.

> Comme on voit dedans le ciel la blanche lune et le soleil
> Ainsi vivait dans le palais auprès de son vieux père la princesse
> Et elle était heureuse près de son père et de sa mère.

But the reality is harder to bear; for the princess must go away.

> Bénis moi, mon père, je m'en vais et plus jamais je ne reviendrai.

And like the first two tableaux, the third also ends with a prayer—to the apostles and to Christ, to keep the wedding pair united. The music carries the voices away as the bride and her friends leave the parental house for ever.

In the fourth and last tableau, the sexes and the two choruses are joined. It is to be thought of, according to Ramuz, as a room with a huge round table, where the guests eat and drink, and through doors at the back one can see the marriage-bed. The jollification begins by likening the couple to two flowers:

> La deux fleurs sur la branche, une rouge une blanche.

But words are often now given over to just cries. There is a delightful section about a goose:

> Qui est arrivée, arrivée? L'oie est arrivée, arrivée?

The bride is now given to the groom with suitable advice. This section is very charming. He must sow linseed; she must wash his shirts and so on and so forth.

In all the continuous percussive sound Stravinsky must have felt the need for some lyricism. The section about the nightingale in tableau one is matched by the more extended section here about the swan and the sea. It begins like another fairy story:

> J'étais loin sur la mer, j'étais loin sur la mer immense.

The orchestration is correspondingly more gentle and provides some relief.

Now a married couple are chosen to go in and warm the bed. This little section should remind us that, despite the tones of resignation and even melancholy, the whole work is really gay and comic. The text is all broken up:

> J'y va. Prends moi. Le lit est étroit. On s'arrangera.

And so on: it is very amusing.

So we come to the last section, where the bride and bridegroom are led in to bed. The doors are closed on them; and the parents settle down with their backs to the bedroom door, and the guests facing them. The bridegroom is heard singing from within of his love. The work ends in a kind of timeless magic.

By the time *Les Noces* was all scored, Stravinsky had become friends again with Diaghilev after a temporary estrangement. Diaghilev confided the choreography of *Les Noces* to Nijinsky's sister, Nijinska. It was first performed in Paris in June 1923, with Ansermet conducting. Stravinsky describes the staging thus: 'The framework of the decor was composed exclusively of back-cloths, with just a few details of a Russian peasant cottage interior . . . the costume [also were] very ingeniously simplified and made uniform.[9]

Unfortunately, when the ballet went to London a month later, *Les Noces* was howled down by the English critics.[10] More shame to them: for the music has outlived them.

---

[9] Stravinsky, *Chronicle of My Life*, 176.   [10] See White, *Stravinsky*, 75–6.

Chapter 6

PURCELL

REDISCOVERY

Holst and Vaughan Williams, and other composers of their generation, were very drawn towards folk-song and the music of the Elizabethans. But it was my generation, including, of course, Britten, that found a new source of inspiration and a fresh example in Purcell.

We were not taught Purcell in the Conservatoire: we discovered him independently for ourselves. When I went to study at the Royal College of Music in London in the early Twenties, Purcell's music was much less played than it is these days. It seems to me incomprehensible now that his work was not even recommended in composition lessons as a basic study for the setting of English. I may have been unlucky, but I think the omission was general. However, when I was 19, I began to conduct small amateur choirs with the object of studying in action, as it were, the English madrigal school—a repertory equally neglected in my Royal College training. Thus, when much later I found out about Purcell, I already had a good ear for the setting of English by his predecessors. Byrd, Tallis, Gibbons, Dowland, were no longer names in a history book, but composers of living music. Through their works, these composers were as alive to me as their great contemporaries Shakespeare, Marlowe, Spenser, and Sidney.

I think it is fairly true to say that the English worship of Handel, and later of Mendelssohn, effectively nullified any possible influence of Purcell. His scores were unavailable, lost from the public gaze, and his music almost unperformed. The Elizabethan composers were also unheard, just as English folk-song was unrecorded. But at the turn of the century, Elizabethan madrigals and Tudor church music were rediscovered and printed, and unmatched riches of folk-song collected, and the Purcell Society itself had already been founded, for the publication of that composer's works in *Urtext* editions.

The personal discovery of Purcell which Britten and I made later led us not only to initiate performances of as much music as possible, but also to issue performing editions through our respective publishers. Eventually, too, we produced recordings of Purcell's music. Altogether, these have demonstrated that Purcell is a European voice, a master in his own unique right.

PURCELL, GIBBONS, AND THE VERSE ANTHEM

Henry Purcell was born in 1659, became organist of Westminster Abbey in 1679, and died in 1695. These dates matter, because they show that Purcell's professional life coincided with the end of the Puritan era, during which church music had been severely curtailed, and the first flowering of the Restoration period, when music, especially for the theatre, received anew the all-decisive royal patronage.

Through his appointment as organist at Westminster Abbey, Purcell became heir, in the most practical and literal sense, to the great, centuries-old tradition of English church music. This music had itself undergone a change consequent upon the Reformation of the Church in the sixteenth century. Two rules of the reformed church were decisive: (1) that everything must be sung in English, not Latin (except in certain cathedrals and college chapels, where Latin was understood); (2) that for greater clarity of the words, the English language should be set always one syllable to a note.

The English Tudor and Caroline composers, right up to the death of Elizabeth I and after, wrestled with the musical problems consequent on these rules. They succeeded brilliantly: both in composing music sensitive to all the nuances of the English vernacular and in simplifying the earlier, florid a cappella Latin style into something quite new and different. For this purpose, they invented the English verse anthem, wherein the cathedral choir was broken down into solos and solo ensembles to contrast with the full choir, and accompanied by consorts of stringed instruments, as well as the organ playing from a figured bass.

One might call the verse anthem the English church cantata. This was the state of English church music when Orlando Gibbons died in 1625 (and I have deliberately omitted the related developments in chamber music of the period—madrigals, string fantasies, keyboard music, etc.).

At this point in English history, politics intervened sharply in public music, in that the successful Cromwellian party, in their fanatical asceticism, declared illegal the public performance of any church music whatsoever. But when the Stuart court returned from exile in 1660, not only was church music restored, but also the pre-Cromwellian court masques and theatrical pieces, which now required even more elaborate music, and music which could only be successfully composed at that time on Italian models. These models reached England and Purcell, coming more exactly from France and Lully. They were irresistible. I myself realized this when I had to conduct a performance of *Dido and Aeneas* in Italian for Swiss Radio. Purcell sung in English sounds chracteristically English; but in Italian it sounds just as natural.

To show both the continuing tradition in church music and the seemingly complete change of temper between Gibbons and Purcell, I'd like to compare two of their verse anthems: Gibbons's anthem to words from Psalm 30, 'Sing unto the Lord', and Purcell's 'My beloved spake', whose words come from the Song of Solomon. Admittedly, by choosing these particular anthems, I've weighted the scales a bit in favour of the difference in temper: for the one is serious, the other gay. It could easily have been the other way round. Nevertheless, in performance, I couldn't, even if I wanted to, make the Purcell sound Elizabethan or the Gibbons Restoration. For they belong to different worlds.

In any case, there are similarities of texture within these anthems that provide some kind of continuity. In each, the verse ensemble (the solo voices chosen to sing the declamatory portion of the anthem) is a quartet: in Gibbons, two countertenors and two basses; in Purcell, one countertenor, one tenor, and two basses. Each has a string accompaniment. But there the resemblance ends. Gibbons treats his string parts, when accompanying the verse soloists, just as if they were themselves voices, in imitative polyphony with the solo singers. Purcell uses his strings only for instrumental ritornelli, and accompanies his verse solos with a basso continuo part for organ, thus enabling these verse soloists and string parts to coalesce into a successful ensemble.

Gibbons divides his verse and full sections more consistently than Purcell, because he has a full choral commentary, so to speak, to each verse section. But Purcell treats his verse ensemble as *the* protagonist of the whole piece and only very occasionally resorts to the full choir for emphasis. Purcell also uses his verse ensemble with absolute freedom. Gibbons, here, is almost mathematical: for the first verse is for two basses, the second for two countertenors, the third for one countertenor and one bass.

In the matter of word-setting they are similar and dissimilar. With both composers we feel that the English words have themselves generated the music to which they are sung. But Gibbons conforms to the rules of the early Anglican reformed church, and sets exactly one syllable to a note. By Purcell's time the rule had been allowed to lapse again, as the taste was then for virtuosity in singing, rather than attention to the biblical meaning. So his setting is more florid.

The verse anthem, as left by Gibbons, is still really within the older polyphonic tradition. The distinctive musical development that occurred between the time of Gibbons and Purcell was the emergence of the continuo accompaniment to a solo voice. In the case of the verse anthem, this meant that the strings could be removed from their role of accompanying the verse solos, for these solos would be clearer, more obviously in contrast with the full choir, if accompanied only by keyboard. And then, too, once the strings *had* been thus separated from the verse solos, they were free to be used as a distinct musical texture of their own—to play a prelude and ritornelli.

In 'My beloved spake', Purcell writes a short string prelude, then lets the four voices begin the first verse. This is commented on, not by the full choir, as in Gibbons, but by the strings. It is the same for the second verse, and the full choir first enters at the end of the third verse, and then just for a single phrase; the strings take over the same music, and the solo voices echo it, so leading to the fourth verse. I don't intend to describe the rest in detail, because all I want is to point out how much more flexible in form and techniques the verse anthem had become by Purcell's time, and especially in his hands.

PURCELL AND THE ENGLISH LANGUAGE

In Gibbon's time, the task before the church composers of making a note-for-note syllabic setting of the English liturgy was still a conscious and vital one. Gibbons seems to have set the seal upon it. Purcell inherited a technique that Byrd, Dowland, and Gibbons had all worked out, and he marries his music to the English language with no further reference to the long tradition of setting Latin. Byrd sometimes set out an English translation to music which he had previously composed to Latin texts. Gibbons, to my ear, at least, is already purely English. But Purcell's spoken English was, of course quite different from Gibbons's. Really, to explore this fascinating subject fully, we probably need to compare Marlowe, say, with Dryden, at the same time as we compare Weelkes or Dowland with Purcell. Even then, we have to remember that the earlier version of the English Bible, which of course persisted and was set by both Gibbons and Purcell, was already old-fashioned to Ben Jonson.

We can experience the change of tone in a passage from Purcell's 'My beloved spake' such as 'flowers appear upon the earth and the time of the singing of birds is come'. The charming musical phrase to the word 'singing' is characteristically Purcell, and it has resonances impossible to find in Gibbons, or in any of the music of his time.

Only Dowland, in my opinion, rivals Purcell in the setting of English. Both had a fine ear for English poetry. Let us consider Purcell's song 'Music for a while'. The first word Purcell sets is 'Music'. Like thousands of English words this is a trochee—long/short. Purcell sets it as such. In 4/4 time, the syllable mu- is a dotted crotchet, the -sic a quaver. Even when he lengthens the mu- to a minim, he ties it over to another quaver, making it longer still, so that the -sic can fill the other side of the short beat.

Heaps of English words are like 'music'. Let us take another—'shepherd': one that is important to Purcell's 'Nymphs and Shepherds'. If one compares Purcell's setting of the word 'shepherd', here, with Handel's, in 'He shall feed his flock' (from *Messiah*), what do we find? At the end of Handel's lovely phrase, the strong syllable of 'shepherd', the shep- is on the weaker bit of the bar, and the weak syllable -erd is on the strong final close. I don't think it's often realized just how much that sort of Handelian usage has harmed our proper sense of the language. We take it for granted because we have heard it from our cradles. I must admit that my own ear, so used now to Dowland and Purcell, receives a jolt, which makes me remember that Handel was an Englishman by adoption, not by birth and tradition. Now Purcell never does the like. However long he may vocalize on the strong vowel of the trochee, he never ends a weak vowel on the strong musical beat, but lets the weak vowel always fall the other side. Listen, for instance, to the word 'wond'ring' in 'Music for a while'. What Purcell really does is to end the musical phrase, however long, always in such a way that the word can be spoken at the very end in this natural rhythm.

Returning for a moment to the word 'music', we can observe that it is partly the need to have the fall from strong to weak that brought about the tradition of the tiny crescendo that gives a nuance to long whole notes, if set to the long syllable of the trochee. For by this means a high pressure can be made with the voice at the point where the short syllable is ready to fall. This tiny nuance helps, in English especially, to soften the impact of the weak syllable if it has hard consonants in it—like the -sic of 'music'.

In Purcell, we have to differentiate carefully in performance the expressive purposes behind his word-settings. With the two 'Hails' at the start of the *St Cecilia's Day Ode* of 1692, for instance, the first is short—a call to the audience—but the second is tied over on to the strong beat, and, to my mind, these demand a different attack. The first should be sung short and strong: and the second begins softer, with the tone growing onto the strong beat, from which can fall the rest of the vocal phrase, 'bright Cecilia'.

Purcell by no means omitted the more naïve forms of word-painting that we find in the vocal music of the Elizabethans, but generally he is after more subtle effects. In the opening chorus of the same ode, the poem continues, after the opening words, with 'fill every heart with love of thee and thy celestial art'. The word which caught Purcell's imagination in this way was 'celestial'. At first he treats it only lightly. But then it is carried up by the voices into the celestial air, and the higher they rise, the softer they should be. In performance, Purcell's vocal music only comes alive when we observe the purpose underlying the treatment of the words. In 'Nymphs and Shepherds', Purcell clearly sets the word 'laughs' to get the effect of laughing, and to sing it in a neutral, flat, legato—as often happens—negates its whole point. I think it's important that performing editions (especially those aimed at amateurs) should draw attention to such matters, for it is technically just as important as the bowing marks in an edition of string music.

Incidentally, I'm not sure whether Purcell was conscious always of which vowels he used for long vocalizations. In the *St Cecilia's Day Ode* (1692), a great proportion of vocalizations are of the vowel *u*—in words like 'flew', 'true', and *u* in 'music', and so on. As far as I can remember, there are relatively fewer vocalizations on the open *a*—that in the word 'charms', which, judging by the way he sets it, Purcell thought to be important.

PURCELL'S THEATRE MUSIC AND THE PURCELL INHERITANCE

Because of the nature of the Elizabethan theatre and the verse drama which needed very little music, composers like Byrd, Tallis, Gibbons, and Dowland wrote nothing directly for the stage; they wrote for the country house and the church. But already, with the death of Shakespeare, and as Ben Jonson was left supreme, the masque began to supplant the drama; and the masque needed a lot of music. This development was cut short by the Puritan Commonwealth, but taken up again and transformed by the Restoration, with demands for incidental music of all kinds, both vocal and instrumental. Purcell came to maturity in the heyday of this theatre, and had all the gifts and techniques it required. He could pour out overtures, dances, arias, *scenae*, choruses, at need—and his works are the one great compendium of inciden-tal music for the English theatre. Handel became his only rival in this, but he wrote to Italian words for the London season of Italian opera. And after Handel there is no one until our own time, unless one counts Sullivan.

I have talked of incidental music for the theatre in Purcell's case, rather than of opera, because this is the truth of the matter. Opera is an aesthetic unity of drama and music, in which the music both adds to and eats up the drama. Purcell was asked to provide this special *operatic* unity of music and drama on only one occasion—*Dido and Aeneas*. Apart from that he wrote for theatrical entertainments in which the *spoken* word was more important—what we would call nowadays a musical—like *My Fair Lady*. Nevertheless, the music contained all sorts of things that were to be found, if at all, only in embryo in Elizabethan madrigals or lute airs.

Let us take the sense of situation in drama, or to be exact, the expression in music of the sense of a situation. The madrigal cannot provide this, but a song can, and in some of Dowland's monologues we are made aware that the singer is giving a personal expression of an almost dramatic situation. This is already an operatic aria in embryo—of the kind where a character gives a personal reaction to some set of circumstances, while the action is, so to speak, held in suspense. The distinction between the expression of emotion, say grief at love betrayed, in a song and in an aria is that one is usually more personal and intimate, while the other is more grandiose and public. This is how Dido expresses her emotions at Aeneas's betrayal in the great lament at the end of the opera. There are many other arias of situation in Purcell's incidental music to entertainments like *The Fairy Queen*. But Dido's lament is such a perfect example that I think it the best piece for me to discuss further.

First of all the situation is quite clear—Aeneas and Dido have been lovers, but Aeneas is called away to found Rome, and not all his eloquence or appeal to divine commands can persuade Dido that she has not been betrayed. After he has gone, Dido decides to end her life. In this desperate situation she sings

the rightly famed lament. It begins 'When I am laid in earth', and those opening words we usually catch. After that we are not always sure of every word
sung, but it is of no tremendous consequence. Firstly, because the situation,
which we appreciate from the drama, is really being expressed in the music:
the music is eating up the words. And secondly, because Purcell, in the second half of the aria, places the words 'remember me' in such a vivid light that
we hear them as though they summed up everything; as indeed they do. This
placing of the key words is something quite out of the range of the
Elizabethans. What his only in embryo in Dowland is now a full-formed creation: an operatic air which is a masterpiece.

Situations occur not only in opera but in oratorios, if they are of the dramatic kind. I like to think I was influenced by Purcellian examples when I
needed to express an aria from some of the relatively simple situations of *A
Child of Our Time*. I am thinking particularly of the air for tenor to a tango-like
bass—an air which had to express the frustrations of the ordinary man temporarily at odds with life. The things that influence one, in a composition of
this kind, are never simple, but always complex. The sense of our time—that
is, in this case, of the period between the world wars—lies musically in the
tango, not in any Purcellian turn of phrase. Purcellian is the setting of the
scene by a short orchestral introduction, and the manner of repeating a simple, easily understood phrase. Such a phrase is that to the first words the tenor
sings—'I have no money for my bread'.

Returning to Dido's lament. As most of us know, this aria is constructed
over a ground bass many times repeated. I use the word 'constructed' deliberately, because the ground bass is a constructional device. The repetitions of
the ground lay out the ground-plan of the piece. To a certain extent Purcell
must always have known how many repetitions of the bass there would be
before he composed the rest of the music that was to go over the top of it.
These constructional devices are one of the mysteries of composition. They
are apparently just mathematical (like the recent preoccupation with serial
devices), yet in the hands of a truly creative composer, like Purcell, they disappear into the *music*, so that we are completely unaware of them. In a case
like Dido's lament the ground bass itself is immensely expressive in its own
right—as are most Bach fugue subjects. We *are* aware, if only subconsciously,
of this wealth of expression at the base of Dido's singing. But other ground
basses are much less important in themselves—as might be a more routine
fugue subject. The accent is then laid directly on the music *above*. With Purcell
the bass is often immediately forgotten in the wealth of melody he composes
above it.

I don't think any of the English composers of my generation who have
studied or much performed Purcell's music can fail to have been influenced
by the constructional power of Purcell's basses. In the first of the ritual dances
in my opera *The Midsummer Marriage*, which represent hunting or chasing in
various symbolic forms, I use a long and in itself expressive bass to exemplify

the hound that pursues. This bass is first given out on the orchestral cellos and basses with drums and harp. When the bass is to be repeated I have, by rhythmical shortenings, compressed it, so that the tension will be slightly increased. And in a second repetition I compressed it still more. The bass is therefore being used constructionally to repeat the musical motions of the chase and at the same time to force them to be smaller or nearer. Under the direct influence of Purcell (though in quite another style from his) even an expressive bass, like this one, can yet disappear in the general music of what is played *above* it: in this case, music for flute and horn, reinforced later with some brass to accompany the dance movements of the running hare, which is hunted. The constructional device is the ground bass; but the expressive quality lies in the whole music that proliferates above it.

There is a feature of Purcell's style of a more special kind worth mentioning. It is his ability to create intensity, particularly in poignant moments, by a sort of harmonic polyphony. I want to speak of it because I can't think of any other feature of Purcell's style which has meant so much to me personally. This poignancy is in Dido's lament, especially in the last ritornello after Dido has ceased to sing. But I think an example from the early string fantasies is better, because it is nearer the source. Much of this intensity and poignancy is to be found in the madrigals of Weelkes and in other Elizabethan music. Purcell did not invent here—he took over a tradition and developed it. The technical means to produce this intense polyphony are chiefly the hanging on to notes in one part so that they make a momentary dissonance with another part before they resolve themselves; and the placing of harmonically unexpected notes at the moments of resolution, so that the music is never quite resolved and still. (It is a method of composing which Wagner used to tremendous effect in *Tristan*.) For instance, the opening of Purcell's four-part Fantasy for Strings No. 4 shows a polyphony developed out of two contrary-moving themes, heard at once together on viola and cello. It is not so intense and poignant as the end of Dido's lament, but it shows the method in great purity.

Exactly this feature of Purcell's style, developed as it was out of the Elizabethans, has become a feature in its turn of my own musical language: a good example occurs in the slow movement of the String Quartet No. 2, a movement which is also a fugue. Whatever other differences of style there are, the features of intensity created in the ways I spoke of in relation to Purcell is virtually the same.

Towards the end of his life Purcell became more and more engrossed in his work for the theatre, for civic occasions like the St Cecilia's Day festivals, and for the court—that is, welcome odes to the Royal family, and such like. Not that all this theatrical and civic music of Purcell is full of choruses; it is not. And let's not forget that Purcell's choruses are not Handelian choruses. There has been a tendency, in England at any rate, to consider Purcell as a sort of junior Handel. This has passed away. Their approach to writing choruses is quite different. Handel's choruses are usually constructed as great vocal fugues. Purcell's choruses are usually enlarged, elaborated madrigals. The fugal chorus is from beginning to end one music, one verse; such as 'He trusted in God that He would deliver him, let Him deliver him, if He delight in him' from *Messiah*. But the madrigal chorus the music changes with the changing verses; a notable example is the Purcell chorus 'Soul of the World' from the big *St Cecilia's Day Ode*. In the final chorus from this Ode, Purcell seems to be reaching forward to greater splendour and clearer form. The shape of this piece is best described as ABCA. A is exhortatory and uncomplicated. B is elaborate, rich, polyphonic. C is short, highly expressive, for solo voices only. Then A comes again. This is still madrigal form—that is, block added to block. But the blocks are so contrasted (and one, of course, is repeated) that we appreciate the simplicity and clarity, as well as the grandeur, of the form.

Chapter 7

BRITTEN

FIRST ENCOUNTERS

I first met Benjamin Britten during the war, when I was musical director at Morley College. We wanted a tenor soloist for the Purcell verse anthem 'My beloved spake'. Walter Bergmann, who was then chorus master at Morley, suggested Peter Pears, recently returned from America. When Pears came to rehearsal, Britten came with him. I can recall the occasion very clearly.

I had in fact seen Britten before the war at the first public performance of *A Boy was Born* at a Lemare concert in the Mercury Theatre, Notting Hill.[1] I had no intuition then that the slim figure walking down the gangway to take his bow before the public would become so decisive and beloved a personality in my life. But I have an unusually vivid mental picture of that moment. The aural memory is much vaguer. It is really only of the Brosa Quartet madly counting quavers in the finale of my First Quartet, also a première!

Though Britten and I met over one of the Elizabethans, our real musical connection was Purcell. It is a rough generalization, but there is some truth in the contention that while a thirty- to forty-year older figure like Vaughan Williams derived special emotional and musical sustenance from the Elizabethans (cf. *Fantasia on a Theme of Thomas Tallis, Sir John in Love*), Britten and I submitted to the influence of Purcell to a degree not seen in English music before. I won't recount what are the points of Purcell we chiefly needed, but certainly we responded to the carry and freedom of his vocal line.

It was also during the war, and not long after I first met Britten, that I was asked by the then precentor of Canterbury Cathedral to hear one of his lay clerks sing. This was Alfred Deller. He sang Purcell's 'Music for a while'. One outcome of this meeting and of the growing friendship with Peter Pears was the first full-scale performance by Morley College of Purcell's *Ode for St Cecilia's Day, 1692*, with the ravishing duet for countertenor and tenor in that work sung by these two incomparable artists and accompanied by a bevy of recorders.[2] I don't remember if Britten was present, but I am pretty sure he was.

[1] 17 Dec. 1934; the first performance had been a BBC broadcast in April the same year.
[2] 31 Dec. 1944, at Friends' House, Euston Road, London.

About this time I wrote my first piece of music for Pears and Britten as a duo. Out of the study of Purcell and Monteverdi had come the urge to write a vocal cantata (as opposed to a song cycle). This piece was *Boyhood's End*, and the first performance was given by them in the Holst Room at Morley College.[3]

Ben later asked me what larger works I had written, if any, other than those he knew. I told him of *A Child of Our Time*, of how I had played it to Walter Goehr some time before, who advised me in the circumstances to shut it up in a drawer, which, being rather patient and literal, I did. Ben had the manuscript out of the drawer at once. In looking through the score, he noticed how, in one of the spirituals, the effect could be greatly enhanced by lifting the tenor solo part suddenly an octave higher. This I entirely agreed with, and so this minute piece of Britten composition is in the score. He persuaded us to venture on a performance; he was already then close to the Sadler's Wells Opera, and talked three of their singers into singing for us: Joan Cross, Peter Pears, and Roderick Lloyd. The fourth, Margaret McArthur, came from us at Morley. In the event, through no fault of these artists, it was an imperfect première[4] under execrable conditions, but inescapably moving. One year later, Britten's own relations with Sadler's Wells bore fruit, with the première of *Peter Grimes*.[5]

BRITTEN AT FIFTY

I will begin with an objective fact. Britten's publishers[6] are producing a catalogue of all his work to date—to his fiftieth year, that is. There are ninety-nine published works as separate items in this catalogue. Ten of these are operas; seven of them are major vocal works for the concert-hall; four are large-scale orchestral works; there are three canticles, two string quartets, not to speak of works for small choirs (a favourite of mine is the *Hymn to St Cecilia*), small groups of all kinds, music for all occasions.

Considering the artistically chaotic period in which we live, without an agreed musical style, so that composers must wrestle with their own language in a manner unknown, say, to Mozart, and considering the tremendous range of subjects, in the widest sense of the word, which Britten has involved himself in, then the sheer scale of his accomplishment is staggering. Here is the first of the facets of his genius. Phenomenal productivity arising from the combination of great gifts with continuous hard work.

Britten's technical mastery is often treated as part of the musical gifts which Mother Nature undoubtedly showered on him. But this mastery is not a gift at all (like the ability in childhood to win chess tournaments from older masters). It is the result of sheer hard work. If anyone can be said to have been

---

[3] 5 June 1943.   [4] 19 Mar. 1944 at the Adelphi Theatre.
[5] 7 June 1945.   [6] Boosey & Hawkes Ltd.

initially responsible for this temper in the critical early years, then it was Frank Bridge. But once that has been said, it still needs to be realized that the hard work is done year in, year out, by Britten himself. By hard work I am not thinking so much of the hours of intense activity, but rather of the pro- longed struggle, even agony, which composition is for Britten. In a letter to me he writes, 'I am having a ferocious time between these public functions and my own work (more and more difficult!) but that's our old problem, isn't it?'. By 'our', he meant that I (who better being so close a colleague?) would immediately understand this problem of creative work as against public pre- sentation. But he also meant by 'problem' the unending struggle within the work of composition itself. And 'more and more difficult!' means just what it says. The older we grow in art and the profounder our sensibilities, the more we find creation—despite all the mastery of experience—difficult.

We can uncover now a further facet of his genius. For if we consider the difficulties, not of the future for him, but simply of the past, we can see that Britten by his very gifts had has full share of the problems bequeathed to us all in this period. There being no single tradition now, each artist forges his links (or blows up his bridges) according solely to temperament and his indi- vidual *kairos*. Britten's *kairos* has never been, even in extreme youth (nor will be in the future) to make his music out of destruction. (I use the word 'destruc- tion' in its healthy affirmative sense.) It is interesting that Britten said of his youthful admiration for Auden, 'Auden was a powerful revolutionary figure. He was very much anti-bourgeois and that appealed.' Yet there is no early Britten work to match Auden's *The Orators*, for example. Britten must make his music out of his own creative gifts in relation *always* to the music of our forebears. So that he is inescapably involved in a fiendish problem of choice. That is, for each work he has to choose (in his finest works only after agoniz- ing struggles) the style and substance afresh and in relation to some tradition. For the purposes of his own music, in nearly every work, his intuitions in this manner have been infallible.

As a third facet of his genius I treasure his lucidity. As Britten said to Murray Schafer, 'Music for me is clarification; I try to clarify, to refine, to sen- sitize. Stravinsky once said that one must work perpetually at one's technique. But what is technique? Schoenberg's technique is often a tremendous elabo- ration. My technique is to tear all the waste away; to achieve perfect clarity of expression, that is my aim.'[7] Britten does not misunderstand Stravinsky, nor does he criticize Schoenberg. He points a finger to himself, because *that* is what he has to be.

Turning now to his productions, there is nothing useful in parading here my likes or dislikes. Nor shall I make any judgement of quality with regard to his works. I am a composer and a deeply attached friend, not a critic. There is also a further reason, which I will discuss in a moment. What I have to say

---

[7] Murray Schafer, *British Composers in Interview* (London, 1963), 118.

concerns style and individual voice. Britten, as everyone knows who listens much to his music, has a marked style of his own. We can always immediately recognize any 'piece of music' by him, and can trace imitations of this style in younger admirers. But every composer with enough personality to possess an individual voice writes works which go further. Of these works we tend to say not merely that this is by so-and-so, but that this is such-and-such a work. (Think of *Tristan and Isolde*—then think of *Meistersinger*.) So, however much Britten grew beyond *Peter Grimes*, there are tones, procedures, orchestral and vocal colours which are more than just Britten in his general style, for they have such a 'Grimes'-ness about them; they are that opera and none other.

For me, though this has not been recognized so generally, the style of the *Spring Symphony* has also this quality. A gaiety and exuberance unique and inimitable. Between these poles of dark and light (*Peter Grimes* and the *Spring Symphony*) is the style of the *Canticles*; flower of his natural piety. We are both of us religious composers—that is, bound, *religati*, to a sense of the numinous—but Britten is more properly Christian.

To attempt an account of Britten's place in contemporary music is to enter on a vexed question, bedevilled by the inability of so many music critics and others to distinguish between the facts of public acclaim and the pretensions (and maybe necessity) of value-judgements. To deal with the facts first. When his own generation comes into the title—that is, when the substantial figures of Stravinsky and Hindemith reside in the memory—then Britten will share the top of the world's acclaim solely with Shostakovich. This is an honour for England (and of course for Russia), and we may 'shine forth' through Britten as a country of no mean musical worth. We want more of this, not less. That is, the world audience for music, and the huge audiences that are to come, can explore and enjoy more such figures. To assess Britten's music in a judgement of value is to my mind pretension, not fact. It will only be a fact when his works are *all* there (we have as yet not the half), and he too must reside in the memory. Yet I am in no way suggesting that critics should not make value-judgements of new music, Britten's or anyone's. That is the burden of their job. We need, I think, more judgements, illuminatory assessments of the general stage of musical affairs; especially, one would think, of the state of the emperor's clothes. But not on the other hand a manic hunt for masterpieces and the one true way announced of God. This is stultifying, especially to the younger English composers struggling to find their individual song. (I make this plea within the birthday tribute to an older figure, because Britten himself would so signally approve my doing so.)

Great disservice has been done to Britten by the indiscriminate coupling of his name with great figures of the past. It cannot be too clearly stated that this can never have emanated from the composer himself. He does not ask himself, 'Am I the —— of my time?' But, 'How can I hammer out these objective works of art which are the proper and full fruits of my gifts in relation to this period?'

OBITUARY

The news of Benjamin Britten's death brought a sense of loss to every musical person of the whole world. To those like myself who knew him closely, the sense of loss is probably no greater. I have memories that go back for a very long period. But I think of him now, in 1945, just after the war, when he had come back from America to England, and I remember walking into the darkened auditorium of Sadler's Wells Opera Theatre, and there was a high sound of violins—in fact, the very opening of the first interlude of *Peter Grimes*—and, with his back to me, this shadowy figure in the orchestral pit, rehearsing the orchestra. And I remember remarking to myself at that time how fantastically professional this young man was who had not only composed this work, but was performing it there with all the authority of a top-ranking conductor. It is difficult for us now, after so many years, to realize what this event, in every sense, meant, not only to us in England but to, I think, the musical world in general. Because, though it did, in fact, happen first in England, the resonances were, in the end, and very quickly indeed, international. But in England itself, the sense of excitement was probably due to the feeling that here, at last, after the very first performance on the stage, was an opera whose professionalism, whose quality, in the best sense of the word, was something which had not been seen in England since the single completed opera, *Dido and Aeneas*, of Henry Purcell, centuries before.

For Britten himself, this triumph meant something more than the immediacy of being an internationally recognized composer. It meant for him that he was now willing in himself, and, indeed, determined to be, within the twentieth century, a professional opera composer. That in itself is an extraordinarily difficult thing to do, and one of the achievements for which he will always be remembered in musical history books is that, in fact, he actually *did* it. For himself, this meant that he had to consider very seriously the question of the economics of opera in modern society, or rather the society of that time, 1945, just after the war, when, as far as England was concerned, it was a period of impoverishment. He considered the matter in great detail and at great length with Peter Pears, the singer, and between them they decided that it was possible to have operas of quality and power, using a very much smaller number of players in the orchestral pit.

In order to do this, the two of them decided they should found the English Opera Group, a small group of professional singers who were, in general, to be accompanied by a brilliant group of up to twelve instrumental players. In order that the English Opera Group should have a permanent place where it could perform the operas written for it, Peter Pears and Benjamin Britten decided that they would begin a festival in Aldeburgh where they lived, and, though the conditions seemed improbable, it is true that within a very tiny building in that old town, this whole series of Britten works was conceived and produced. Indeed, this series contained, for me at least, one masterpiece that equals *Peter Grimes*, in the larger opera-house, and that is *The Turn of the Screw*, to the libretto out of Henry James.

Nearly as fascinating as the whole series of operas, to my mind, is the whole series of song cycles. These were written, generally, for Peter Pears, and one must realize that this close and intimate relationship produced from Britten some of the most tender, beautiful music that he ever wrote. I first heard them together during the war at a very early, if not the first, performance of the *Michelangelo Sonnets*. I can remember again, as a composer, being struck by this extraordinary musicality in both composition and and performance: with an additional sense of surprise, indeed, almost bewilderment, that these songs were written to Italian words, with a fantastic sense, so far as I could hear, of the relation of the music to the Italian. So it is really no surprise that within this series of works for voice and piano, or voice and small numbers of instruments, Britten also wrote music not only for English, but for French, German, and even Russian texts.

I would also say that this seems to me the way in which we should appreciate this composer, as being a figure who lived all his life totally within his native country, but who always had a professional and international attitude to the music of his time. And surely we can see that his pacifism and his feelings about international war sprang from something of the same source, and that, sooner or later, this passion concerning the things that human beings did to each other during the two great wars that he had lived through would issue in some profound work of art. I am referring, of course, to the *War Requiem* which he meditated on many years before it was actually performed.

I want to say, here and now, that Britten has been for me the most purely musical person I have ever met and I have ever known. It always seemed to me that music sprang out of his fingers when he played the piano, as it did out of his mind when he composed. I am sure that the core and centre of his great achievement lies in the works for voices and instruments.

Through his extraordinary musicality and fantastic technical equipment, Britten was probably one of the finest accompanists on the piano of anyone of his generation. Anybody who heard Pears and Britten, year after year, do their annual recital at the Aldeburgh Festival or, luckily, heard them during the great tours they took right round the world, has a memory which, I feel, is ineffaceable. But I think that all of us who were close to Ben had for him something dangerously near to love. And it gave us, perhaps, an almost anguished concern for what might happen to this figure.

It seems to me that certain obsessions belonged naturally to the works of art which he produced. I don't think it matters at all that they may not in any way have belonged to his personality. I refer to a deep sense of cruelty upon people, cruelty as a suffering. A sense, I think, also of the fragility of all existence, leading him to a sense of death. He had a special sensitivity, I am sure, for the works of Henry James and the whole period running from 1890 to

1920, during which a figure like Thomas Mann was writing. The penultimate opera, *Owen Wingrave*, had been in Britten's mind as an intended opera years and years ago, probably even before he returned to England from America. In *Owen Wingrave*, the artistic obsession with cruelty and death is clear for us to see, but a sense of death was sharper still in *Death in Venice*, the last of all the operas. Here is a work of extraordinary tenderness, and I think all the love which he had for his singer flowed out into this work. But there was a sense, with those of us outside the immediate circle, of apprehension: an apprehension which was deepened as we knew of his illness. The apprehension is totally fulfilled, and we are left with a sense of sorrow and loss.

Chapter 8

HOLST

When Holst's daughter, Imogen, and I were students at the Royal College of Music in the early 1920s, Holst was at the centre-point of his public success. This success had been occasioned by the appearance in 1919 of *The Planets* (without 'Venus' and 'Neptune') and in the following year *The Hymn of Jesus*. Both works were publicly performed in London by the Royal Philharmonic Society. *The Hymn of Jesus* was immediately acclaimed as a masterpiece. According to *The Times*, Holst had 'achieved the position, rare for an Englishman, of being a really popular composer'. Such success disconcerted him: he wrote to a friend, 'Woe to you when all men speak well of you!' But for those of us embarking on a musical career at that time, it was all part of the exciting spectrum of English musical life—later to be described as a 'second Renaissance' in English music.

With the young Adrian Boult (who conducted the first performance of *The Planets*) actively interested in the new music of the time, with Hamilton Harty at Manchester and Dan Godfrey at Bournemouth, and later with Malcolm Sargent conducting the Sargent–Courtauld concerts (a wonderful series, as I well remember), our national musical life was beginning to thrive. The Royal College of Music under Sir Hugh Allen was in many respects far from the stuffiness associated with such institutions. We sang performances of *The Hymn of Jesus* and the *Ode to Death* very few years after their first performances. There being no established opera-houses then, we gave the first public performances of Vaughan Williams's *Hugh the Drover*. Allen had confidence in the big English figures coming to the fulfilment of their powers, Holst and (senior to him by two years) Vaughan Williams; a confidence they deserved. And Allen always acted upon such confidence. I myself and three other students in Sargent's conducting class had to conduct the RCM string orchestra in a movement from Holst's *St Paul Suite* in the presence of the composer. After the concert, Holst sought each of us out to thank us. I recall the great frankness and sincerity of his eyes. That momentary meeting is associated in my mind with an occasion later when, in the BBC Concert Hall at Broadcasting House, after Bartók had performed on the piano in one of his works, my eyes crossed with Bartók's. There was the same intensity of outward vision, as though eye looked into eye quite immediate and unclouded; yet there was the same second sense of an inward vision springing from some pristine and untouchable imaginative life.

Holst worked himself to death (perhaps literally) in his dealings with hundreds of students at the Royal College, at St Paul's School, Morley College, and wherever. For all that, in his composition, he was like Bartók, principally a solitary. No one, I am sure, had more sense of the need for the living relations of new music to its means of expression and to its public; yet, when he said that he was compelled to compose in the way he did, always leaving one vision, one style, for yet another, he was absolutely accurate and without pose. Holst didn't always succeed with his innovations. At the first performance of *The Perfect Fool*, I was aware that he had not really solved the problem of integrating dance into opera (something that concerned me right the way through my own career as an operatic composer). The dances themselves, so brilliant and vivid, found their true home in the concert-hall. But in the theatre, they unbalanced the effect of the work.

The Planets and *The Hymn of Jesus* quite quickly became part of our musical history; *Egdon Heath* took rather longer. The issue is already implicit in *The Planets*. Whatever seminal power the ideas of astrology had for Holst personally, the resultant work, which we know as *The Planets*, is received by us, his public, as a work of musical art unconditioned as to its understanding and enjoyment by any ignorance of or hostility towards astrology we may profess. The grandeur of the artistic conception is quite objective and real. The music to this grand design is a suite of varied movements in a style whose impressionism is more Russian than French (to my ears). Within it we can distinguish the accidents of dress and the originalities. 'Mars', with its simplicity of form, direct but novel rhythm and gravely portentous movement of heavy brass, has never dated: on the contrary, the two world wars that succeeded its composition have reinforced its sense of relevance.

At first, 'Venus the Bringer of Peace' might not seem to have this compelling power. For his musical image here, Holst appears to have leant too readily on the Housmanism that was a pervasive feature of the English musical scene; manifest in Butterworth's *A Shropshire Lad* and in settings of Georgian lyric poetry in general, it reached its apogee in Vaughan Williams's *Pastoral Symphony*, introduced at a Royal Philharmonic Society concert by Boult, but three years after *The Planets*. With the hindsight perception offered by Paul Fussell's *The Great War and Modern Memory*,[1] the pastoral idyll can now be seen as an essential psychological counterbalance to the horrors of the trenches, replacing them with an imagined Arcadian ideal. (Churchill, haranguing Siegfried Sassoon for his pacifism, declared: 'War is the normal occupation of man,' but then added: 'War—and gardening!'[2]) These opposite poles seem to be deeply embedded in the English sensibility. (According

[1] Paul Fussell, *The Great War and Modern Memory* (New York and London, 1975); see esp. ch. 7 'Arcadian Recourses'.

[2] Ibid. 234.

to Fussell, 'Recourse to the pastoral is an English mode of both fully gauging the calamities of the Great War and imaginatively protecting oneself against them.'[3]) Holst's 'Mars' and 'Venus' articulated these twin polarities; his Hardy-inspired *Egdon Heath* tried hard to fuse them.

Comparing *The Planets* with Stravinsky's *Firebird* suite, we find the same paradox between the pictorial nature of the techniques and the deeply held beliefs of both composers in the non-representational nature of music as such. There is the same rootedness in national and European traditions and the same sense of an original and exploring mind. The impressionist technique demands a continual invention of ever fresh passages of music and of new sound: blocks often built up on repeated rhythms or motifs. Stravinsky found these sounds more often than Holst, but when in *The Planets* we reach 'Saturn, the Bringer of Old Age', we know that Holst was destined to be a Protean character, again like Stravinsky. 'Saturn' looks musically forward to Holst's development, just as 'Venus' looks musically back. (*Egdon Heath*, I feel, was to be born of 'Saturn'.) By Protean, I mean the compulsion to change from and be enriched by experience and to discover new content and new styles. If Holst had lived to a great age, I think he would have been a musical Picasso.

What he did manage, even early on, however, was the sort of odd inter-mingling of disparate ingredients which, when also properly cohesive, attests to the quality of a vision. I feel that Holst reached this level in *The Hymn of Jesus*. It is wonderfully daring: I well recall the difficulty we Royal College students had singing those rich passages where the two main choruses go their separate ways, tonally speaking—as in 'To you who gaze, a lamp am I; To you that know, a mirror'. If Holst went back to the basic sources of religion in this piece, it was not merely a process of delving into the past, in his choice of text (from the Apocryphal Acts of St John) or through the incorporation of plainsong: more important, he reinstated the link between dance and religious ecstasy. *The Hymn of Jesus* plays with musical space, just like Tallis in his *Spem in Alium* or, more recently, Giles Swayne in his epic for amplified voices, *Cry*. With such a work, Holst transcended his time, his location, his roots, showing himself a true visionary.

[3] Ibid. 235.

Chapter 9

HINDEMITH AND
LUDUS TONALIS

Hindemith's *Ludus tonalis* was one of his most substantial compositions of the early 1940s. Written for piano solo, it comprised a set of twelve fugues, with eleven linking interludes and a postlude which are mirror images of each other. (If you turn the last three pages of the printed copy upside down, imagining the clef signs and accidentals the right way up and in their accustomed places, then they would read as the first three pages.) On the title-page, Hindemith has given it the following subtitle: *Studies in Counterpoint, Tonal Organisation and Piano Playing*.

As to the last of these matters, piano playing, I am not competent to judge, and this is probably not in general its greatest interest, except in the interludes, which are pure intermezzi. They perform the same function as the comic scenes between the acts of *opera seria*, out of which *opera buffa* arose, or as the masques at the end of each act of Purcell's *The Fairy Queen*. Their function is to provide respite from the more serious matter of the work, and as such, they fulfil their purpose admirably. Three of them are genre pieces, with the titles, 'Pastorale', 'March', and 'Valse'. A further one is marked 'Scherzando', and two others 'Fast' and 'Very Fast', demanding a good deal of nimble fingerwork.

The core of *Ludus tonalis* is its set of twelve fugues, which invite comparison with the fugues of Bach's *Well-Tempered Clavier*. As far as I can judge, Hindemith does not use a more complicated contrapuntal apparatus than Bach. He uses resources that are simply adequate to his purpose, which did not include (I imagine) the extension, or quasi-operatic elaboration of the eighteenth-century fugal tradition which you find in late Beethoven. One device common to innumerable earlier fugues is strikingly absent from Hindemith's, and that is the true countersubject, designed to be sounded with every entry of the subject after the first. A beautiful Bach example would be the C minor fugue in the *Well-Tempered Clavier*, Book 1. There is no technically comparable fugue in *Ludus tonalis*. Perhaps we need to have Bach's continuity of key in order to appreciate such invertible counterpoint. Such a device is not impossible in an idiom of today; but to be effective, it needs variety in the melodic components to be combined. Our weakness, as Hindemith's, may lie there.

A canonic fugue such as Bach's E flat major (Book 2), in which the canons are exhausted almost mathematically, also has no parallel in this work. Hindemith uses canon frequently, and most other similar contrapuntal devices, but his fugues are necessarily not part of a lifetime's output of such forms, to culminate in an *Art of Fugue*. The first fugue in *Ludus tonalis* is a beautiful but very condensed triple fugue. Bach's triple fugue in F sharp minor (Book 2) is as extended and developed as Hindemith's is condensed.

Now Bach, in writing *The Well-Tempered Clavier*, wanted to show the immense advantages harmonically of equal temperament, whereby every possible key becomes equally available. Thus he twice wrote a prelude and fugue in each possible key, and in both modes, major and minor, starting from C major and C minor. But in practice we do not use key so indifferently. Even Bach begins his series on C, not on C sharp. And Mozart, half a century or so later, kept only a comparatively small group of traditionally 'homely' keys for everyday use: C, G, D, A, F, B flat, E flat, and so on, and avoided the 'strange' keys of B, C sharp, F sharp, and others, except for special reasons. Later still, Wagner, whom we think of as much more fluid, chromatic, and tonally unfettered, knew quite well the difference between using C major for the overture to *Die Meistersinger* and using a key signature of six flats for the prelude to *Götterdämmerung*.

Hindemith has chosen his twelve tones, or keys, in a special order designed to exemplify his theoretical approach to this problem, as he argues it in his book *Unterweisung im Tonsatz*.[1] He propounds a theory of distance and corresponding tension; or, to use the metaphor already introduced above, the 'homely' and the 'strange'. His twelve fugues proceed from the nearest to the farthest, from the 'most homely' to the 'most strange'. The order, emerging as a harmonic series out of a fundamental, is: C, G, F, A, E, E flat, A flat, D, B flat, D flat, B, F sharp. However, Hindemith uses no named modes, major, minor, or any other; his choice amounts to a series of tone-centres rather than of keys. I can see no theoretical reason why the series should not begin, as Bach's could have done, on C sharp (or anywhere else). But in fact, Hindemith begins it on C, apparently thereby acknowledging, if only unconsciously, another and more traditional sense of the homely and the strange. Actually, *if* one began the Hindemith series on F sharp as the prime tone, then C, in equal temperament, would become the most strange. But this *theoretical* possibility would be counter to our accumulated associations with the homeliness of C major.

In the postlude, Hindemith set himself a problem. He wanted to return to C, the home, after the twelfth fugue in F sharp, the strange. His solution is both ingenious and moving. He modulates already in the prelude from C to

[1] Paul Hindemith, *Unterweisung im Tonsatz*, i. *Theoretischer Teil* (Mainz, 1940). Trans. Arthur Mendel as *The Craft of Musical Composition*, Book I: *Theoretical Part* (London, 1945).

F sharp (thus carrying out the sequence of fugues in miniature), ending on the dominant of F sharp—that is, C sharp. From this note he, so to speak, slips down a semitone to C natural—and so begins the first fugue. The G sharp in the bass clef (which ends the prelude) becomes C sharp in the treble clef for the beginning of the minor postlude, and thus the way back to the final C is begun. For me, the beautiful twelfth fugue in F sharp and this returning postlude are the artistic high-water mark of the whole work.

My general impression of this composition was of Hindemith's strong sense of tradition and great cultivation of sensibility. Someone pointed out that Hindemith is a 'great observer' rather than an originator. Certainly, he observed the fugal tradition minutely, and that is something. In so far as his music exemplifies the ideas put forward in *The Craft of Musical Composition*[2] and his little textbook of two-part counterpoint,[3] then it is also valuable; and the latter book is indeed to be recommended to those students who find themselves drawn into the contemporary revival of linear musical styles.

---

[2] Paul Hindemith, *Unterweisung im Tonsatz*, i. *Theoretischer Teil* (Mainz, 1940). Trans. Arthur Mendel as *The Craft of Musical Composition*, Book I: *Theoretical Part* (London, 1945).

[3] Hindemith, *The Craft of Musical Composition*, Book II: *Exercises in Two-Party Wiriting*, trans. Otto Ortmann (New York, 1941).

Chapter 10

SHOSTAKOVICH

Shostakovich's *Testimony*[1] was addressed to his countrymen, not the West—which is Shostakovich's name for Europe and America. He was a Slavophile, not a Westerner. He disliked the West intensely, and he seems concerned in this book to make certain truths known to a future generation of Soviet composers. In order to do this, he felt that he must send his manuscript illegally to the West, so that after his death—since the manuscript, if discovered in Russia, might have been destroyed—it could be 'returned' for a kind of 'publication'. The mechanism is that the Russian version of the manuscript would be beamed back to Russia by radio and there picked up and transcribed by devoted listeners who type it on to samizdat. It's a method which in principle has been used in Russia since Tolstoy. It was even for security purposes used by Krushchev.

The process may seem strange, but it is natural enough in dealing with any form of censorship. In my student days, for example, the two major literary works banned in England by the censors were Joyce's *Ulysses* and D. H. Lawrence's *Lady Chatterley's Lover*. The manuscripts of these were sent to France for publication, and then brought back in printed form to England illegally: that is how my generation read them. The difference with Russia would seem to be only a matter of degree. Nevertheless, it is surely pusillanimous for a major state like Russia to be unwilling to allow publication of *Doctor Zhivago*, which has already been read by everyone who wishes to read it in samizdat. *Testimony* is being read in Russia in this way already.

I had two 'non-meetings' with Shostakovich. The first would have taken place in 1949. This was a period when, after the war, the Communist powers were attempting a series of international conferences on peace. There had been one in Warsaw, and there was to be a more spectacular one in New York. It was announced that Shostakovich was to be present in New York, and he himself in *Testimony* gives an account of his appearance there.

I was surprised to receive an official invitation to this conference, since, as a Trotskyite, I had been debarred previously from all contact with the Stalinist faithful. Nevertheless, it seems to have been felt that, since I had been

[1] Shostakovich, *Testimony: The Memoirs of Dmitri Shostakovich*, ed. Solomon Volkov, trans. Antonia W. Bouis (London, 1979).

sent to prison as a pacifist, my dilettante Trotskyism could be safely over-looked. Some ex-Trotsky friends attempted to persuade me that I should go to New York in order to ask Shostakovich questions concerning the notorious 1948 decree of Zhdanov on the arts. This would have made Shostakovich appear a political coward in the most public manner possible. I refused. I explained that if I went to New York at all, I should try to ask questions which would show Shostakovich that I understood the meaning of Siberia. This was regarded as strange at the time, since all the present disillusionment in left-wing circles with the Communist regime had not begun. It was probably eas-ier for me, both because of my Trotskyist affiliations and pacifist convictions. Thus I always knew that both Hitler and Stalin were monsters, though one was the enemy and the other was the ally.

In New York Shostakovich was in fact asked the questions. With his head down he answered them all as Stalin had ordered. Shostakovich describes his experience in New York:

People sometimes say that it must have been an interesting trip, look at the way I'm smiling in the photographs. That was the smile of a condemned man. I felt like a dead man. I answered all the idiotic questions in a daze, and thought, when I get back it's over for me.[2]

The moral question as to what answers he was expected to give comes in the book in the generally elliptical manner in which he speaks of these things. He speaks through another person. The most moving and personal account is in his description of Meyerhold's last theatrical production:

Just before the Theatre of Meyerhold was shut down, Kaganovich [a Communist party leader and brother-in-law to Stalin] came to a performance at the Theatre. He was very powerful. The Theatre's future depended on his opinion, as did Meyerhold's future.

As was to be expected. Kaganovich didn't like the play. Stalin's faithful comrade-in-arms left almost in the middle. Meyerhold, who was in his sixties then, ran out into the street after Kaganovich. Kaganovich and his retinue got into a car and drove off. Meyerhold ran after the car, he ran until he fell. I would not have wanted to see Meyerhold like that.[3]

It is quite clear that people of Shostakovich's integrity were unaware of what they were doing, and I am certain that the constant necessity to act in this manner within Russia itself agonized him to the very end. He made this crys-tal clear, in his elliptical manner, by a similar story concerning Akhmatova, the marvellous poet who, a generation older than Shostakovich, had such great courage. Her poet-husband Gumilyov was shot quite early on in the purges, and her son was taken to Siberia. Stalin demanded that she should

    [2] Shostakovich, *Testimony: The Memoirs of Dmitri Shostakovich*, ed. Solomon Volkov, trans. Antonia W. Bouis (London, 1979) 152.
    [3] Ibid. 60.

write a 'celebratory' ode in his honour if she wished him [her son] to live. Akhmatova and Zoschenko, a satirist and playwright and close friend of Shostakovich, were forced to meet a delegation of tourists:

The old trick, to prove that they were alive, healthy and happy with everything, and extremely grateful to the Party and the government.

The 'friends' with meal vouchers in their hands couldn't think of anything cleverer to ask than what Zoschenko and Akhmatova thought of the resolution of the Central Committee of the Party and Comrade Zhdanov's speech. This is the speech in which Akhmatova and Zoschenko were used as examples. Zhdanov said that Zoschenko was an unprincipled and conscienceless literary hooligan, and that he had a rotten and decayed socio-political and literary mug. Not face; he said mug.

And Zhdanov said that Akhmatova was poisoning the consciousness of Soviet youth with the rotten and putrid spirit of her poetry. So how could they have felt about the resolution and speech? Isn't that sadistic—to ask about it? It's like asking a man into whose face a hooligan has just spat, 'How do you feel about having spit on your face? Do you like it?' But there was more. They asked it in the presence of the hooligan and bandit who did the spitting, knowing full well that they would leave and the victim would have to stay and deal with the bandit.

Akhmatova rose and said that she considered both Comrade Zhdanov's speech and the resolution to be absolutely correct. Of course, she did the right thing, that was the only way to behave with those shameless heartless strangers. What could she have said? That she thinks she's living in a lunatic asylum of a country? That she despises and hates Zhdanov and Stalin? Yes, she could have said that, but then no one would have ever seen her again.

The 'friends' of course could have bragged about the sensation back at home, 'among friends' . . . And we would have all suffered a loss, we would have lived without Akhmatova and her incomparable late poetry.[4]

(I would like to say that I have total sympathy with Akhmatova and by implication with Shostakovich. It is also clear that I would never have had probably more than one-fifth of Akhmatova's courage.)

Has the book changed my view of Russia or of Shostakovich? *Testimony* tells us nothing new about the general condition of Soviet intellectual life before and after the war—nothing that one might not have gathered from, say, the two volumes of memoirs by the widow of Mandelstam or those of Galina von Meck. Some circumstantial details are, of course, different, and only serve to accentuate the fact of its being written for Shostakovich's countrymen, who would know all the numerous subsidiary figures of whom he speaks. Neither does the book change my limited understanding of Shostakovich, though it certainly fleshes out my previous guesses.

Some of one's intimations of the truth have come always from the music itself. To give a personal example: I first heard Shostakovich's Eleventh Symphony only about four or five years ago. This symphony is supposed to be concerned with the events of the 1905 revolution. I was quite sure when I

⁴ Ibid. 156.

heard it that the use of 1905 was a kind of political alibi, since this was a matter of known revolutionary history. The music to me was self-evidently about Shostakovich's own experiences in the continual catastrophe of his life. This he confirms:

I wanted to show this recurrence in the Eleventh Symphony. I wrote it in 1957 and it deals with contemporary themes even though it's called 1905. It's about the people, who have stopped believing because the cup of evil has run over.[5]

What is new to me is his categoric statement that he knew this to be entirely understood by his public. The music must remain his only true memorial, and this because it is a music which, carrying the message of humanity under stress, has crossed all frontiers to speak to the world, though experienced by a composer of a dedicated patriotism.

My second 'non-meeting' was in 1968, in the autumn following the invasion of Czechoslovakia. I was rung up by someone at the Russian Embassy in London to ask whether I would agree to go as guest of honour to the Moscow meeting of the Congress of Soviet Composers. Once again I refused; partly because I was very busy at my own composition, but also from some instinct. The Congress, of course, took place. Kosygin and Brezhnev were present at the opening plenum (according to the account in *The Times*). Shostakovich began the whole affair by reading a special resolution of thanks to the Red Army for their heroic deeds. Presumably he might once more have asked us to comprehend, by reference to Akhmatova. Yet it must appear strange that he would still feel that way, since Stalin was dead, the thaw had taken place, and he had an impregnable position in Russian society. Could he not have refused? The explanation lies in his deep agony of spirit between his love of Russia and her great history and his experience of its present corruption (his own word). Like Solzhenitsyn a generation later, he felt a duty to write the truth down for the generation to come. But when Solzhenitsyn asked him to sign some public protest, he refused. He was moving towards his death, profoundly embittered; and at least according to his editor, Solomon Volkov, he felt himself out of touch, even rejected by the very young composers. So we must comprehend.

I am glad I did not go to Moscow. I would not have wanted to see him like that.

---

[5] Shostakovich, *Testimony: The Memoirs of Dmitri Shostakovich*, ed. Solomon Volkov, trans. Antonia W. Bouis (London, 1979) 5.

Chapter 11

CHARLES IVES

Charles Ives's music became known in Britain very gradually—mainly through discs and BBC broadcasts. Most of his work has been recorded, and is discussed in many books on music and monographs. One of the best and most influential was Wilfrid Mellers's *Music in a New Found Land*,[1] which illuminated many connections between American history, literature, and music. What emerges from all this is a sense of Ives's place in the formation of an American tradition, if such a national tradition were thought at all possible or viable in our age. (The problems of an English, or British, national musical tradition in relation to a comparable area to the west, and to me much smaller, but more intensive region of Europe to the east, are different and, for the moment, much less clear-cut.) For instance, James Goodfriend has written thus on Aaron Copland and Charles Ives as representative American composers:

There is no false magic in this. It rests on the fact that there are certain things today common to virtually all of us (Americans), not ethnic or racial qualities, but the stuff of everyday experience, of growing up in some part of this country. Just about every American, at some point in his life, will have eaten a hot dog and Southern-fried chicken and Thanksgiving dinner, heard the music of a Broadway show, a Negro spiritual, a hymn, a mountain tune, a square dance and a cowboy song, watched a parade, seen a Western movie, chewed on a straw or a pine needle, read or heard a bit of Emerson or Thoreau, drunk a malted milk, sung 'My country, 'tis of thee', and had a thousand and one other experiences that together make up life at this time and this place. Both Ives and Copland dipped their hands into this enormous stock of American sound and experience, and each made a personable and viable music of it.[2]

If we add Gershwin to this list of names, we do indeed come close to the real popular (in the sociological sense) basis of American music. Because Gershwin equally dipped his hand into the 'enormous stock of American sound' and equally made a 'personal and viable music of it'. (A notable omission from Goodfriend's list of American sounds is jazz.)

Now, because of the spoken language and the early development of

[1] Wilfrid Mellers, *Music in a New Found Land* (London, 1964).
[2] Sleeve-note for Ormandy recording of *Three Places in New England* (CBS Records).

literature in the colonial period, American writing has always had English literature as its earlier tradition. But the universities in America are chiefly German in tradition, not English. And the music schools have been entirely German. This is part of the reason why Schoenberg and Hindemith fitted into America so easily, and perhaps one reason why Bartók didn't. The only other great academic musical figure has been Nadia Boulanger. Nobody English at all, apart from Holst, whose stay at Harvard University lasted only six months because of illness (amongst his pupils was Elliott Carter).

Ives lived and worked right outside this American-German musical world; and, quite apart from his experimental methods, this, as well as his own 'Sunday-composer' attitude, made his music difficult at first for his countrymen. It still makes his music unacceptable to those—and they are many—who remain hung up in the narrow world of Schoenberg and Webern and their present-day epigones. It would not be proper for me as an Englishman to give advice to Americans as to where their true traditions lie. After all, with the great immigrations from Europe of the nineteenth century, America has many more ethnic groups than WASP and Negro.

German music might literally transplant to the United States along with the Germans. But, though the ethnic groups—like the New York Jews, for example—are far bigger, longer-lived, and tougher than the melting-pot theory would take account of in the short run, I have the feeling that, in the long run, Goodfriend's description of American life as presenting an enormous stock of common sounds and experience as 'stuff' for the composer is the right one. Ives, Gershwin, Copland have all responded to it in their varying ways.

Ives was a New Englander, and has been called 'pragmatic, level-headed'. He was an insurance executive. 'I have experienced a great fullness of life in business,' he wrote. 'You cannot set an art off in the corner and hope for it to have vitality, reality and substance.' And again: 'My work in music helped my business, and my work in business helped my music.' But if Ives found a complementary relationship between his business and his art, there is also, I think, a complementary relationship, within the music itself, between the externally derived sounds and experiences (brass bands, hymn-tunes, Fourth of July jollifications, historic occasions of the War of Independence, etc.) and the inner sensibilities, intimations of the spirit, in the tradition of the literary flowering of New England before the Civil War. This dichotomy between inner tenderness and outer toughness runs through all American experience—there is, for instance, a longing for primal innocence even within the violence of the frontier. I find this tradition fascinating, though often alien. (At the risk of its being merely a play on words, I hazard the remark that perhaps the true English tradition is opposite—outer tenderness and inner toughness.)

Like all such dichotomies within the psyche, individual or collective, the American dichotomy can generate enormous forces, destructive or creative. Thus Black Power and the literature that expresses it are absolutely caught up in this ambivalence. But with Ives the ambivalence is not so extreme or so violent. For all that he belongs within the total American experience, he is also bound within the limitations (if that is the right word) of his New England heritage and his period. His apprehensions should be set beside the extraordinary remark of Emily Dickinson: 'and the noise in the pool at noon excels my piano'.[3] This half-sentence might be an exact description of the tiny moment of visionary, almost silent sound which comes at the end of Ives's *Fourth of July* after the *fff*s of the multiple brass bands. These often minute visionary moments are difficult to bring off in performance just because they are so intense, so short, and yet so inwardly tender.

In practice we usually try first to find our way to Ives by thinking of him as an American experimenter before his time. We wonder at his collages of sound, his complexes of cross-rhythms, his dissonances, his transcendental difficulties of performance (as with the *Concord Sonata*). But the 'noise in the pool at noon' is what all the noise of the collages and the cross-rhythms and the dissonances are to uncover. I do not think any American music does this with the power and vision of American literature. The literary tradition is, of course, much older. Ives is already two generations beyond the flowering of New England. So he is a pioneer (in American music), not a late cultivator. His experiments can become uncouth, his philosophical transcendentalism can overwhelm his art. (This is nearly the case in *The Unanswered Question*.)

In the *Three Harvest Home Chorales* Ives is trying to break up the rigidities and banalities of New England church music by means of tonal and rhythmical experiment. They are set for choir, organ, and brass. The original manuscript was lost early in this century, and it is not known how much Ives rewrote them in his later revision. *General William Booth Enters into Heaven* is a setting of Vachel Lindsay's poem, which Ives first composed as a solo song and later arranged, with the collaboration of John Becker, as a piece for solo voice and small orchestra (with choir voices occasionally used as a kind of off-stage chorus). This second version is the better. Ives's purpose here is to lift the usual, obvious, and even sentimental music of Salvationists ('Are you washed in the blood of the Lamb?') by dramatic force to a true visionary level. It is thus, in small, an epitome of everything that Ives was aiming at: to accept the local, the contemporary, the immediate, and so transform it, or contrast against it, that we obtain glimpses of a visionary, even transcendental reality.

[3] Emily Dickinson, letter to Thomas Higginson, 25 Apr. 1862: 'They are better than Beings—because—they know—but do not tell—and the noise in the Pool, at Noon—excels my piano.'

Part III

TRADITIONS AND TEXTS

Chapter 12

ARCHETYPES OF CONCERT MUSIC

In the present period, the traditional titles for instrumental forms have often been found confusing. Small wonder that younger composers have tended to eschew such titles altogether, the impulse of the avant-garde being to exclude all received procedures or nomenclature. In any case, actual received terms such as 'symphony', 'concerto', 'sonata', and 'suite' really are imprecise terms for the music written today. They need re-examination and re-definition. Such imprecision and the confusion that it causes are not absolute; nor should the rejection of received titles be automatic.

SYMPHONY

I feel that much of the confusion that may arise when a contemporary instrumental work is called a 'symphony' is due to the fact that we have habitually two differing uses of the word, implying two contrasting conceptions. Further, we are generally unaware of this division in use, and pass from one conception to the other unawares.

What is meant by a symphony? Firstly, it implies a *historical archetype* from which we depart and return—for example, the so-called middle-period symphonies of Beethoven. Secondly, there is the *notional archetype*, permitting endless variations to the end of time—for example, the Mahler symphonies, or those of Charles Ives or Lutosławski. It is all too tempting to say that Mahler's are not true symphonies at all. This was a common enough opinion before the 1960s, when world-wide appreciation of that composer had hardly begun its extraordinary surge. The older view was that the Mahler symphonies did not conform to our historical archetype of the moment. Alternatively, we might say that Mahler (or Ives or Lutosławski) gave the symphony new and valid forms; and in so doing, we momentarily abandon the conception of a historical archetype for that of a notional archetype.

A nice public example of this occurred in three BBC television programmes with the London Symphony Orchestra, entitled *The Twilight of the Symphony*. The conductor, Leonard Bernstein, introduced the programme himself in interview. Each programme contained one work: Sibelius's Symphony No. 5, Shostakovich's Symphony No. 5, and Stravinsky's *Le Sacre du printemps*. The title of the series clearly implied the historical archetype—that at some time in the past, which Bernstein did not specify, the symphony had a noon. Unfortunately, the interviewer (probably because he was never clear in his own mind about it) never pressed Bernstein on this point. But he did bring out admirably the inherent confusion—unconscious, I guess—by pressing Bernstein to say whether, then, the three chosen modern works were in his opinion symphonies at all—especially *Le Sacre du printemps*—and whether the works as music exemplified a cultural twilight *in toto*. Bernstein said that all the works were symphonic in some sense, and all were positive musically. This answer, of course, implied the notional archetype—that even an avowed ballet score like *Le Sacre* could justly find a place in a television pro-gramme concerning the symphony, because it could be said to exemplify, as Bernstein thought, the kind of musical piece we might call 'symphonic'.

This was Bernstein's view, of course. It might call *Le Sacre du printemps* 'sym-phonic', but I doubt if I would want to call it a 'symphony'. Not because I have a true (for me) historical archetype to which I refer it and dismiss it, but because I dismiss it with reference to my notional archetype, which is proba-bly not the same as Bernstein's. My notion is no more valid, finally, than his.

CONCERTO

With 'concerto' for title, we have an added problem, in that the use of the word changed quite radically between the early and late eighteenth century. Thus the *Concerti grossi* of Vivaldi and Handel were suites of short instrumen-tal movements generally using binary form, and as such indistinguishable from dance 'suites' as such; and this format was just as common in, say, the harpsichord sonatas of Domenico Scarlatti. 'Concerto' as used by Mozart and Beethoven meant not a suite of movements but an extended three-move-ment display vehicle for solo instrument virtuosity, accompanied by an orchestra. The movements used all the characteristic forms of this later period, in a wide range of intriguing new variants. 'Concerto' remains a term referring to display pieces, and 'concertante' a term definitely signalling this approach.

Thus when Bartók devised the title *Concerto for Orchestra*, he implied, once we had seen what the music was, two negatives and two positives. Negatively, since there was no solo instrument, it was not a standard display concerto; and since it was not a deliberate return to eighteenth-century classicism, it was not a concerto in the older sense. Positively, however, through its succes-sion of five movements, it suggested that it had the suite in some sense in mind, and also that the orchestra itself might be a display instrument.

ORCHESTRA

The term 'orchestra' is itself ambivalent: that is something most composers this century have tended to acknowledge; and it is, incidentally, the failure to understand this that often bedevils the attempts of arts councils and other such bodies, desperately imposing their own absurdly bureaucratic solutions upon an inherently—and positively—chaotic orchestral scene. To speak of 'Bach's orchestra' is perhaps a little pretentious, because it can only mean an ensemble of instruments beyond chamber music—that is, a notional archetype of the orchestra. Those who have made statements like 'Bach would have written for the orchestra of today had he heard it' are moving over to the idea of a historical archetype—what has come to be known as the standard symphony orchestra.

In the late twentieth century this idea of a fixed, Standard Orchestra with a capital O, has broken down. Revolutionary figures such as Schoenberg, Stravinsky, and Bartók, in their early days, all wrote exciting, new-sounding pieces for this 'standard' orchestra. But, of course, its very standardness came finally into question. Its marvellous internal balance and homogeneous blend of sonority got in the way. Eric Walter White has told how Stravinsky, having become dissatisfied with the standard orchestra after *Le Rossignol*, spent nine years searching for the right ensemble for *Les Noces*;[1] and listening to the three versions in succession (as I once did at a superb concert by the London Sinfonietta) is illuminating. Stravinsky's espousal of new instrumental combinations in the post-First World War period was dictated partly by outside circumstances (hence the tiny, but distinctive group required in *L'Histoire du soldat*), partly dictated also by self-imposed restrictions (hence those works in which wind instruments predominated, such as *Symphonies of Wind Instruments*, *Mavra*, the Octet for winds, and the *Concerto for Piano and Winds*). As White has mentioned, Stravinsky became interested also in the concertante treatment of single instruments and small groups of instruments. And in his later works the orchestra was treated as a collection of chamber music groups. White concludes, 'every time he wrote a full-scale composition, he deliberately rethought his orchestra.'[2]

This is, in fact, quite probably where we composers have all now arrived. And it is a situation that brings with it social and acoustic problems. What we term the standard symphony orchestra developed during the nineteenth century, and concert-halls were built to match the size and volume of the ensemble and to house the proportionate audience. If composers now change the volume of their orchestral ensemble for every piece, then clearly the concert-halls do not match up. The celebrated orchestras of Berlin, London, and the United States tend naturally not to be enamoured of the new demands upon

[1] See Eric Walter White, *Stravinsky: The Composer and his Works* (London, 1966), 561–2.
[2] Ibid. 562.

them. The general public still lives for the Orchestra with a capital O. They may be slow to accept the changing face of concert music, but not for ever.

In my own case, I was slow to understand and act upon the general considerations outlined above. My *Concerto for Double String Orchestra* (1938–9) indicates, by its very title, some awareness of the problems, though the solutions are far from revolutionary. In calling the piece a 'concerto', I was harking back to the *Concerti grossi* of Handel, which I knew and loved. I attached myself partly to a special English tradition—that of the Elgar *Introduction and Allegro* and Vaughan Williams's *Fantasia on a Theme of Thomas Tallis*, both of which intermingle the intimacy of the solo string writing with the rich sonority of the full string ensemble. I did not regard the two orchestras as vehicles for concertante writing, such as might be found in the concertino groups of Handel's *Concerti grossi*: they were far more to be considered as antiphonal groups. But the musical forms deployed in my Double Concerto were those of Beethoven: a succinct dramatic sonata allegro, a slow movement virtually modelled on the song–fugue–song layout of the Andante of Beethoven's String Quartet in F minor, Op. 95, and finally a sonata rondo with coda.

My Symphony No. 1 (1945) was the culmination of a long period of struggle with classical sonata forms in the Beethovenian sense, within the context of the musical life I lived at that time. That is to say, I still started with a dramatic sonata allegro laid out on a big scale. But I was already trying to add to the forms of the other movements. The slow movement was thus a set of mirror variations on a long ground bass. I could not have come to this conception without the prolonged preoccupation of that period of my life with the music of Purcell. So once more it is clear that I was reaching back behind the Beethoven period to older traditions. In this sense I was perhaps acting out a decayed neo-classicism. The third movement, the scherzo, indeed reached further back still. I had observed how Pérotin wrote vocal trios all in triple time in which, after a few measures of plainsong in crotchets, the voices took off in a flying hocket on a chosen vowel in bumpy quavers. Yet the effect of these hockets was always to have a very strong accent on each bar. This allied itself in my mind with the presto crotchets of some Beethoven scherzos, which equally have an accent to each bar. Thus I saw what seemed to me a new material for a symphonic scherzo, and, of course, the bare, stark quality of the Pérotin allied itself easily to the starker sounds of my own music (starker, that is, than I had used before). This experience of agreement almost between late medieval or very early Renaissance sounds and contemporary sounds is common to many composers influenced in this way.

For the finale, I called upon my natural flair for polyphony and counterpoint and wrote a large-scale, unorthodox double fugue. But all along, despite the freedom with which I used the orchestra, I was using the standard symphony orchestra, as I had studied it in Cecil Forsyth's manual, *Orchestration*,[3]

---

[3] Cecil Forsyth, *Orchestration* (London and New York, 1914).

with the addition of the instrumental balances enunciated by Rimsky-Korsakov, that in a forte sonority, one trombone or one trumpet equals two horns or four woodwinds or one line of the string body.

By the time I returned to the problem of orchestral music with my Symphony No. 2 (1956–7), I had completed a long opera, *The Midsummer Marriage*. Although I found the symphonic problems as intractable as ever, the work became a sort of turning-point. On the surface, the work seemed like a more concentrated example of neo-classicism, despite the use of broken tone-clusters in the slow movement and a scherzo entirely in additive rhythm. But of course the fact that this scherzo was in additive rhythm was symptomatic of the change happening inside. I was at last ridding myself of the historic archetype of the symphony and moving decisively towards the notional archetype.

Before I could test out further this change of emphasis, I needed to write another opera, *King Priam*. The dramatic nature of this opera forced me radically to reconsider the standard orchestra. I began to realize that the sound of the standard orchestra had become so strong a historic archetype that contemporary music written for it gets inevitably drawn back in history by analogy to the period when the archetype was produced. To put it melodramatically, and perhaps rudely, this may not have mattered to Shostakovich, but it mattered to me. So I had systematically to consider an alternative.

First, it seemed clear enough that Stravinsky had shattered the Rimsky-Korsakov balances, showing (as with much music from earlier periods) that any instrument can equal any instrument in forte sonority if played in the necessary way. Also, with a contemporary of mine like Messiaen, what was clear was the excitement that kinds of unusual instruments could lend to the non-standard orchestra. There is no dearth of examples from all over the world of this general process. But I had to take a rather more personal step. I had begun as a composer with an intense love of the string quartet, of which I had at that stage written three. I had also written three pieces for string orchestra. I realized that the use of the string body within the standard orchestra was thus the crux. This body is historically the string quartet blown up, as it were, so that there is a terrifically strong historic archetype embedded within it. I was at last ready to let go of this archetype and replace it with a body of stringed instruments whose number and layout would be entirely conditional on the piece to be composed. Essential to this understanding was the realization that there were to be no first or second violins, but just violins. Once I had reached this point, in *King Priam*, it was never a problem thereafter to emulate Stravinsky as described above: 'every time he wrote a full-scale composition, he deliberately re-thought his orchestra.'

When the opera was finished, I turned once again to instrumental music, completing a Second Piano Sonata (1962), then a new *Concerto for Orchestra* (1962–3). The Concerto is a three-movement work with obvious references to both *concerti grossi* and display concertos. But where the Double Concerto used only Beethoven-type classic forms, the *Concerto for Orchestra* dispensed with a first-movement dramatic sonata allegro—testing, indeed, what I envisaged as advances in dealing with contemporary symphonic form and the nature of the contemporary orchestra.

I had, of course, rethought the orchestra specifically for this work. The change is already quite radical in the first movement. Its nine concertini—or groupings of solo instruments—had to embody three musical functions. The first three (flute and harp, tuba and piano, three horns) were concerned with melodic line. The second three (timpani and piano; oboe, cor anglais, bassoon, and double bassoon; two trombones and percussion) were concerned with rhythm and dynamic punch. The third (xylophone and piano, clarinet and bass clarinet, two trumpets and side-drum) were concerned with virtuosity of speed. It took at least a third of the movement to display all this section material. The three 'development' episodes are not of the kind associated with the historic archetype of Beethoven. They are in reality chiefly a matter of effective juxtaposition and 'jam sessions', with the concertini never changing their component elements throughout the movement. That juxtaposition, those superimpositions, or jam sessions, could not be random: and the composer's skill can be measured in terms of the exact lengths and proportions of each return, in shortened or extended form, of the materials, and in the choice of elements for superimposition.

The slow movement brought the strings into play for the first time. Here again I specified in the score a small string body—not a scaled-down string section of a symphony orchestra with a conventional balance between violins 1 and 2, violas, cellos, and basses, but a group of stringed instruments which divide up in various ways and produce, when they do in fact play together, a balance of their own. The overall number is left to the discretion of the conductor, but an optimum might well be six or eight violins, four violas, five cellos (one generally playing solo), and four double basses. If this number is for any reason increased, the proportions should still conform. The purpose of this set of proportions was to keep the light from the dark. The light violins are never asked to match in weight the dark violas, cellos, and double basses. I specially wanted the sound of a small group of violins playing almost concertante and capable of great virtuosity.

In the finale I used mixed ensembles of strings and winds. Thus the six or eight violins played rapid triplets against a single trumpet in forte sonority. Then, at a repeat, the dark lower strings were added below in harmonically hard-sounding chords. On another repeat, the two-part string chords were replaced by the two trombones in other chords. Lastly, some idea of the placing of the forces in relation to each other needed to be specified in order to get the best ensemble. My plan developed from the need for the piano to be as close as possible to all the instruments it played with (see figure).

For younger generations of composers—especially those growing up after the Second World War—it has been possible to take the present position of

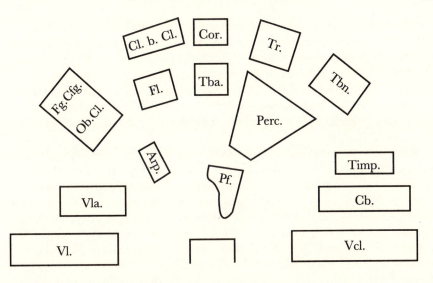

the non-standard orchestra in their stride. They have been born free from the hangover of the old historic archetype. They accept the present condition that no fresh historic archetype of the Orchestra with a capital O has been settled. The temptation to try and establish in its place another kind of model—the Schoenberg *Chamber Symphony* model roughly followed by the London Sinfonietta, for example—may be seductive for some, but not for me. For any re-definition needs to take into account a complementary liberation from the historic archetypes of symphony and concerto, or of symphonic and concertante music. This liberation is difficult to manage, and is not evaded by the use of literary and other fanciful titles.

If, from the *Concerto for Orchestra* onwards, I began to think only in terms of notional archetypes, I soon became aware that others had been there before me. This awareness became most acute with my Third Symphony. Initially, its conception was independent of any past model. In 1965, attending an Edinburgh Festival concert, I heard some music by Boulez—much of it very slow, almost immobile. I found myself saying that if ever I wanted to use that kind of music, I would have to match it with something extremely sharp, violent, and certainly speedy. In retrospect, I realize that I had gone from the sounds coming to my ears from the outside world to the interior world within my own body. As ever, the music outside constructed a protective shell which the inner creative activity seems to favour. I experience this most commonly while composing at the piano, which entails surrounding my ears with a piano approximation of, say, the orchestral or vocal score I am working on. Here the external shell and the interior imaginative activity are seemingly congruous. When a conception or an idea springs unbidden into the mind, as here, during a concert (or, as sometimes happens to me, when sounds in nature—for example, wind on big trees in leaf—make the protective shell), the interior musical imagination creates only momentarily and in very broad sweeps. At this concert, I merely turned to my neighbour, Karl Hawker, and said 'The Third Symphony has begun.' There followed the usual years of prolonged but only occasional formulation and consideration, while other compositions were being written, and the symphony itself did not reach the desk until the spring of 1970.

What had happened meanwhile was that the polarities I had experienced, between the outside immobile music I had heard and the fast music I imagined might be set against it, engendered the metaphors for a symphonic conception. They were to be present from the start of the work. I sought and found, eventually, hard chords which I compared once to an aircraft waiting to start and take off—energies of compression as against the energies of explosion in the music to follow it. But these polarities enlarged in scope to those of day and night: two halves of an extended continuous movement, forming part I of the work as a whole, the slow second half of this part incorporating a kind of musical image of the night sky and the great ocean moving beneath it.

By the time the work reached the piano desk stage, I had already written the text for the blues that were to figure later in the work. What brought me to this point of introducing a dramatic, vocal element into the symphony was a realization that the polarities I was exploring in Part I were fundamental to my temperament: that while I cherished the ideals of Beethoven, of Goethe, of Jefferson, I was living in the twentieth century, which had seen two world wars, numerous revolutions, the concentration camps, the Siberian camps, Hiroshima, Vietnam, and much else. Affirmation had to be balanced by irony. That irony surfaced in the symphony at first as a series of instrumental blues, an archetypal expression of anguish understood the world over. Incidentally, I found on investigation that the blues, whether sung or simply played, were always thought of in terms of dialogue. A voice sings to an instrument, and vice versa, or two instruments sing to each other. At this stage I was unwilling to contemplate a vocal finale; it seemed to me that Beethoven's solution in the Ninth Symphony was too easy to follow—he wrote variations which attached themselves, as it were, to certain lines of Schiller's poem. What steered me eventually towards a vocal finale was the chance hearing of a BBC radio programme comparing different interpretations of Mahler's *Das Lied von der Erde*. I realized that when he came to plan his settings of Chinese poems translated into German, Mahler wanted to articulate the songs as a specific shape. The end result was a symphony—first movement, slow movement, a scherzo comprising three songs, and then a finale. I began thus to plan and organize lyrics that would have a shape—of human beings moving from innocence to experience. The first three of the four songs are blues or blues-derived—slow, fast, slow—with strophically planned verses:

I

As I drew nurture from my mother's breast
As I drew nurture from my mother's breast
I drank in sorrow with her milk.

As I stood upright on my father's knee
As I stood upright on my father's knee
I drank in sorrow with his kiss.

Blood of their blood
None of their bone
What then is me that was not them?

II

O, I'll go walking with my nostrils
quivering and my eyeballs
flushing and my mouth
round open laughing and my tongue,
My tongue on fire.

O, I'll go whirling with my armpits
glistn'ning and my breast-buds
shaking and that navel,
which my mother left me,
luxuriously dreaming,

O, I'll go prancing with my toe-tips
flying and my knee-bones
jerking and my thighs,
with what between there lies,
My thighs aflame.

III

I found the man grown to a dwarf.
After the circus, in his tent, he said:
So many take me for a doll.
  I gave him milk and kisses.

I found the girl born dumb and blind.
She stroked my hand and tap-wrote in the palm:
I feel but cannot see the sun.
  I gave her milk and kisses.

I found the beautiful moronic child.
His smiling eyes shone bright; he said:
Nothing; for his mind is lost.
  I gave him milk and kisses.

As I lay down beside my mate,
Body to body,
We did not heed the sorrow.

Ah, merciful God, if such there be,
Let him, let her, be born straight.
But if no answer to the prayer.
   We shall give milk
   We shall give kisses.

The fourth song was more of a dramatic *scena*, bringing the polarities of the present into focus. I was impelled here to refer musically and verbally to Schiller's 'Ode to Joy' as sung by the chorus in Beethoven's Ninth. For I had looked up Schiller's poem to discover what, in fact, Beethoven had not set—a considerable amount, in fact. In Schiller's poem everybody is accepted in the brotherhood of man—this sacred band of people—but you have to fulfil certain qualifications. One is that you were either married or had some sort of friend. If you were alone, however, you were ordered to leave, weeping, from the holy circle—you were outside the brotherhood of man altogether. This aroused my interest: even in that extraordinary period of affirmation, there were exclusions. While I thrill to the affirmations as I hear them in Beethoven's Ninth, I can't but help recall these exclusions, which I could not tolerate. Blake had pin-pointed the same problem. To his period's belief in natural law—the belief, which underpins Jefferson's magnificent opening of the American Declaration of Independence—Blake asked: 'What true law of equity can be found in a nature that has produced both the Tyger and the Lamb?' Or, as he put it once in an aphorism, 'One Law for the Lion and Ox is Oppression.' Again, to those who still held to the Christian Creed, he exclaimed: 'How can you believe both in Nobodaddy-Jehovah, who demanded 1,000 Amalekite foreskins as a sacrifice, and an all-forgiving Jesus?' The answer in our own day is that we cannot. It is better for us to accept the Tyger and the Lamb, Jehovah and Jesus, as enduring states of our common humanity—hence my line, 'My sibling was the torturer'; now one, now the other, is in the ascendant. What is 'out of date' in Schiller's concept of joy is any romantic notion of its universality and inevitability. All that has happened since, in aid of various political utopias, has but deepened the disillusion. Yet, if now is our season in hell, then when we occasionally celebrate, as we must, and if we can, we do so from a deeper need and with a sharper pang. So, in the fourth song of my finale, I at first transformed Schiller's couplet

Alle Menschene werder Brüder
Wo dein sanfter Flügel weilt

and then confronted it with the evils of the present; following which, I permitted myself a burst of what I afterwards called Nobodaddy rhetoric (impossible to any true poet!) preceding some dream of the peaceable kingdom. The most difficult thing was not to let the ironies overwhelm the affirmations. 'Though the dream crack, we will remake it' had to be put down as perhaps a dream—as such an absolute necessity, if we are to go on living. The words of Martin Luther King himself lent it plausibility:

IV

They sang that when she waved her wings
The Goddess joy would make us one.
And did my brother die of frostbite in the camp?
And was my sister charred to cinders in the oven?

We know not so much joy
For so much sorrow—
Though my fine body dances;
Nor so much evil—
Though I sometimes be good.
My sibling was the torturer.
He takes his place.

So if the worm was given love-lust,
Let him stay patient in his place.
But if the cherub stands b'fore God,
Let him demote himself to man,
Then spit his curses across the celestial face
Though he be answered (Answered!?)
With annihilation from the whirlwind.

It is our agony
We fractured men
Surmise a deeper mercy;
That no god has shown.

I have a dream
That my strong hand shall grip the cruel
That my strong mouth shall kiss the fearful
That my strong arms shall lift the lame
And on my giant legs we'll whirl our way
Over the visionary earth
In mutual celebration.

What though the dream crack!
We shall remake it.
Staring with those startled eyes at what we are—
Blood of my blood
Bone of my bone
We sense a huge compassionate power
To heal
To love.

The bringing together of the purely instrumental first part of the symphony and the dramatic second half forced me into a position where I had to acknowledge Beethoven's Ninth Symphony as, in fact, an overwhelming historical archetype of itself. Firstly, I had to think out how and where the voice would emerge in part II. I began by putting down a kind of scherzo, a *mélange* of five 'musics' (I suppose I had been listening to Charles Ives!), whose interplay was carefully planned to develop into a fantastic jam session which suddenly stops—just like that. I wanted to emulate Beethoven at this point and make my own gear change to another set of possibilities using the voice. But I was unable to do so. Beethoven's own transition, a blaring piece of *Schreckenmusik*, was too strong: I couldn't do anything better than quote what he had done and extend it in my own way. From there it was a natural step to integrate further elements from Beethoven into the later sections of the piece. And at the very end, I wanted to preserve the underlying polarities, concentrating all the violence into strong, sharp, rather acid wind chords, but matching them with string chords, representing some kind of compassionate answer from behind.

With each of my main compositions for the concert-hall since the 1970s, my initial premiss has been a notional rather than historical archetype. At the same time, having observed how Beethoven's notional archetype in his Ninth Symphony could become a historical archetype, I felt able to lean on past precedent to some extent when I wrote Symphony No. 4. Here I began a sequence of pieces that condensed every aspect of the music into a single movement, in particular, searching out new ways of intermingling the dramatic and the abstract. I heard Colin Davis talk about Sibelius's Seventh Symphony as a 'birth-to-death' piece, and that seemed just right for the symphony I wanted myself to compose. I knew too that others—Strauss in *Ein Heldenleben* and his other symphonic poems, Elgar in *Falstaff*—had successfully embraced a whole cycle of experience within a single-movement design. Thus, the symphony I now planned had an abstract framework, paying homage to the historical symphonic archetype with an introduction and exposition, slow movement and development, scherzo and trio, recapitulation and coda. Interspersed with these main sections were subsidiary episodes of a more divagatory type—like episodes in a rondo or the fresh ideas being brought into play in a seventeenth-century fantasia. The last of these moved as far away as possible from the main thematic material, elaborating upon an actual Gibbons string fantasia that I had previously used in the *Divertimento on Sellinger's Round*. The intriguing task I then faced was how to integrate this back into the design as whole. The outcome, thus, was a continuous seven-section piece, with main and subsidiary lines of thought.

The shape and contents of the score were, however, no less determined by extra-musical considerations. Back in the 1920s, I had been taken to the Pitt–Rivers Anthropological Museum in Dorset, and there was shown an early film, speeded up, of a birth of a foetus (maybe that of a rabbit). At successive stages, it shook and became two and then four and so on. That creation image remained stored up in my memory, and eventually suggested the character of the introductory ideas in the symphony. I also envisaged marking various stages in the unfolding of the music with breathing effects, so that there would be the gentle sound of an organism coming to life at the start, a gradual expiration at the end, and something of the character of a violent storm in the main central climax. The mosaic schemes used in previous works could also figure prominently, partly because they helped define the contours and horizons of the orchestral sonority. Thus, after the opening introduction, three main ideas are introduced, featuring the strength and brilliance of the brass, the dance-like energy of the strings, and the lyricism of the woodwind. These are combined to produce a climax rounded off by a poetic passage on the horns: a sequence that reappears twice subsequently, with the horn passage raised by a tone each time. In this work, as in Symphony No. 3, the block-like construction of the work and its dramatic or extra-musical component helped me to find the right way to end: a sequence of repeated episodes, which are overtaken by the breathing. Standard final perorations, even solid cadences, were not to my temperament (listening to one or two in my earlier pieces, I am unsettled by them).

Renewing the concerto I found rather more difficult. Although I had previously written a piano concerto (1956), I was not terribly in sympathy with the late Romantic confrontation of soloist and orchestra. What interested me more was the idea of using more than one soloist, which I first tried out in the *Fantasia Concertante on a Theme of Corelli* (1953). When I eventually decided to write a triple concerto, with violin, viola, and cello soloists, what attracted me was the possibility of demonstrating the various sharp contrasts in sonority as between these three stringed instruments. Outside baroque music, however, the historical models for double and triple concertos are relatively few and far between. Beethoven's Triple Concerto is clearly a concerto for piano trio and orchestra: and I was clear that my concerto would not be for string trio and orchestra—the three players were to be real soloists, not a chamber music ensemble. Here, as with Mozart's Sinfonia Concertante for violin and viola (K. 482) and Brahms's Double Concerto, what exercised my mind was the problem of avoiding tedium with lengthy multiple expositions, as everyone gets his chance to state and comment upon the main thematic ideas. Between Symphony No. 4 and the Triple Concerto, I composed a Fourth String Quartet—another continuous single-movement design, although it has four main sections. Near the end of this, I wanted to answer a final outburst of violence with an overwhelming vision of lyricism and radiance: hence the passage reproduced in Ex. 12.1, with its unusual textural layout of first violin and cello singing ardently in their highest registers, second violin a decorative line somewhere in between, and double-stopping viola at the bottom. This gave

Ex. 12.1 *String Quartet No. 4*

me a strong clue as to how the three soloists in the concerto might make a distinctive impression when playing together for the first time—hence my rewriting of part of this episode from the quartet (see Ex. 12.2). This ensemble passage thereafter became an important reference point in the concerto, returning at the end of the first movement and at the end of the work. I also found that the spacing of the soloists could be emulated later—for example, in the opening theme of the central slow movement.

The next decision was the manner in which the soloists would introduce themselves. Normal expectations would be: cello, viola, violin, or violin, viola, cello, and there was the risk that the viola might be overshadowed. I therefore began the concerto with three cadenzas, the first of them giving the viola full prominence, with violin and cello responding to it. This sequence could also be recapitulated later on in the concerto. The differentiation between

Ex. 12.2 *Triple Concerto*

soloists thus established could be extended to the orchestra, so that the mosaic scheme of thematic characters that ensued seemed logical; also other orchestral soloists (notably flute and bass oboe) could become important obbligato partners.

The structure of the concerto followed historical precedent with a fast–slow–fast sequence of movements, but included linking interludes that helped signal the change of mood within the movement to follow. Thus the first interlude prepared the way for the reflective, nocturnal slow movement, whereas the second one suggested a gradual transformation from night into day; indeed, here I felt impelled to quote some of the dawn music from the concluding scene of *The Midsummer Marriage*. Debussy's *Ibéria* has a similar kind of structure.

Not long before I actually sat down to write the Triple Concerto, I visited Java and Bali. I had first been attracted to gamelan music when I heard some on records in the 1930s, and imitated its gong-sonorities in my First Piano Sonata. Now, hearing several kinds of gamelan music live, I sensed the relevance of its decorative procedures to my own work. Thus, in the concerto, apart from extending the orchestral palette with the sonorities of gongs, bells, and other pitched percussion, I included one or other Balinese-modelled episodes as landmarks in the design. One such was the refrain that concludes the exposition of the first movement, in which the main thematic line is in the centre of the texture, with other instruments surrounding it with shimmering repeated notes and similarly patterned lines (see Ex. 12.3). This ritornello idea became useful to mark the end of the first movement and, in a gradually fragmented version, the entire work.

The confidence to try and revitalize the symphony orchestra and established genres of composition like the symphony and the concerto undoubtedly derived in part from the experience of writing for the theatre. Extending further the stylistic scope of the mosaic schemes I had used in *King Priam* not only enabled me to give *The Knot Garden* its special flavour, but prepared the ground for the jam sessions of the scherzos of Symphonies Nos. 3 and 4. When, in my eighties, I dared envisage a fifth opera, *New Year*, its character entailed a radical rethinking of the orchestral component involved. The close integration of dance into the action necessitated a musical style drawing closely upon various forms of the vernacular: this suggested a pit orchestra more like that of a Broadway or West End musical—with electric guitars, homogeneous groups of wind, including three saxophones, an extensive percussion component, and fewer strings. Above all, for the first time in twenty-five years or so, I excluded the piano, which had previously seemed essential for its sheer versatility: I had used it to accompany operatic recitatives, as a potential soloist, as a useful means of reinforcing other sonorities, and as a way of boosting the rhythmic and percussive impact of the music. Although I didn't extend all the sonic innovations of *New Year* to the concert-hall, thereafter I made a point of not including a piano in the orchestra for *Byzantium* and *The Rose Lake*. My piano period was over!

What I discovered, however, from *New Year*, were possibilities for a new kind of orchestral luminosity using the minimum number of players. Despite the cornucopia of fresh colours in the scoring of this opera, the textures are

Ex. 12.3 *Triple Concerto*

often limited to two or three parts, the aim being a very distilled kind of lyricism. With the mosaic-style scoring of the *Concerto for Orchestra*, I had explored the notion of using the orchestra as a collection of chamber ensembles and soloists. This also brought with it a potential for heterophony, which I was able in three subsequent works—*Byzantium*, String Quartet No. 5, and *The Rose Lake*—to make a special feature. In particular, *The Rose Lake*, while scored for a large orchestra that includes six horns, three trumpets, two harps, and an array of percussion, contains relatively little for the fullest complement of performers. The substitution of such chamber music intimacy for the powerful orchestral rhetoric of works like the Third and Fourth symphonies also entailed replacing the conventional timpani with the less robust but telling and pointed sonorities of roto-toms.

For many decades I had insisted on writing my own texts for large-scale works, rather than using existing poetry or dramatic texts or words specially conceived by a poet or dramatist. It thus seemed perverse, to many people, that I should now propose to set to music an entire Yeats poem, 'Byzantium'. In retrospect, a number expressed surprise that I had not chosen to set Yeats's earlier poem, 'Sailing to Byzantium' (1927), whose vivid images have perhaps more obvious musical implications:

> . . . The young
> in one another's arms, birds in the trees,
> —Those dying generations—at their song,
> The salmon-falls, the mackerel-crowded seas,
> Fish, flesh, or fowl, commend all summer long
> Whatever is begotten, born and dies.
> Caught in that sensual music all neglect
> Monuments of unageing intellect.

My approach to the composition of *Byzantium* was, in fact, somewhat different. I was not writing a song, a dramatic *scena*, or a cantata, or one or other known genre of vocal music: rather, I was impelled to create a work that was *sui generis*. Instinct led me towards the invention of another notional archetype of vocal music for the concert-hall, whatever that might entail. My starting-point was indeed an attraction to the actual structure of 'Byzantium'—a five-stanza format which led me straight off to plan a continuous work in five sections. Furthermore, the advantage, it seemed to me, of this particular poem over its predecessor was its sheer compression and condensation, allowing me, the composer, to apply techniques of musical extension. 'Byzantium' was, in sum, an artefact: an artistic object in which all the emotion of the artist had disappeared inside. One might compare it with a Brancusi sculpture, where the artist's subjective emotions have disappeared in the work, and nothing is left but the polished metal. The extension processes I had in mind here implied, moreover, a virtuosity of performance that became the prime intention—virtuosity above all for the singer.

Each stanza of Yeats's poem has a rhyme scheme of four short lines, each pair with rhymed endings of different sorts. Immediately, with the first line 'The unpurged images of day recede', it meant that I could extend and repeat the word 'recede'. Throughout I was mesmerized by special images. At the core of the poem, the third and fourth stanzas contain the contrasting images of song and dance: not the actuality of song and dance, but images of them. The golden bird sings better than the actual bird (and my vocalizing extension allowed it to do so); the dance is a dance of 'flames begotten of flame'— here again the 'dance' and 'trance' rhymes in the poem suggested linked musical extensions.

What appears for the first time in the poem with the final stanza is the sea: not the sea rippling by the shore that appears in Yeats's earlier Innisfree poetry, but a powerful symbolic force; and hence the concentration of Yeats's imagery:

> Those images that yet
> Fresh images beget
> That dolphin-torn, that gong-tormented sea.

These final lines always fascinated me. Now, the challenge of their internal rhymes, and particularly the convergence of the mythological and the actual at the very end, prompted the return of the opening music of the piece and a final ambivalent resolution. The musical ingredients are almost naïve: but it is their fusion that counts.

Listening to Solti rehearse *Byzantium* with the Chicago Symphony Orchestra, I was almost unable to concentrate on the music being played: what set me off was the wondrous range of orchestral colours being deployed, which now geared me up to write another orchestral work! As it happened, the initial impetus to do so—the *Einfall*—had come sometime earlier. During a holiday in Senegal, late in 1990, with a young architect friend, Graham Modlen, we were recommended to visit a small lake, known as Le Lac Rose, where at midday the impact of the sun was such as to transform its whitish green colour to whitish pink. I have always loved lakes; and in earlier days I visited several— particularly those of the English Lake District and in Switzerland and Italy. At the beginning of Frazer's *The Golden Bough* there's an evocation of a tiny lake in Italy, Lake Nemi, with its Temple of Diana and her nymphs: this is the context for his account of the sinister ancient ritual of kingship, wherein a priest is pursued around the lake by an adversary, who kills him and takes his place, then in due course is himself pursued and killed. The frontispiece to Frazer's book was a black and white print of Turner's early painting of Lake Nemi: recently I acquired a print of Turner's later, rather better painting of the lake, and it remains a favourite. As things now turned out in Senegal,

Graham and I reached Le Lac Rose at midday, just in time to see it turn a marvellous translucent pink. The sight of it triggered a profound disturbance within me: the sort of disturbance which told me that the new orchestral work had begun.

Two possible historical archetypes might be borne in mind in relation to *The Rose Lake*: Beethoven's 'Pastoral' Symphony and Debussy's *La Mer*. Notwithstanding the titles to their various movements, the essence of both is a kind of symphonic construction: a five-movement design in Beethoven's case; three movements of so-called 'symphonic sketches' in Debussy's. The descriptive or evocative elements in the Debussy are perhaps more concealed than they are in the Beethoven. But both are concerned with expressions of feeling rather than pictorialism; and with both, the extra-musical is generalized. In my work, the external image is specific, referring to an actual lake in an actual place and an actual visual transformation that I could translate as the central feature of the piece. But how in fact could this be done, in musical terms? There was no instant answer. But the idea that took shape gradually was that some kind of lyric utterance would burgeon within the design, initially polarized against a sharper, more pungent element, but ultimately reaching a climactic stage where song reigned supreme.

The outcome was that I was able to formulate a musical structure whose main stages I risked identifying with captions: 'The lake begins to sing', 'The lake song is echoed from the sky', 'The lake is in full song', 'The lake song leaves the sky', and 'The lake sings itself to sleep'. All this may sound naïve; but, in fact, the titles signify an important dimension to what might otherwise be baldly summarized as a continuous five-part composition (like *Byzantium*), in essence a set of variations. The descriptive captions finally suggested an overall subtitle for the piece: 'A song without words for orchestra'. While the initial emergence of the lyricism and its climactic outpouring are not hard to imagine, the echoing of the lake song from the sky became a matter of canonic imitation (a bass clarinet melody echoed a bar and a half later by flute); the reverse happens when the lake song leaves the sky (high violins echoed by cellos). Overall, one can think of the piece as also manifesting a progression from dawn to dusk.

With both *Byzantium* and *The Rose Lake*, I was stretching to some degree my ability to invent new notional archetypes of concert music: that, and the effort of producing an ultimate refinement of orchestral language, has proved, at my advanced age, a tremendous physical strain. Now, the very thought of trying to go further is enough to bring me out in spots!

Chapter 13

T. S. ELIOT AND
A CHILD OF OUR TIME

It was quite by accident that I came into contact with T. S. Eliot. Yet soon he was to turn into a sort of artistic mentor. I met him through Frank Morley, an American colleague of Eliot's. Morley was seconded from Harcourt Brace, the New York publishers, to Faber & Faber in London, where Eliot worked in the afternoons. Morley's younger son, Oliver, then about 6, while musically very gifted, was virtually inarticulate verbally. If he spoke at all, he would make remarks like: 'That dog barks in B flat.' This was a real headache for the family. Morley asked W. H. Auden for advice. Auden recommended me, as someone musically well versed and interested in psychology. Thus it came about that Morley visited me at my tiny cottage (two up, two down) in Limpsfield, Surrey, on his way home to Crowhurst, further south down the road. The notion was that I should 'teach' Oliver at the piano about his obsessively beloved music, in order to tempt him to speak. Terms were discussed and agreed: and all the time I could see through the window, mooching about the minute grass frontage, the famous figure in the clerical hat—Eliot himself.

Through Oliver, I got to know the Morley family. On summer weekends, I bicycled over to enjoy some vicarious family life—only to find that Eliot, who had rented rooms nearby (they were soon known as Uncle Tom's Cabin), also turned up at the house proper. On such occasions, he divested himself of his poet's mantle and helped Morley's wife in her domestic duties, both in the kitchen and in the garden (where once I found him studiously picking black currants). After supper in the evenings we all played monopoly. Eliot was, in fact, quite good at monopoly. The problem was always Oliver. If Oliver ever lost, it was simply calamitous. Eliot bore with it all, good-humouredly. (Oliver, I ought to mention, had an amusing side to his nature. He loved to show off—most of all, by standing on his head. Once I took him to hear Schnabel play a recital of late Beethoven piano sonatas. In the interval, Oliver did a head-stand in the foyer!)

Although we had no professional involvement, I managed to talk to Eliot extensively then about the nature of poetry and drama: matters which were deeply occupying his own mind at that time (i.e. 1936–8). Our talks took place later in his room at Faber & Faber's. I would indicate that I'd like to see him, and he would generally invite me to tea. At these tea-time conversations he (above all others) helped me clarify my notions of the aesthetics of theatre and opera. Unwittingly, he became my spiritual father. Sometimes he even guided my reading. For instance, it was through Eliot, later, that I came to read and identify closely with Yeats. Gradually, after the war, I saw less of him, for one reason or another. I remember one late encounter at a lunch party given by the Sitwells (one of several which I attended, where a surprisingly tolerant attitude was taken to my irreverent leftist views). Eliot had just returned from Sweden, where he had been awarded the Nobel Prize. Drily, he told of his discomfiture when, just before dinner with the King, he had received back his only spare underwear from the laundry, in an impossibly shrunken state. On his return to England he had to buy replacements, and parted with an appalling number of clothing coupons!

My last meeting with Eliot was in Edinburgh, at one of the performances of the first production of *The Elder Statesman*, in 1958. I found myself sitting beside him. Both of us were unaccompanied, so we were able to talk freely. I chided him gently, I recall, for going so far away from the poetic language of *The Family Reunion* to the near-prose of the subsequent plays. Would he move back once more towards poetry? He said it was possible. If that was truly in his mind, it was not in his fate.

In the early days, before the war, I must have known Eliot better than I can now recall; for when I came to write *A Child of Our Time*, I plucked up courage to ask him if he would provide a text. This he agreed to do, as long as I gave him a precise scheme of musical numbers and an exact indication of the number and kinds of words I considered necessary for each musical section. I returned home to do just this for him, because I saw at once what he meant. In oratorio or opera, the musical schemes must be paramount, if the work is to live. I had not read Susanne K. Langer at that time, but taught, in part, by Eliot, I instinctively appreciated her dictum: 'Every work of art has its being in only one order of art; compositions of different orders are not simply conjoined, but all except one will cease to appear as what they are.'[1] So that, while drama eats up all incidental music and painted stage sets, music, in Langer's words, 'ordinarily swallows words and action creating (thereby) opera, oratorio, or song'.[2]

This, then, was the reason why Eliot demanded that I, as the musician, prepare a musical scheme, before he as a poet did anything whatsoever. Also, since he knew as well as I did that narrative recitative needs many words, while a vocal fugue may use next to none, he asked for precise directions concerning the numbers and kinds of words. As he expressed it: 'I need my homework set for me.'

---

[1] Suzanne K. Langer, *Problems of Art* (London, 1957), 85.   [2] Ibid.

I put down on paper for Eliot a 'scenario' under the title 'Sketch for a Modern Oratorio'[3] (the final title for the piece had not then appeared). Eliot considered this sketch for some weeks, and then gave me the surprising advice to write all the words myself. He felt that the sketch was already a text in embryo (as, in fact, it was), and whatever words he, Eliot, wrote would be of such greater *poetic* quality they would 'stick out a mile'. While remaining true to his belief in the primacy of the *musical* imagination in opera and oratorio, he considered the *poetically* imaginative words of a real poet to be often unnecessary.

Thus it was that I began the somewhat unusual task for a composer: to invent or find the necessary words for my own musical scheme.

Set down coldly like this, it might almost appear as though the musical scheme which the composer needs is to be conceived as absolutely independent of his dramatic or other verbal material. But the issue is only one of *primacy*. In the case of *A Child of Our Time* the inner feelings, which could be expressed only in some artistic image, were finally given objective substance in the musical scheme of an oratorio. But the dramatic and even philosophic material which the music had to 'swallow' was entirely embedded in the gradually forming musical apprehensions from the very start. A great deal of this fusion of words and music is of necessity traditional. Or rather, there are certain constructive or functional practices which are basic and unchangeable. If the dramatic material requires narrative, then this part of the musical scheme will be fundamentally different from the musical correlative to the contemplation or expression of a single situation or emotion. The one is recitative and the other aria; and if they are to play their proper functional or constructive parts in the scheme, they will be, at any rate, analytically recognizable as such.

Narrative or contemplation, recitative or aria, whether for solo voice or for a chorus, these then are the basic functions in any and every scheme of oratorio. Being quite clear on the matter, I found it easier, when I came to prepare this homework for Eliot, to sketch out an embryo text, where of course my proposed words were already at one with my musical scheme.

But from music of the past, I also knew of two local traditions of arrangements which had always fascinated me. The scheme of Handel's *Messiah* and the scheme of the Lutheran Passions. The shape of *Messiah* is tripartite. The first part is all prophecy and preparation. The second part is epic: from the birth of Christ to the second coming, judgement, millennium, and world's end. The third part is meditative: chiefly, the words of St Paul. Incomplete performances grievously impair this wonderful shape. But I have always observed and admired it. I decided to accept this format for *A Child of Our Time*, by keeping a first part entirely general, restricting the epic material to a second part, and using a third part for consequential comment.

---

[3] See Ch. 14 below.

The scheme of the Lutheran Passions is of course more unitary, based as it must be on the liturgical gospel set for Passion Sunday. Within that unitary scheme the traditional musico-verbal functions can always be distinguished: narrational recitative, descriptive chorus, contemplative aria, and finally the special Protestant constituent of the congregational hymn. I wanted to use *all* these functional practices within the tripartite shape borrowed from *Messiah*.

The obvious difficulty lay over the congregational hymn. A modern oratorio based on sensibilities of emotion expressive of inner and outer events in Europe and America between the world wars and destined for the concert-hall, not the church, cannot merely use the metaphorical language of liturgical Christianity. Christian hymns could not speak to agnostics or Jews; Jewish hymns could speak to the general concert-hall public even less. For to 'speak' in this sense is to do the operation which much-loved hymns do to the appropriate congregation of the faithful. But in what sense at all are listeners in a concert-hall a congregation of the faithful?

For some time I was at a loss. Then one never-to-be-forgotten Sunday, I heard a singer on the radio sing the Negro spiritual 'Steal Away'. At the phrase, 'The trumpet sounds within-a my soul', I was blessed with an immediate intuition: that I was being moved by this phrase in some way beyond what the musical phrase in itself warranted. I realized that in England or America everyone would be moved in this way, forcing me to see that the unique verbal and musical metaphor for this particular function in this particular oratorio had been found. But it was not until after the world war which soon supervened that I could test in performance the fact that the Negro spiritual presented no expressional barriers anywhere in Europe. Nor maybe anywhere in the world.

I sent to America for a collection of spirituals,[4] and when these came, I had an experience possibly similar to those of the Lutheran composers. I opened the collection, and found that it contained words and tunes for every dramatic or religious situation that could be imagined. I chose five spirituals, therefore, for their tunes and words, which provided the exact 'congregational' metaphor for five calculated situations in my scheme.

The next question, that of presentation, meant a further purchase from America: this time recordings of a cappella performances of spirituals by the relatively conventional Hal Johnson Choir (whom I remembered from the sound-track of the film *Green Pastures*)[5] and by the 'hot' vocal group called the Mitchell Christian Singers. These latter went in for cross-rhythmical counterpoint by the spoken voice, as well as a great deal of blues-provoked ambiguity of pitch. Fascinating though this disc was, I had to forego such extreme methods of presentation, if only for the sake of the normal European concert-hall choir. I also realized that I would have to purify the harmonies and clarify the contrapuntal texture.

---

[4] See Ch. 14, n. 16 below.   [5] See Ch. 14, n. 15 below.

I did not need to use Negro material for its own characteristic flamboyance, its nostalgia, or its rhythmic exhilaration (all of which are elements Gershwin uses powerfully in *Porgy and Bess,* for instance). I had to elevate this musical vernacular to take charge of feelings of a rather higher order without at all losing its immediacy of impact and appeal. This did not just mean purging the conventional harmonies of sentimentality: but rather in apparently excluding all harmonies whatsoever. I accepted the underlying conventional chord of the added seventh particular to each spiritual, and often sought variety only through rhythmic counterpoint and by playing off tonal masses of choral sound against solo-voiced leaders. The harmonically static choruses, thus, at the five critical points, provided a peculiar contrast to the much more harmonically ambiguous music of the other numbers. They became periods of rest.

Having got so far, I had to accept also that this virtue of emotional release supplied by the spirituals had to be paid for by allowing the popular words and music to affect the *general* style, within which the 'sophisticated' parts of the oratorio had to be written. I used the interval of a minor third, produced so characteristically in the melodies of the spirituals when moving from the fifth of the tonic to the flat seventh, as a basic interval of the whole work— sometimes on its own, sometimes superimposed upon the open fifth below the note. These intervals (minor third, fifth, and flat seventh) could lead on the one hand to a kind of sliding chromatic fugue (cf. no. 5, 'Chorus of the Oppressed'); and on the other, to a Kurt Weill-like tango (cf. no. 6, tenor solo, 'I have no money for my bread'); or even to a dance-like accompaniment (cf. no. 27, alto solo, 'The soul of man'). Initially, there was a good deal of press criticism concerning the propriety of turning the popular into something sophisticated in this way. Subsequently, however, the spirituals have been seen as an integral and essential part of the work, and the transitions to them are regarded as effective.

When I took the sketch to Eliot, I had already decided upon the five spirituals, and observed their brand of folk-poetry. There were first and foremost specific references to the Bible:

> Go down Moses,
> Way down in Egypt land;

echoes of the Apocalypse:

> The trumpet sounds within-a my soul;

homely phrases such as

> Nobody knows the trouble I see

and

> I'm goin' to lay down my heavy load;

and wonderful, poetically fresh metaphors like the line from 'Deep River',

I want to cross over into camp-ground,

which particularly stirred me. As with the Negro melodies, therefore, when I came to take stock of how I could best indicate to Eliot the kind of words I imagined suitable, I turned first to the verses of the spirituals, and noted the various metaphors I have listed above.

The taking stock was actually more elaborate. I tried to set in order all the considerations of musical and dramatic shape (*Messiah* and the Passions) and all the considerations which I had so long pondered concerning the dramatic and philosophic material itself. After such prolonged deliberation, I was now ready to lay down a viable scheme of numbers with their lengths and kinds, ready even to indicate by actual words what I meant. Since I was always expecting that Eliot's words would replace mine, I wrote my words on every right-hand page of the manuscript book and wrote an explanation of what I was intending on every left-hand page.

Comparing the sketch with the published work, it is clear that I was able to set down straightaway a musico-dramatic scheme (of three parts, each containing several numbers) which could remain unchanged. I prefaced each part (but especially Part I) with a chorus which I considered functionally as a kind of 'Prologue in Heaven' on the lines of Goethe's *Faust*: that is, everything seen in the most general terms in relation to the cosmos. I then proceeded inward from that point. In the overall tripartite scheme, the same inward movement takes place from the general to the individual, from Part I to Part II (and then out again in Part III), as happens within Part I itself. In tabular form, it looks like this:

I The overall pattern
   Part I   The 'situation' in general terms: from cosmic to human
   Part II   The effects of the 'situation' on an individual human being
   Part III   Meditations on this drama; moving outward again toward the
              generally human

II The outward–inward–outward movement of the scheme of part I, which
   was to echo the same rhythm as between the three parts:
   1 Choral overture: the 'cosmological' position
   2 Alto solo: a generalized argument; with alto considered as personifi-
      cation of the soul, whether of the world or of man
   3 A scene of question and answer between chorus and alto concerning
      the argument (This and the two numbers above made up my idea of
      a 'Prologue in Heaven'.)
   4 Bass solo: narration of the general human situation in our time; the
      bass considered (to quote the 'Sketch') 'as a father-God figure'
   5 Choral fugue: for which I first wrote no words, simply writing,
      'Chorus of the Oppressed'; the chorus personifying the generally
      human

6   Tenor solo: statement of the ordinary man within this general mass;
     i.e. (in terms of my theme) his cry of anguish
7   Soprano solo: statement of the ordinary woman; her cry of anguish
8   A spiritual: the first hint of comfort, at least in simple generalized
     terms

If we look back for a moment, first at the overall pattern, we can see that if
each part began with a prologue-chorus, then the choruses would be in relation to each other as well as in relation to the coming part each prefaced.
Using the final text, this is how they read:

Part I   The world turns on its dark side. It is winter.
Part II   A star rises in midwinter. Behold the man! The scapegoat! The
           child of our time.
Part III   The cold deepens. The world descends into the icy waters.
           Where lies the jewel of great price.

From the above finished example, the problems of writing or constructing
one's own text to one's own musico-dramatic scheme can be seen quite easily. Thus, having decided on the function of the choral overtures and having
decided that musically each was 'to be a short constructed chorus on a "text"
or two "texts", to last about a minute or more' (to quote from the instruction
to Eliot for Chorus 1),[6] the verbal problem reduced itself from the nebulous
to the particular—to that of style and metaphor.

Eschewing the poetic, which seemed to be inappropriate to the theme, I
wanted a style of short statements, whether of story or comment. I called this
style to myself 'lapidaric'. Remembering the poet Wilfred Owen, killed in the
First World War, who had always seemed close to me in spirit, I thought of
two lines from one of his prophetic poems:

           War broke. And now the winter of the world
           With perishing great darkness closes in.[7]

I joined this notion of seasons in history with personal experience concerning
the 'dark' and the 'shadow' in Jung's terminology, and then wrote for Eliot
the two texts of Chorus 1 in my own over-simple words:

           The world turns on its dark side.
           It is winter.[8]

On the opposite left-hand page, I explained discursively for Eliot what I
needed, and quoted the lines from Wilfred Owen. I proceeded in this way for
every number. I considered carefully the function of the proposed number, its
duration, and so forth; invented or borrowed words that could stand as example; and wrote an explanation. Where I could think of no example, I wrote
only the explanation and left the right-hand page free.

---

[6] See p. 118 below.   [7] See Ch. 14, n. 2 below.   [8] See Ch. 14, n. 3 below.

Now once Eliot had persuaded me that the sketch had a viable shape, in his opinion, and that I myself had already done much of the strictly verbal work, I had to get down to filling up the gaps and the words. Not being a poet but a composer, I took endless advice, whether for whole phrases or simple words. I also hunted around in literature. Thus, for the short text needed for the choral fugue, 'Chorus of the Oppressed', I eventually twisted a sentence from Isaiah to read:

When shall the usurer's city cease?[9]

And I was excited, I remember, when I made use of an anonymous 'folk' expression in a later declamatory chorus, 'Let them starve in No-Man's-Land!' 'No-Man's-Land' had a fine ring to it, expressed exactly what I wanted, and joined itself admirably to the Negro metaphors, such as 'I want to cross over into camp-ground, Lord'. Much less successful, in my opinion, were the occasional indigestible psychological metaphors which produced phrases like

I am caught between my desires and their frustration as between the hammer and the anvil[10]

But the psychological jargon gave one tremendous phrase which is the motto for the whole work:

I would know my shadow and my light,
so shall I at last be whole.[11]

The seasonal metaphor supplies the final words (before the last spiritual):

It is Spring.

Summing up, regarding this matter of shape and text, it seems to me that the composer works with himself as librettist in much the same way as he would work with a poet. However, unless he is willing to give over the whole conception of shape to the poet, he *must* prepare the poet's homework, in something like the manner of my sketch for Eliot.

[9] See Ch. 14, n. 11 below.   [10] See p. 175 below.   [11] See Ch. 14, n. 56 below.

Chapter 14

SKETCH FOR A MODERN ORATORIO[1]

---

[1] See pp. 110–16 above.

PART I

1.

This is to be a short constructed Chorus on a 'text', or two 'texts'. To last about a minute or more. Enough to set the mood of descent. The metaphor of winter and spring is perhaps a necessary one, as will be seen later.

> ('War broke. And now the winter of the world
> With perishing great darkness closes in.')[2]

---

[2] Wilfred Owen, 'The Seed'; see n. 5 below.

PART I

1.

CHORUS.
The world turns on its dark side. It is winter.[3]

---

[3] Final layout:

The world turns on its dark side.
It is winter.

2.

This solo is 'rhythmic translation', either a sort of recitative, or sung speech, rising to specific points of expression by the slight use of purely musical means. The alto voice is conceived as a personification of the soul, the anima, descended into the deeps of chaos, whence she has drawn the gods after her. The great price paid for the necessary advance in empirical science is the severance of the spiritual union with the anima. Hence the accumulation of unconscious, dark, destructive powers that burst up in man as a disease, war, revolution, and so forth. Man, by bringing the gods down from heaven, has brought them into his own passions and body. As yet he does not comprehend this, and so the 'Living God' is a gnawing pain in the vitals. This section is as yet simply a statement of the position; the prologue in heaven.

(The time is 2 or 3 minutes.)

2.

ALTO SOLO.

The Promethean intellect has measured the heavens with a telescope and driven the gods from their empty thrones. But the soul, from the depths of chaos, watches the gods return to man as vultures feeding on the liver. The living God consumes within and turns the flesh to cancer.[4]

---

[4] 'Man has measured the heavens with a telescope, driven the gods from their thrones. But the soul, watching the chaotic mirror, knows that the gods return. Truly, the living God consumes within and turns the flesh to cancer.'

See n. 46 and 48 below: cf. Jung: 'Our intellect has achieved the most tremendous things, but in the meantime our spiritual dwelling has fallen into disrepair. We are absolutely convinced that even with the aid of the latest and largest reflecting telescope, now being built in America, men will discover behind the farthest nebulae no fiery empyrean; and we know that our eyes will wander despairingly through the dead emptiness of interstellar space. Nor is it any better when mathematical physics reveals to us the world of the infinitely small. In the end we dig up the wisdom of all ages and peoples, only to find that everything most dear and precious to us has already been said in the most superb language' (*Collected Works*, trans. R. F. C. Hull, xi/1 (London, 1959), 16).

3.

This dialogue is all 'rhythmic translation'. The chorus is conceived of here as mankind in general. The alto is still the world soul. The paradoxes are beyond the mass of men, so they feel a sense of powerlessness before the events (the Sept. crisis, etc.)—they feel the spiritual impulses in an untempered form, out of all control, as seeds before the wind. The association to the war and the general upheaval is in Wilfred Owen's lines:

> But now the exigent winter, and the need
> Of sowings for new spring, and flesh for seed.[5]

(Time: 1 to 2 minutes)

This more or less ends the feeling of 'the prologue in heaven', and may need an instrumental interlude[6] before the next singing.

---

[5] 'The Seed'. In the second draft of this poem, entitled '1914', these lines became:

> But now, for us, wild Winter, and the need
> Of sowings for new Spring, and blood for seed.

'The Seed' was published in *The Poems of Wilfred Owen*, ed. with memoir and notes by Edmund Blunden (London, 1931); the later version, '1914', appears in *The Collected Poems of Wilfred Owen*, ed. with introduction and notes by C. Day Lewis (London, 1963).

[6] See n. 7 below.

3.

CHORUS *SCENA* WITH ALTO.[7]

CHORUS.   Is evil then good?
           Is reason untrue?

ALTO.   Reason is true to itself;
           But pity breaks open the heart.

CHORUS.[8] We are lost.
           We are as seed before the wind.
           We are led to a great slaughter.[9]

---

[7] Linked to the previous number by an instrumental interludium.
[8] Linked to the previous section by an instrumental interludium.
[9] This line became 'We are carried to a great slaughter'.

4.

This is 'rhythmic translation', probably recitative like the narrator in the Bach Passions. (Time is about 1 minute.)

The bass solo is a father-God figure, appearing as the narrator in the first part and as the boy's uncle in the second part.

The alto solo, in the same way, will appear as the boy's aunt in the middle part.

The bass describes the division in the commonwealth that corresponds to the division in the individual and general psyche.

4.

BASS SOLO: THE NARRATOR

Now in each nation there were some cast out by authority and tormented—a human symbol of the vile thing.

Purges in the east, lynching in the west, Europe with a cancerous growth
in the vitals.

And a great cry went up from the people.[10]

---

[10] 'Now in each nation there were some cast out by authority and tormented; made to suffer for the general wrong. Pogroms in the east, lynching in the west; Europe brooding on a war
of starvation. And a great cry went up from the people.'

5.

This should be a constructed chorus on an appropriate text (in the manner of the populace at the foot of the cross in Handel's *Messiah,* who sing a terrific fugue to the words: 'He trusted in God that He would deliver him, let Him deliver him if he delight in Him'). The bitterness of the oppressed will be expressed in the musical construction, as long as the text itself contains also some verbal expression of the cry.

(Time: 2 or 3 minutes, enough to stabilize the musical movement in counterpoise to the realistic descriptive solos, etc.)

5.

CHORUS.

(Chorus of the oppressed)[11]

[11] Chorus of the oppressed

When shall the usurers' city cease,
And famine depart from the fruitful land?

6.

This is 'rhythmic translation' again.

The tenor and soprano soloists are conceived of here as the personification, humanization of the common man and woman (young). The metaphor should be homely, proletarian, warm, and human—as a foil to the abstractions of the soul and the Father-God. The man tells of his psychological split self which appears to him, and actually is on a certain plane the frustrations of his condition in the commonwealth. He has lost the relation to his soul, to the impersonal things, hence the feminine, the women have demonic power (or he has an infantile fixation, etc.). He projects the anima on his womenfolk, with devastating personal misunderstandings and complexes. But the imagery used should be entirely personal, practical, and homely, so that the ordinary man listening, still embedded in concretizations, can feel himself truly expressed and understood. Without this coming down to earth, the oratorio would fail of its purpose.

(Time: 1 to 2 minutes)

6.

TENOR SOLO.[12]

'Starvation of body and mind is eating into my spirit.

I am caught between my desires and their frustration as between the hammer and the anvil.

> Women have hold on my entrails,
> how can I grow to a man's stature?'[13]

---

[12] This has an extended instrumental introduction and postlude.

[13] I have no money for my bread;
I have no gift for my love.
I am caught between my desires
and their frustration
as between the hammer and the anvil.
How can I grow to a man's stature?

7.

('Rhythmic translation')

The soprano voice is the young mother comforting her children; her doubts and fears. She experiences the same false dichotomy between instinct and the oppressed circumstances. Her sense of it is practical—wages, war. The imagery again must be homely, simple, and warm, so that the clear young voice sings free and high; a sort of inverted cradle-song, that is also a personal expression of fear and uncertainty.

(Time: 1 to 2 minutes)

7.

SOPRANO SOLO.

'How can I cherish my man in such days, or become a mother in a world of destruction?

How shall I feed my children on so little wages?

How can I comfort them when I am dead?'[14]

[14] How can I cherish my man in such days,
Or become a mother in a world of destruction?
How shall I feed my children on so small a wage?
How can I comfort them when I am dead?

8.

Here the oratorio reaches the modern universal musical symbol. The setting will be in the style of the singing to 'Green Pastures',[15] e.g. a strong line of the spiritual and a choral descant at the back using probably the solo voices as well.

---

[15] Film (Warner Bros., 1936) based on *The Green Pastures—A Fable in Dramatic Form* by Marcus C. Connelly (London, 1930).

8.

CHORUS AND SOLOISTS: A Spiritual[16]

1.   'Steal away, steal away, steal away to Jesus!
Steal away, steal away home—
I ain't got long to stay here.[17]

My Lord, he calls me, he calls me by the thunder.[18]
The trumpet sounds within-a my soul,
I ain't got long to stay here.

2.   Steal away, steal away, steal away to Jesus!
Steal away, steal away home—
I ain't got long to stay here.

Green trees a-bending, po' sinner stand a-trembling,[19]
The trumpet sounds within-a my soul,
I ain't got long to stay here.'

---

[16] From *The Book of American Negro Spirituals*, ed. James Weldon Johnson (New York, 1925; London, 1926).

[17] 'ain't' becomes 'han't' throughout the spiritual.

[18] 'he' becomes 'He' in this line.   [19] 'po'' becomes 'poor'.

PART II

9.

This is a short constructed chorus as at the start of part I. In Handel's *Messiah* the second part, which follows on the joyful prophecies, starts with a grave and solemn chorus on a text which begins: 'Behold the Lamb of God . . . etc.' Something of the same feeling is wanted here. After the argument the drama begins.

A Child of Our Time is the title of a story by a young German writer (von Horvath, d. 1936) on an allied subject, and is the sort of title needed for this oratorio.[20]

(Time: ½ to 1 minute)

---

[20] Odön von Horvath (b. 1901, d. 1938, *not* 1936), *Ein Kind unserer Zeit* (1938).

PART II

9.

CHORUS.
The action unfolds.

Behold the man! the scapegoat, the child of our time.[21]

---

[21] A star rises in mid-winter.
Behold the man! The scapegoat!
The child of our time.

10.

This is 'rhythmic translation'—like no. 2.

The narrator becomes in part II closer to earth, less distant and 'god-like'.

(Time: ½ minute)

10.

BASS SOLO: THE NARRATOR

And a time came when amid the universal tyrannies and oppression one race became the symbol of persecution.[22]

---

[22] 'And a time came when in the continual persecution one race stood for all.'

11.

This is a dramatic chorus such as Bach used in the Passion music for similar exclamatory choruses. It tends to 'rhythmic translation' rather than repetition of words. It is short. The desperate questions of the persecuted will be interjected into the violence of the incitations of the persecutors.

(Time: 1 minute)

11.

DOUBLE CHORUS OF PERSECUTORS AND PERSECUTED.

'Away with them!
Curse them! Kill them!
They infect the State.'

'Where? How? Why?
We have no sanctuary.'[23]

---

[23] CHORUS 1. Away with them!
Curse them! Kill them!
They infect the state.

CHORUS 2. Where? Why? How?
We have no refuge.

12.

This is 'recitative' again, as in no. 10.

(Time: ¾ minute)

12.

BASS SOLO: THE NARRATOR

Where they could, they fled from the terror.

And among them a young lad escaped secretly, and was kept in hiding in a great city by his uncle and aunt.[24]

---

[24] Where they could, they fled from the terror.
And among them a boy escaped secretly,
and was kept in hiding in a great city.

13.

This is a declamatory chorus, like choral recitative, possibly in unison singing. It is the point at which the oratorio gets nearest to the danger zone of political polemic. Yet it is nothing newer than the scribes and pharisees before whom Pilate washed his hands! Its inclusion has to be made possible, I think, by a calm and dispassionate treatment. Time will soften the blows which fall nearest home!

(Time: ¾ minute)

13.

CHORUS OF THE SELF-RIGHTEOUS.

We cannot have them here in our just Empires. They shall not work, nor draw a dole.

Let them starve between the frontiers.[25]

---

[25] We cannot have them in our Empire.
They shall not work, nor draw a dole.
Let them starve in No-Man's-Land!

14.

Recitative, as in no. 10.

(Time: ¼ minute or less)

following straight into:

14.

BASS SOLO: THE NARRATOR

And the boy's Mother wrote him a letter, saying:[26]

---

[26] 'And the boy's mother wrote a letter, saying:'

15.

This is 'rhythmic translation' as in the *scena* no. 3. At this point all the soloists take on human form, but the boy and the mother are the two least detached from the consequences of their actions, in the Buddhist sense. The mother cannot foresee the terrible consequences of her letter, nor detach herself sufficiently from the past which compels her to send it. The boy likewise. The uncle and aunt are wiser as befits their closer association with their transcendental ancestry in part I and part III.

(Time: 1½ to 2 minutes or more)

15.

SCENA: THE BOY'S MOTHER, HIS UNCLE AND AUNT, AND THE BOY

MOTHER (soprano).   O my son, I am near to death in the terror of our race. There is no pity, only demented frenzy. Help me!

BOY (tenor).   Mother, Mother! What can I do?

AUNT (alto).   Be patient. Your young life should not be thrown away in futile sacrifice.

UNCLE (bass).   You are one against the world. You must accept the impotence of your humanity.

BOY (tenor).   But my mother . . . I must save her.[27]

---

[27] Solo Quartet: The Boy's Mother, his Uncle and Aunt, the Boy

MOTHER.   O my son! In the dread terror
they have brought me near to death.

BOY.   Mother! Mother!
Though men hunt me like an animal,
I will defy the world to reach you.

AUNT.   Have patience.
Throw not your life away
in futile sacrifice.

UNCLE.   You are as one against all
Accept the impotence
Of your humanity

BOY.   No! I must save her.

16.

A spiritual, describing the boy's anguish of mind and the general contemporary anguish of soul.

(Time: 2 minutes)

16.

CHORUS: A Spiritual[28]

> Nobody knows de trouble I see, Lord,[29]
> Nobody knows de trouble I see,
> Nobody knows de trouble I see, Lord,
> Nobody knows like Jesus.
>
> O brothers, pray for me,
> O brothers, pray for me,
> O brothers, pray for me, an' help me to drive ole' Satan
>   away.[30]
>
> Nobody knows de trouble I see, Lord,
> Nobody knows de trouble I see,
> Nobody knows de trouble I see, Lord,
> Nobody knows like Jesus.
>
> O Mothers, pray for me,
> O Mothers, pray for me,
> O Mothers, pray for me, an' help me to drive ole' Satan
>   away.
>
> Nobody knows de trouble I see, Lord,
> Nobody knows de trouble I see,
> Nobody knows de trouble I see, Lord,
> Nobody knows like Jesus.

---

[28] See n. 16 above.
[29] 'de' becomes 'the' throughout the spiritual.
[30] 'an' ' and 'ole' ' become 'and' and 'old' throughout the spiritual.

17.

This is narrative 'recitative' with observations by the anima, e.g. the alto voice. It is the province of the anima to observe the compulsive movements of the *alter ego*, which indeed are personified so often in her form.

(Time: 1 minute or a little longer)

17.

SCENA: DUET——BASS AND ALTO

NARRATOR. The boy becomes desperate
in his mental agony.

ALTO. The fate is drawn.
The dark forces threaten him.

NARRATOR. He goes to the Consulate.
He is met with hostility.

ALTO. His other self rises in him,
demonic and destructive.

NARRATOR. He shoots the official . . .

ALTO. But he shoots only his dark brother . . .
And lo!   he is dead.[31]

---

31 ·

NARRATOR.   The boy becomes desperate in his agony.

ALTO.   A curse is born.
The dark forces threaten him.

NARRATOR.   He goes to authority.
He is met with hostility.

ALTO.   His other self rises in him,
demonic and destructive.

NARRATOR.   He shoots the official—

ALTO.   But he shoots only his dark brother—
And see . . . he is dead.

18.

Recitative, as no. 14.

(Time: ¼ minute or less)

18.

BASS SOLO: THE NARRATOR

And a terrible vengeance was unleashed.[32]

---

[32] 'They took a terrible vengeance.'

19.

This is a short constructed chorus like no. 5 in part I.

(Time: 1 minute or so)

19.

CHORUS: THE POGROM[33]

---

[33] The text became:

> Burn down their houses! Beat in their heads!
> Break them in pieces on the wheel!

20.

Recitative as in no. 18.

(Time: ¼ minute or less)

20.

BASS SOLO: THE NARRATOR

THE NARRATOR.

> Men's entrails were wrung
> by what was done.
>
> There was bitterness and horror.[34]

---

[34] Men were ashamed of what was done.
There was bitterness and horror.

21.

A spiritual of anger.

(Time: 1¼ minutes: followed perhaps by a short musical interlude to mark the height or depth of the drama)

21.

CHORUS: A Spiritual[35]

> Go down, Moses,
> 'Way down in Egypt land;
> Tell ole' Pharoah,[36]
> To let my people go.
>
> Go down, Moses,
> 'Way down in Egypt land;
> Tell ole' Pharoah,
> To let my people go.
>
> When Israel was in Egypt's land,
> Let my people go,
> Oppressed so hard they could not stand,
> Let my people go.
> 'Thus spoke the Lord', bold Moses said,
> 'Let my people go',
> 'If not, I'll smite your first-born dead',
> 'Let my people go.'
>
> Go down, Moses,
> 'Way down in Egypt land;
> Tell ole' Pharoah,
> To let my people go.

---

[35] See n. 16 above.
[36] 'ole' ' becomes 'old' throughout the spiritual.

22.

This is a solo like no. 6 in part I.

It describes the boy caught in the outer and inner prisons of the law. He thinks of his missed life, like Owen's dead soldier:

> Whatever hope is yours,
> Was my life also; I went hunting wild
> After the wildest beauty in the world
> Which lies not calm in eyes, or braided hair,
> But mocks the steady running of the hour,
> And if it grieves, grieves richlier than here.
> For by my glee might many men have laughed,
> And of my weeping something had been left,
> Which must die now.[37]

It is very quiet in tone, warm and simple, distilling some of the 'pity of war', which Owen wished expressed.

(Time: 1 to 1½ minutes)

---

[37] 'Strange Meeting'.

22.

TENOR SOLO: THE BOY

> My dreams are all shattered
> in a ghastly reality.

> The wild beatings of my heart are
> being stilled; day by day——minute by minute.

> The sky and the earth are for those
> beyond these prison walls.

> Mother, Mother! Goodbye.[38]

---

[38] My dreams are all shattered in a ghastly reality.
The wild beating of my heart is stilled; day by day.
Earth and sky are not for those in prison.
Mother! Mother!

23.

This, and the previous number, correspond to the two homely solos in part I.

The accent is more poignant, but the metaphor is just as personal and direct.

(Time: 1 to 1½ minutes)

23.

SOPRANO SOLO: THE MOTHER

O my son! What have I done to you

What will become of us now?

The springs of hope are dried up, and a
continual pain aches in a mother's heart.[39]

---

[39] What have I done to you, my son?
What will become of us now?
The springs of hope are dried up.
My heart aches in unending pain.

24.

This describes the inner and outer state of mankind in general. It sums up the statement in no. 2 of part I. The irrational elements in ourselves have got to be reckoned with, even integrated into some new synthesis, if a way through is to be found.

'Peace' is the symbol of this new synthesis, as 'armed peace' or 'War' is the symbol for the effort to solve the problem by neurosis and the tension of the opposites.

(Time: ½ minute)

24.

ALTO SOLO.

The dark forces rises everywhere:
the shadow of universal war.

Men's hearts are heavy
They cry for peace.[40]

---

[40] The dark forces rise like a flood.
Men's hearts are heavy: they cry for peace.

25.

This spiritual describes the common human need for some spiritual certainty, for 'peace'. The way through is only dimly felt, not as yet understood. In fact there is only the awareness of the deep need and sometimes only from the unconscious, while the conscious mind persists along outworn political cliches, etc.

(Time: 1 to 1½ minutes)

25.

CHORUS:[41] A Spiritual[42]

O, by an' by,—by an' by—[43]
I'm gwinter lay down my heavy load,[44]
O, by an' by—by an' by—
I'm gwinter lay down my heavy load.

I know my robe's gwinter fit me well,
I'm gwinter lay down my heavy load,
I tried it on at the gates of hell,
I'm gwinter lay down my heavy load.

O, by an' by,—by an' by—
I'm gwinter lay down my heavy load,
O, by an' by—by an' by—
I'm gwinter lay down my heavy load.

O, hell is deep an' a dark despair,
I'm gwinter lay down my heavy load,
O, stop po' sinner & don't go dere!—[45]
I'm gwinter lay down my heavy load.

O, by an' by,—by an' by—
I'm gwinter lay down my heavy load,
O, by an' by—by an' by—
I'm gwinter lay down my heavy load.

[41] Chorus and Soprano Solo.
[42] See n. 16 above.
[43] 'an' ' becomes 'and' throughout the spiritual.
[44] 'gwinter' becomes 'going to' throughout the spiritual.
[45] 'po' ' and 'dere' become 'poor' and 'there'.

PART III

26.

This short constructed chorus is like the ones at the opening of part I and part II, no. 1 and no. 9.

It turns again towards the imagery of part I:—'But now the exigent winter and the need Of sowings for new spring — etc.' The descent into the water is a universal dream symbol of the present day.

Ein protestantischer Theologe träumte öfters denselben Traum, er stehe an einen Abhang, unten lag ein tiefes Tal und darin ein dunkler See. Er wusste im Traum, dass ihn immer etwas abgehalten hatte, sich dem See zu nähern. Diesmal beschloss er, zum Wasser zu gehen. Wie er sich dem Ufer näherte, wurde es dunkel und unheimlich und plötzlich huschte ein Windstoss über die Fläche des Wassers. Da packte ihn die Angst und er erwachte.

     Dieser Traum zeigte Ihnen die natürliche symbolik. Der Traümer steigt in seine eigene Tiefe hinunter und der Weg führt ihn zum geheimnisvollen Wasser. Under hier geschiet das Wunder des Teiches von Bethesda: Ein Engel kommt herunter und berührt dass Wasser, welches dadurch Heilkraft erlangt.
     . . . Den Weg des Wassers der immer nach unten geht, muss man wohl gehen, wenn man den Schatz das kostlose Erbe des Vaters, wieder heben will.[46]

     (Time: 1 minute)

---

[46] C. G. Jung, *Über die Archetypen des kollektiven Unbewussten*, in *Eranos-Jahrbuch 1934* (subtitled *Ostwestlichen Symbolik und Seelenführung*), ed. Olga Fröbe-Kapteyn (Zurich, 1935), 195–6. This essay was later revised and published in *Von den Wurzeln des Bewusstseins* (Zurich, 1954), then was translated by R. F. C. Hull in the *Collected Works of C. G. Jung*, ix/1 (London, 1959). The passage quoted by Tippett is translated therein as follows:

     A Protestant theologian often dreamed the same dream: He stood on a mountain slope with a deep valley below, and in it a dark lake. He knew in the dream that something had always prevented him from approaching the lake. This time he resolved to go to the water. As he approached the shore, everything grew dark and uncanny, and a gust of wind suddenly rushed over the face of the water. He was seized by a panic fear, and awoke.
     This dream shows us the natural symbolism. The dreamer descends into his own depths, and the way leads him to the mysterious water. And now there occurs the miracle of the pool of Bethesda: an angel comes down and touches the water, endowing it with healing power.
     . . . We must surely go the way of the waters, which always tend downward, if we would raise up the treasure, the precious heritage of the father. (17–18; the italics are the translator's)

PART III

26.

CHORUS.

The cold deepens.

The earth descends into the icy waters, for there lies the jewel of great price.[47]

---

[47] The cold deepens.
The world descends into the icy waters,
where lies the jewel of great price.

27.

This alto solo of the anima corresponds to no. 2 in part I. She propounds the modern paradoxes. When misconceived and suppressed, she is like an impassioned woman, and man is compulsively animated. The problem of coming to terms with her is the problem of a creative impulse beyond good and evil. Yet behind this chaotic face lies another, full of meaning—the *illuminificatio* of the alchemists.

Es enstehen allmählich Dämme gegen die Flut des Chaos, denn das Sinnvolle scheidet sich von Sinnlosen und dadurch dess Sinn und Unsinn nicht mehr identisch sind, wird die Kraft des Chaos durch die Entnahme von Sinn und Unsinn geschwächt, und der Sinn mit der Kraft des Sinnes und der Unsinn mit der Kraft des Unsinnes ausgerüstet. Damit ensteht ein neuer Kosmos.[48]

In Blake's drawings, when Job reaches the point at which he cannot distinguish the action of God from the action of Satan, the Divine Mercy shows him the mystery of rebirth into a new synthesis.[49]

(Time: about 1 minute)

---

[48] Jung, *Über die Archetypen des kollektiven Unbewussten.* The passage quoted is translated in the *Collected Works*, ix/1, as follows:

Gradually breakwaters are built against the surging of chaos, and the meaningful divides itself from the meaningless. When sense and nonsense are no longer identical, the force of chaos is weakened by their subtraction; sense is then endued with the force of meaning and nonsense with the force of meaninglessness. In this way a new cosmos arises. (ix/1.31)

[49] See *Illustrations of the Book of Job. Invented by William Blake: reproduced in facsimile from the original New Zealand set made about 1823–4. With a note by Philip Hofer* (London, 1937). See also review of this edition by Evelyn Underhill in *Time & Tide*, 8 Jan. 1938, pp. 46–7; the following passage is relevant:

The Moral Christian . . . must pass from the state of innocence into the anguish of Experience—the only path to full spiritual life. The forces of cosmic violence are unloosed against him; Satan does his worst. Job's world is shattered. He is successively tortured in body, mind and spirit . . . till that extreme of interior dereliction is reached in which he can no longer distinguish between the action of Satan and the action of God (Plate XI).

. . . Then it is, when the terrible night of the soul is fully established and his own nothingness fully revealed, that the Creative Wisdom in its awful majesty and beauty—the real God, whom he had never known before—answers Job 'out of the whirlwind'. There is disclosed to his astonished and purified sight the mystery and splendour of the heavenly and earthly creation; when 'the morning stars sang together, and all the Sons of God shouted for joy'.

. . . It may well be that the modern world is destined to follow Job's path from 'this life to that which is to come'; and to endure something analogous to that stripping and dereliction, as the preliminary of rebirth.

(According to some leading Blake scholars, these reduced-size colour versions of *The Book of Job* illustrations were not made by Blake, but by a member of his circle of friends.)

27.

ALTO SOLO.

The soul of man is impassioned
                like a woman.

She is old as the earth and beyond
                good and evil, the sensual garments.

Her face will be illumined
                like the sun. Then is the time of his
                deliverance.[50]

---

[50] The soul of man is impassioned like a woman.
  She is old as the earth, beyond good and evil,
  the sensual garments.
  Her face will be illumined like the sun.
  Then is the time of his deliverance.

28.

This *scena* is like no. 3 in part I.

The paradoxes are extended in dialogue form. Patience is born in the *voluntary* withdrawal. The 'man of destiny' is conceived as a possible name for the Dictator or his counterpart. The 'man of destiny' reaches out towards the collective powers of God, and receives the opposing projections of the Devil. Such perversions of our human origin and fate bring their own self-destruction, which simple people may even rejoice in. The boy reached up likewise to make a judgement in God's name and cannot uphold the contradiction of such judgement with his human flesh. The way out is not along such paths. 'Render unto Caesar the things which are Caesar's, and unto God the things which are God's.'[51]

[51] Matt. 22: 21.

28.

SCENA: CHORUS AND BASS SOLO

BASS.   The words of wisdom are these;
               Outer cold means inner warmth,
               the secret fermentation of the seed.

CHORUS.   How shall we have patience for the
               consummation of the mystery? Who will
               comfort us in the going through?

BASS.   Patience is born in the tension of
               loneliness. The garden lies across the desert.

CHORUS.   Is the man of destiny then master of us all?
               Shall those cast out be unavenged?

BASS.   The man of destiny is apart, cut off from
               fellowship.
               Only time may heal and the simple-hearted
               exult.

CHORUS.   What of the young lad, what of him?

BASS.   Justice is cold and abstract.
               He is ground to powder in the clash of powers.
               He too is apart like God, though his flesh is
               human.[52]

52

BASS.   The words of wisdom are these:
               Winter cold means inner warmth,
               the secret nursery of the seed.

CHORUS.   How shall we have patience of the
               consummation of the mystery?
               Who will comfort us in the going through?

BASS.   Patience is born in the tension of loneliness.
               The garden lies beyond the desert.

CHORUS.   Is the man of destiny master of us all?
               Shall those cast out be unavenged?

BASS.   The man of destiny is cut off from fellowship.
               Healing springs from the womb of time.
               The simple-hearted shall exult in the end.

CHORUS.   What of the boy, then? What of him?

BASS.   He, too, is outcast, his manhood broken
               in the clash of powers.
               God overpowered him, the child of our time.

29.

After the preceding *scena* there will probably be a short musical interlude[53] to mark the 'moment of silence' before the final awareness. The tenor and soprano still stand for the distinctively human figures. When all these texts have been sung, the chorus repeats them in a swelling ensemble. We have reached the point where man must dare to know himself, cost what it may.

'After such knowledge: what foregiveness? . . .'

'Think
Neither fear nor courage saves us. Unnatural vices
Are fathered by our heroism. Virtues
Are forced upon us by our impudent crimes.
These tears are shaken from the wrath-bearing tree.'[54]

---

[53] See n. 55 below.   [54] T. S. Eliot, *Gerontion.*

29.

GENERAL ENSEMBLE: CHORUS AND SOLOISTS[55]

TENOR.   I would know my dark side
             and my light, so shall I at
             last be whole.

BASS.   Then courage, brother, and dare the
             difficult passage.

SOPRANO.   Here is no final grieving
             but an abiding hope.

ALTO.   The moving waters renew the earth.
             It is spring.[56]

CHORUS REPEATS AND ENLARGES.[57]

---

[55] Introduced by an instrumental praeludium.

[56] TENOR.   I would know my shadow and my light,
                  so shall I at last be whole.

     BASS.   Then courage, brother, dare the grave passage.

     SOPRANO.   Here is no final grieving,
                  but an abiding hope.

     ALTO.   The moving waters renew the earth.
                  It is spring.

[57] Chorus and Soloists.

30.

This is the generalized expression of the hope of the new spring.

30.

CHORUS AND SOLOISTS: A Spiritual[58]

> Deep river, my home is over Jordan,
> Deep river, Lord,
> I want to cross over into camp-ground, Lord,
> I want to cross over into camp-ground, Lord,
> I want to cross over into camp-ground, Lord,
> I want to cross over into camp-ground.
>
> Oh, chillun, Oh, don't you want to go,
> To that gospel feast,
> That promised land,
> That land where all is peace?
> Walk into heaven, and take my seat,
> And cast my crown at Jesus' feet, Lord,
> I want to cross over into camp-ground, Lord,
> I want to cross over into camp-ground, Lord,
> I want to cross over into camp-ground.
>
> Deep river, my home is over Jordan,
> Deep river, Lord,
> I want to cross over into camp-ground, Lord,
> I want to cross over into camp-ground, Lord,
> I want to cross over into camp-ground, Lord,
> I want to cross over into camp-ground.[59]

[58] See n. 16 above.   [59] 'Lord' is added to the last line.

Chapter 15

THE NAMELESS HERO:
REFLECTIONS ON
A CHILD OF OUR TIME

When any of you hear *A Child of Our Time* for the first time, the most obvious thing to strike you will be the five Negro spirituals, which come at certain important moments in the story. I might call this the folk element in the work—folk-music and folk-poetry. The spirituals are appropriate only because the whole oratorio is not so much the record of an individual or personally peculiar experience, but of a common, or folk experience. What our forefathers might have called, even, a mythological experience. There are indeed ancient myths very similar to the underlying story of *A Child of Our Time*. Mythological heroes usually had names, though not really personal ones. (Apollo, for instance, probably means the wild apple.) But contemporary myths just have no names. *A Child of Our Time*, from its very title, has the anonymity of 'The Unknown Soldier', on the faceless Cenotaph. There was once a real story behind *A Child of Our Time*, just as there was a real soldier, whose body is buried at Westminster Abbey. We can *never* know the Unknown Soldier's *name*—and whoever in fact played out the drama of *A Child of Our Time* to its tragic end, there is no name in the oratorio text.

In my opinion this text is happiest when what it has to say could be said by folk idioms. This is so even of the solos:

> I have no money for my bread.
> I have no gift for my love . . .

is better in every way than the lines which follow:

I am caught between my desires and their frustration as between the hammer and the anvil.

One feels that the psychological terminology (desires and frustrations) has not been absorbed into our common speech. But sometimes the folk idioms fall pat with an almost terrifying actuality. The self-righteous expressing their eternal refusal to be moved by the anguish of the outcasts, sing these three lapidaric sentences:

> We cannot have them in our Empire.
> They shall not work nor draw a dole.
> Let them starve in No-Man's-Land!

Every outcast, be he unemployed or refugee, feels the implacability and the desolution of the 'No-Man's Land'—a folk idiom born, in fact, from the common experience of both sides on the Flanders battlefields.

There are disadvantages of course, too, arising from this use of folk idiom. For instance, the verbal style becomes so condensed, and yet the words so simple and clear, that we note the mechanics of the repetitions in the music, which has so often to meditate, by repetition, upon these sentences, in the traditional manner. We are so used to the repetitions of 'Every valley', for example, that we do not think about them, and suffer rather the danger of forgetting the text altogether. Very few people now know how, let alone why—that is, dramatically why—the words of *Messiah* were compiled as they were. But the text of *A Child of Our Time* is far too close to us for that. I can believe that if I were to recompose the work now, in the light of my experience of performances, I might try to disguise these repetitions by artifice. But, on the other hand, something of the naked simplicity might go. In any case the question is vain.

The pre-eminent advantage of this folk-style wording lay in the means it gave to incorporate the folk-verse of the spirituals into the text, without undue strain. Naturally this was only possible in our own language, in English. (Though the consequent difficulties in translation into French and German have in fact been triumphantly overcome.) For so many English idioms have sprung, at one or more remove, from the Bible, and that is the source of most of the Negro poetry; the trumpet that 'sounds within-a my soul' is the same trumpet of *The Pilgrim's Progress*, when Mr Greatheart had safely crossed the river: 'And all the trumpets sounded for him on the other side.[1] Probably some of the imagery of *Pilgrim's Progress* is older even than the Bible—for instance, the waters into which the hero descends. *A Child of Our Time* makes use also of primeval seasonal imagery. The opening chorus of each part is conceived as observing the drama from some point in interstellar space.

> The world turns on its dark side.
> It is winter.

Only gradually does the camera approach our planet and hover over Europe. Even time undergoes that same condensation, slowly moving from the general past to the immediate present and the particular drama. In this telescopic view our period seems restless and violent. Spring seems a long way off.

Although the story of *A Child of Our Time* is indeed tragic, there's no attempt to spotlight the horrors. The artistic method is not a realistic one. It's assumed that we all nowadays know these horrors by heart—they can be read of in the

---

[1] John Bunyan, *The Pilgrim's Progress*, part II.

papers. In *A Child of Our Time* the tragic events are brought before us just long enough to reproduce the appropriate emotions in the relative tranquillity of recollection so that we may ask of them their message. But except for the 'Chorus of the self-righteous' and one spiritual, which I have deliberately headed 'A spiritual of anger', there is no attempt to moralize.

But the desire to moralize is very strong, and to appear to desist from it seems unnatural. So that it was difficult, at least during the war, to believe that *A Child of Our Time* was really intent on other things. One or two English critics thought I had glossed the realities of violence because I am a pacifist; another execrated the oratorio because he considered it an irresponsible plea for political assassination. This latter nonsense was the more stupid, and difficult to imagine on the Continent, where even music critics have all been too close to concentration camps not to know the sort of provocation people may have. But the gravamen of my charge against this criticism (and it's for this reason that I refer to it) is that it misunderstands the method—which brings the events before us in recollection, not to judge, but that by terror and pity we may be moved to stop equating intellect with spirit, and to 'break open the heart'. It's nothing less than the rebirth of the inner imaginative world that is sought. To plough the dark ground of our disorders that we may sow new seeds—to 'harrow hell'.

Now Christ 'harrowed hell' as a triumphant God—triumphant indeed, because as man he went the way of a barbaric death—but none the less victorious.

> Lift up your heads, O ye gates,
> And be ye lifted up ye everlasting doors
> And the King of Glory shall come in.[2]

A child of our time, be he professed Christian or agnostic, has to harrow his hell with less confidence and with humility, armed though he be with every god-like scientific weapon. And maybe there is, no longer, final escape for any of us through a vicarious scapegoat, though the attempt of us all—individuals, races, nations, and ideologies—to find one whom we may tear to pieces for our sins is one of the actualities of this oratorio.

'Behold the man! The scapegoat! The child of our time!' For surely that is the deepest evil of our day? Every division, every war, threatens to become a moral crusade. And the greatest danger point is when our self-righteousness overcomes our fear.

> Odour of blood when Christ was slain
> Made Plato's tolerance in vain
> and vain the Doric discipline.[3]

Because it had to, *A Child of Our Time* receives its peculiar effect from the power of this evil. A mephistophelean power that pricks us upward, as well as

---

[2] Ps. 24: 7.　　　[3] W. B. Yeats, 'Two Songs from a Play', II.

plunging us in catastrophe. The devil is always the wicked other man (our 'dark brother') for *you* and *me*—but it is you and me, of course, for *them*. They will show tenacity and courage and heroism too.

There are two scenes in the oratorio when the four solo voices have a sort of conversation. These scenes make two of the pivotal points of the work. The first one comes at the moment of decision which precipitates the drama itself. The boy (the nameless hero) is moved to such passion by the agony of his mother under the terror, that he sweeps aside all reason and prudence proffered by his uncle and aunt, and declares his challenge: 'I will defy the world to reach you.' For it's the ineluctable fate of mankind to engender tragedy by heroic passion. Nothing in the oratorio suggests that this will ever be different.

But, when the four soloists come together again, at the very end, the plane has been shifted to an examination of the nature of this passion, the nature of our inner life from which the 'dark forces' spring. It may be that the width and intensity of the present continuing catastrophe forces on *all* of us a fresh questioning, a renewed searching, born of our anxiety. But I think there will be a few whose destiny it will be to undergo whatever initiation is demanded as the price of the power to decipher the message. Our nameless hero, no longer even the daily outcast who shoots at authority but one of an even stricter anonymity, will make for us a new declaration, reaching out to some reborn humanism within the bitter ideologies.

> I would know my shadow as my light
> So shall I at last be whole
> Then courage, brother, dare the grave passage.
> Here is no final grieving but an abiding hope.
> The moving waters renew the earth.
> It is spring.

In a programme note to an early performance of *A Child of Our Time* I once wrote:

Because an oratorio, like an opera, has a story and ideas, these forms are impure musically as compared with symphonies and sonatas. But the impurity can also become the cause that we are moved the more deeply, moved beyond analysis or consciousness of that which moves us.

This seems to me particularly true of *A Child of Our Time*, for two reasons: first, that the story, the idea, behind the oratorio (man's inhumanity to man) is deeply relevant at this time; and second, because the music is simple, even occasionally naïve. But a naïvety which is not embarrassing, which is indeed part of the proper means for letting the oratorio speak immediately and to everyone.

It's clear that an idea so permanent and deep as 'man's inhumanity to man' could have been the subject of an opera equally as of an oratorio. Indeed, at the very beginning I thought it was to be an opera on the Easter Rebellion in Dublin in 1916 and the consequent shootings. But that passed—really because the story proved intractable; and because I came to realize that I wanted to present the matter contemplatively rather than dramatically. This is the essence of the difference between oratorio and opera. Both use stories. But opera must present the drama and the characters in action; while oratorio only refers to the events of the drama in order, having refreshed our memory of them or brought them to our notice, to consider their moral implications.

In the traditional Christian Passions, the events are described to us by a narrator in recitative, and with the help of interjection by the chorus, while the moral comments are given to soloists in extended arias. The subject-matter of these arias is simply: how should the Christian soul behave in relation to the event just described? The acquiescence and affirmation of the congregation is provided by selected verses of appropriate hymns or chorales.

When I decided to treat the matter of the pre-war Nazi pogroms as an oratorio, I turned first of all to this traditional pattern of the Passions. But I also turned to the tripartite division of *Messiah*, in which part I deals solely with prophecies and things general, while part II deals with history, from the birth of Christ to the Last Judgement, and part III deals solely with metaphysical comments mostly taken from St Paul. This three-part division works out for *A Child of Our Time* in the following way. Part I deals with the general state of oppression in our time; part II presents the particular story of a young man's attempt to seek justice by violence and the catastrophic consequences; while part III considers the moral to be drawn, if any.

But while the traditional forms of oratorio do lie behind *A Child of Our Time*, they are somehow turned and twisted to carry the charge of our contemporary anxiety. I can explain this best by quoting the half-line of verse from Eliot's *Murder in the Cathedral*, which heads the score like a motto. It runs: 'The darkness declares the glory of light.'[4] The chief point is that this quotation is itself a kind of quotation—from the Psalms: 'The heavens declare the glory of God.'[5]

Eliot has twisted the well-worn words, and by so doing forced them into our time. I have played this trick, if that is the right word, on both words and music. It appears, too, even in the spirituals. For if the five spirituals, which come at appropriate moments during the work, act as modern chorales, in that we *all* are moved by them beyond the power of the tunes as mere music, yet the spirituals themselves have turned and twisted Bible language into a modern dialect; the stories they tell of the Bible Jews are used to comfort Negroes in the bitterness of oppression, and I use these Negro spirituals to symbolize the agony of modern Jews in Hitler's Europe. It makes a powerful,

---

[4] T. S. Eliot, *Murder in the Cathedral* (London, 1935), final chorus speech.
[5] Ps. 19: 1.

condensed poetic image. Not only did the spirituals give me a kind of spirit-level folk-poetry to which the rest of the text had to conform, but so also did the music.

Just before the fatal act of violence which the young protagonist of the oratorio feels forced to commit in his desperation, he leads the choir in the spiritual 'Nobody knows the trouble I see, Lord'. In the chorus of the spiritual, the tune is given to all male voices, the counter-tune to the women. In the verse the leader is left on his own, and the high voices of the choir thrown up into the air behind him. I partly learnt this method of setting from recordings of Negro choirs. Now the syncopations and implied beat of that music are what we find in jazz. This was an added reason why I found the spirituals so apt to my hand. Because I was convinced at the time I wrote it—twenty-five years ago—that modern oratorio of this direct kind should try to make use of the popular musical vernacular, in the same way as the words made use of general contemporary expressions like 'They shall not work nor draw a dole / Let them starve in No-Man's-Land'. But the vital consideration must always be whether this musical (or literary) vernacular can be purified, enhanced, de-sentimentalized enough to carry the charge of deeply serious artistic emotions.

To exemplify how far this was possible in relation to a jazz-derived music, or rather how far I managed to go, it is worth listening to the opening of an alto aria out of the last part: 'The Soul of man is impassioned like a woman'. It is a dance—as though the spiritual 'Nobody knows' had produced from within itself a kind of sacred gaiety. There is no question but that this music is jazz-derived (with of course other influences behind it as well), but it is also unquestionably individual music of its author. I did not have to mitigate my serious style one whit. One of the very simple metaphors I used to convey the sense of 'no final grieving' (to quote the soprano) was the age-old one of the seasons. The opening chorus of all has only the words: 'The world turns on its dark side. / It is winter.' When I reached the end of the work, I let the alto (then the choir) sing: 'The moving waters renew the earth. / It is spring.' I had written the whole text already before the last war. The music began as the war began. Spring (in the poetic sense) was hard to imagine. At all costs I didn't wish to produce mere 'pie-in-the-sky'. But finally the imaginative necessities forced a spring into the music. Before the final spiritual, 'Deep River', I let the four solo voices sing together, vocalizing over a pedal bass and accompanied by all the orchestra. It is spring: but spring with an ache in it.

I had to attend a performance of *A Child of Our Time* a few years back, in Germany. Someone pointed out to me that two-thirds of the young choir and about half of the audience would hardly have been born when the events from which the oratorio sprang took place. It is I, who, when I hear the piece, go back to those terrible events, the rise of Hitler and the concentration camps; but younger people find in the piece, as equally terrible, a relevance to today. When I wrote the work, I was so engulfed in the actions of the period, I never considered its frightening prophetic quality. But it seems that the growing violence springing out of divisions of nation, race, religion, status, colour, or even just rich and poor is possibly the deepest present threat to the social fabric of all human society.

In the oratorio this violence is presented in archetypal form, a simple murderous shot of protest, followed by retaliatory mass vengeance. It seems possible (within the mood of the piece) to have some understanding of the shot, though there is no condonation. It seems harder to feel understanding for the mass vengeance (and that is why I named 'Go Down, Moses', 'a spiritual of anger'). But though the oratorio refers to political events, it is not about politics. And though the oratorio is concerned with man's rejection of whole groups of his fellow men, it is not about acts of protest. (I should like to say in parenthesis that when I wrote the piece, there seemed only one kind of shot, aimed at the obvious tyrant. But alas, now, when a shot rings out around the world, its aim can as easily be Gandhi or Martin Luther King or John F. Kennedy.)

The oratorio, as is proper, is not dramatically descriptive, but contemplative. The events are presented to us for contemplation only, that we may stand back for the events to induce the deeper emotions which might cross the gulfs of division: compassion, tolerance, acceptance of our 'shadow', as of our 'light', absolute refusal of any stereotype of division that prevents the expression of our total humanity.

Yet, in saying all that, I risk making *A Child of Our Time* sound more didactic than it really is. That is to say, I was committed when I wrote it: to all those rejected, cast out, from the centre of our society on to the fringes; into slums, into concentration camps, into ghettos. But in actual composition of the work, while never denying, I think, this personal commitment, I got drawn by the work itself towards some deeper commitment which needed to embrace both sides: the self-righteous and the rejected. And yet with passion, and not an inert neutrality. This passion, in all the senses of the word, springs from the archetypal nature of the drama as the oratorio presents it. When the chorus ask: 'What of the boy then, what of him?', they are answered by 'He too is outcast, his manhood broken in the clash of powers. God overpowered him, the child of our time.' This answer is terrible; but the use of the word 'God' is in no way inappropriate. We grope our way towards compassion and understanding, because the shock of the collective tragedy is so great each time any part of the archetypal drama of violence and division is re-enacted.

Chapter 16

THE MIDSUMMER MARRIAGE

DRUM, FLUTE, AND ZITHER

I picked up once off a book barrow in Berne a mid-nineteenth-century brochure, which was a set of lectures given by a von Stein about the theatrical relations of Schiller to Goethe. I have an idea that the lecturer was the son (or grandson?) of Goethe's Frau von Stein, but I have lost the brochure and cannot be certain. In any case the tone of voice was of someone very close to the Weimar circle.

As I have not read Schiller properly or seen his plays, I found all von Stein had to say about him interesting and new. Von Stein examined Schiller's idea that one of the roles in a drama might be a collective personality, not an individual. Schiller, he said, called his play 'Wallenstein's Lager', instead of just 'Wallenstein', to emphasize that the camp is to be apprehended as playing just such a collective role. I suppose this struck a chord in me, because it echoed my own preoccupations with the intense sense of place, the temple on its wooded hill, of *The Midsummer Marriage*. More interesting was a discussion of what Schiller had intended in *William Tell*. How he had intended the scenery of Switzerland to play in some degree a collective role, to mirror the events of the drama. Schiller never went to Switzerland. He fed his imaginative picture of Swiss landscape on Goethe's letters to Weimar during his, Goethe's, Swiss journey. Thus Schiller imagined the lake of the four cantons (Lake of Lucerne) as abruptly whipped up by the mountain wind from a placid stillness to a violent storm, which as rapidly subsides. Schiller wished this storm, seen from the room of a cottage on the stage, or from the auditorium of the theatre, to be the visual prelude to the dramatic action of *William Tell*, which has the same rise and fall.

Later in the play, when the men take the famous oath by night on the Rütli, Schiller wanted the men to leave the stage after the oath, and for the sunrise to be effected scenically to an empty stage. Von Stein stated that Schiller's stage direction in this instance was never followed because it could not be. It is not viable theatre to have a sunrise acting a role, even if the sunrise seemed to echo in Nature the psychological moment of the human drama.

What struck me forcibly is that this effect not viable in spoken theatre might quite well be viable through music in the opera-house. It is clear that Wagner thought so too. The music to the opening of *Rhinegold*, the fire music at the end of *Valkyrie*, or the great interlude of Siegfried's journey to the Rhine are astonishing examples of what music can do that scenic effects on a silent stage cannot do.

But there are other subtler forms of extending, or fulfilling, stage situations by music, which are not of this Wagnerian kind. 'Drum, Flute, and Zither' starts off by examining something of the sort implied by some late Yeats stage directions. Unlike Schiller, Yeats asks for music. What sort of music is he really asking for?

The attempt to probe this question brought a whole series of questions in its train. As so often happens to me, the consequent essay is tight packed with ideas, which are perhaps only held together by the arbitrary fact that they were in my mind in this connection. Yet there is a kind of central theme: the way in which an ancient Greek theatrical experience, which seems to imply this special music that fulfils situations, was quite lost and then in some sense found again.

First I must define my terms—which means beginning with music; but a special sort of music, which carries us into the theatre. And not into any theatre, but especially into the theatre of the Renaissance, and of the Greeks and of some moderns. A theatre, at least in the Greek period, which sprang up somewhere, sometime from rituals of various kinds, so that a primitive hieratic element stubbornly remains after all the poetic and theatrical work that the authors have heaped upon the traditional material. Hence the title of this section, for that already reaches out towards the definition of this special music, in that the instruments—drum, flute, and zither—are emblematic of rhythm, of melody, and of accompaniment, which is what I take it Yeats thought when he referred always in his later plays to the musicians sitting down by, or taking up, the drum, flute, and zither as a kind of theatrical ritual.

Yeats gave only the slenderest indication of what he expected the musician to do with these instruments. But he wrote words for them to sing; sometimes as themselves, and sometimes as characters of the drama enacted from the back of the stage—voices, songs, of a queen dancing, of a severed head. When the musicians are asked to sing songs to words Yeats has written for them, then (as we read the play) we assume we know what Yeats meant music to do, even thought the melody to the words is absent. When the music is to be instrumental only, more is left to our imagination—except perhaps where the theatrical situation is such that the situation itself makes the music. I mean of course this special music of the theatre. It is most easily discussed from an example. After the murder of Cuchulain in Yeats's last play *The Death of Cuchulain*, there is such a musical moment. Cuchulain has unwittingly fought with his own son and killed him. Maddened by the tragedy, he fights with the sea till exhausted towards death by loss of blood. At the end, a blind beggar, who has been promised twelve pennies for Cuchulain's head, taps his way on to the stage till his stick reaches the bound hero. And now I quote direct from the printed play:

CUCHULAIN.   You have a knife, but have you sharpened it?

BLIND MAN.   I keep it sharp because it cuts my food.
(He lays bag on ground and begins feeling Cuchulain's body, his hands mounting upward.)

CUCHULAIN.   I think that you know everything, Blind Man. My mother or my nurse said that the blind know everything.

BLIND MAN.   No, but they have good sense. How could I have got twelve pennies for your head if I had not good sense?

CUCHULAIN.   There floats out there
The shape that I shall take when I am dead,
My soul's first shape, a soft feathery shape,
And is not that a strange shape for the soul
Of a great fighting-man?

BLIND MAN.   Your shoulder is there,
This is your neck. Ah! Ah! Are you ready, Cuchulain!

CUCHULAIN.   I say it is about to sing.
(The stage darkens.)

BLIND MAN.   Ah! Ah!
(Music of pipe and drum, the curtain falls.)

Now, though Yeats has not written out the music for the pipe and drum, we are not disconcerted when we read the play, for we can imagine the overtones and undertones of the situation drawn out to a melody, beaten in a rhythm. We—that is more possibly I as a composer—might be more disconcerted in the theatre when actual music is sounded. For the melody and rhythm of theatrically poetic situations like the death of Cuchulain are imagined by us, I think, as expressing the otherwise inexpressible. It is not merely that Yeats stops his poetry and writes a stage direction for music; it is also that the music he wants is the ineffable perfume of the 'soft, feathery shape' of Cuchulain the other side of death. And I have deliberately mixed my metaphor between sound and smell for a reason which will appear later.

I suggested above that, at least in the Greek theatre, there is a primitive hieratic element, springing perhaps from rituals of various kinds, which stubbornly remains after all the poetic and theatrical work done by the dramatists upon the traditional material. I am thinking now of the generally accepted views of the ritualistic origins of Greek tragedy and comedy; the mystery of— to quote—'life enflamed by death'. Music and dance are traditionally inseparable from this mystery, if ever men try to present it, whether it be Euripides or Yeats. From our evolutionary point of view we regard Euripides as nearer in time to the period of ritual, and Yeats as nearer to enlightenment. So that stubborn primitive and ritualistic element in Yeats can seem affectation if we believe only in an evolutionary immanence of the spirit. But for Yeats himself the spirit had qualities, affirmations beyond any evolution within history, though Yeats no more than Euripides denied history for an exclusive fundamentalism.

However, for the moment, all that I have in mind is the extent to which music (in this special sense as I have just described it) and dance are used to present to us the poetic, theatrical moment which is out of time and beyond death.

Yeats was influenced by the Japanese as well as the Greek theatre. In Japan, music and dance within the stage play are even now the theatrical apparatus of an unbroken tradition generations old. A recent visitor in Japan described it thus: 'Sometimes an orchestra sits in tiers at the back of the stage or in front of a painted screen. The musicians kneel, sitting on their heels, a row of zither players, half a dozen men with small hour-glass-shaped drums, and an old man with a shrill flute.' The Yeats stage orchestra is more economical, reduced in fact to three players, one for each sort of instrument, but in kind the same. It is much more difficult to be sure that our operatic orchestras in pits before the stage are only a multiplication of drum, flute, and zither. That would be an unhelpful simplification. Western music, at least since the convention of opera, moved quite away from the stubborn primitive, hieratic element, as did all the sister arts. Operas became possible which were almost, if not quite, rationalist; almost, if never quite, realistic. But the origin of opera in the late Renaissance lay in no desire to exclude the transcendent or religious experience from the stage. It seems to have been chiefly a belief that the coarse and uncivilized elements (as the famous group of amateurs in Florence round Count Bardi saw them) in the theatre of that time could be purified and tempered by the moral virtues of the ancient world. This was certainly the conscious aim: to extend the Renaissance victories over the medieval crudity (but of course entirely within Christian tradition) into the realm of the theatre.The consequences of what they were not conscious of came, of course, later, and cannot be imputed to their wickedness. They were lettered Christians with a civilizing intention, and opera, which became the very whore of Babylon to other Christians later, equally lettered as they, was merely the result of their attempt to revive the technique of the ancient stage. They believed that the highly serious and moral tone of the Greek tragedies was bound up with the use of heightened speech—that is, sung speech. So far as I know, they did not investigate the nature of the special music which can present to us the poetic, theatrical moment which is out of time. They did not, for *that* purpose, break down all music into the constituent parts of rhythm, melody, and accompaniment. They did not, therefore, in any Yeatsian sense, ask for drums, flutes, and lutes in their features. They used them to underpin some of the theatrical situations—and it was a task the musicians enjoyed. But their more important innovation was the raising of stage verse beyond incantatory speech into recitative and song. And what they made suddenly possible by so doing was to have not only theatrical relations between the various moments of a drama, but also musical. There became apparent, independent of the degree of conscious awareness of the audience, a pattern of keys and modes and measures and vocal registers. Within a century, or less, this musical pattern had so far outstripped in interest the dramatic pattern, that the plays themselves were reduced to sterility. Every reform of the opera, whether by Gluck, Wagner, or Verdi (perhaps in the end even by so ambiguous a figure as Bertolt Brecht)—every reform has been directed, though carried out by the composers not the librettists, towards raising the dramatic interest again to equal the musical interest. Thus the opera could become for a period once more an attempted unity between pattern of music and pattern of drama. But for one reason or another it never stays there. It is not merely that critics and public conspire to reduce opera to vocal and instrumental accomplishment (much as dramatic critics and public might try to reduce the interest of stage plays to the acting), but rather from *force majeure*. The more the primitive, hieratic element gave way, in every sphere where European spiritual life had flowered, before the newer fascinations of scientific rationalism, brilliant discoveries, excellent hygiene, and other values, the less the theatre, as mirror of manners, needed the special music for moments of poetic transcendence; and the music of instrumental and harmonic virtuosity was, at any rate for a time, admirably suited to a more materialist age. So without some change in the relations between the values given to the world of technics and the world of the spirit, it is difficult to see how critics and public can do anything but be inexorably drawn to virtuosity of performance, even without any conspiracy at all. It is the virtuosity which is mirror of such virtue as our age of precision instruments possesses. Even where the primitive, hieratic element is stubborn enough to remain, the lack of collective interest means that it is bloodless and debased, primitive in the pejorative sense; while what passes often for spiritual experience within the realistic theatre is merely the morbid.

But that is to anticipate. The proper next step in my argument is to look more closely at the Greek theatre which the Renaissance desired to emulate. Having already named Euripides along with Yeats, I shall take a Euripides play for example: the *Hippolytus*.

One must imagine the customary Greek open-air theatre, with the doors at the stage back and the orchestra in front with the ritual altar to Dionysus. But we need to see two further altars in the mind's eye, probably on either side of the stage itself, and perhaps each topped by a statue of the goddess to whom the altar has been dedicated: on one side Artemis, on the other Aphrodite, the goddesses of chastity and of desire. But an ennobling chastity and a frank desire. Although we can easily imagine these statues as stone personifications of enduring but contrary human states, that is not really enough. There is a divine element in each, chastity and desire transcending the limitations of the human or of history. Or rather, the sculptures proclaim that humans, within the exalted joys of chastity or desire, can find moments out of time and immortal. Thus when the *Hippolytus* starts, we hear, as though the statue had come to life, the goddess Aphrodite herself speaking in her own person, coming to tell us that the flower of young manhood, Hippolytus, Theseus's son, enjoys such transcendent moments; not however in the worship of herself, Aphrodite, through the consummation of desire, but in the worship of Artemis, through the passion of chastity. Further, so near is Hippolytus to his goddess, the man is guilty of pride. Aphrodite will therefore take revenge, and she describes the methods by which she will do so. So we virtually know the plot when Aphrodite's voice then ceases.

Now, it would be immeasurably interesting to know how the divine voices were staged by the Greeks. Was such a long speech as Aphrodite's prologue delivered in any way differently from the traditional long speech of the messenger? Even if the school of scholarship is correct which holds Euripides for a sceptic, laughing at his gods and goddesses, the question remains for the tradition of divine speeches before scepticism appeared. But it cannot be answered. It is easier to see how things went in the scene following, when Hippolytus enters with a chorus of youths, going straight by the altar of Aphrodite to lay his garland on the altar of Artemis. For the verse itself changes, in that Hippolytus and the chorus chant (I can think of no better word) a lyric.

Here the matter is unambiguous. For if the audience is to *feel* the passion of Hippolytus's absorption in his chaste divinity, on which the whole drama depends, then the laying of the garland must convince. And it is at this necessary moment that the verse assumes the music of poetry. 'πότνια, πότνια, σεμνοτάτα,' the chorus begins. Thus, beyond any curious question as to how the Greeks spoke, chanted, or sang their verse, it is clear that in this scene the special dramatic significance of the tragic hero's relation to his experience of transcendence was expressed by poetry. Even if Euripides as man was himself sceptical of transcendent experience personified in the Greek traditional Olympian forms, as dramatic instrument he had to present his hero's predicament as real. For myself, I am prepared to argue that Euripides was affirmative towards his hero's belief, because otherwise the poetry itself should ring false. Indeed, I do not think a later play, like the *Bacchae*, has any dramatic point at all, unless Euripides had likewise, at least at the moment of writing, an affirmative relation to that terrible religious mystery: 'life enflamed by death'. However, to discuss the special problem of Euripides I have no competence, while to propound the critical heresy that the poetry is not independent of the belief is once again to anticipate. I must return to the story.

To Hippolytus, when he learns of his stepmother Phèdre's incestuous desire for him, the knowledge is an unspeakable horror. And so the inevitable tragedy supervenes. But before the mangled but still living Hippolytus is brought back to the stage to die, Artemis, the goddess of the other statue speaks in *her* voice. From her, Theseus learns the truth—too late. When the blinded Hippolytus is carried on, Artemis comforts him. He begins his answer with the words: 'O, divine perfumed breath'; probably sensing Artemis as a transcendent paradigm of his own 'soft, feathery shape', the other side of death. But Artemis, as immortal goddess, may not look on death, and she withdraws. It is the father, Theseus, who holds up the son, as he sees the gates of Hades open.

It is a curious experience to pass abruptly from Euripides to Racine, to set the *Hippolytus* beside *Phèdre*. For it is a great deal more than the change of title—than the shift of dramatic emphasis from the man to the woman; or even than the possibility that a chaste hero cannot ever be to French taste. (Racine gives Hippolytus a lover.) One has to begin at the beginning, for the most striking difference is that in *Phèdre* there are no divine voices. Aphrodite and Artemis do not appear.

This was not at all because Racine had no religious feelings, no belief in transcendence. On the contrary, as he makes clear in his preface to *Esther*, he could not represent Aphrodite and Artemis as real goddesses, because he believed them to be false. He believed, on the other hand, that the Bible was the word of God. It needs a little theatrical history to get this point straight. *Phèdre* was first given in 1677. But the cabal against it and its author was so distressing and unmerited that Racine withdrew from the theatre and wrote nothing for twelve years. It was not only dissatisfaction with the theatrical life around the court which silenced Racine; he was also distressed by the equivocal position of a Christian author writing tragedies on pagan subjects. He still believed probably (like the Renaissance before him) that there was a civilizing and ethical force in the return to ancient classical subjects. But if, as I hold, Euripides could not make dramatic sense of Hippolytus unless he convinced his audience that Hippolytus really experienced a sense of the divine in the image of Artemis, neither could Racine. There is an ambiguity about Racine's hero. For while, true to the Euripidean or Senecan model, he makes his Hippolytus a virgin, he also makes him confess, at the moment of the play's beginning, to a first love. So his refusal of Phèdre's incestuous appeal is not the immediate, absolute reaction of the proud worshipper of chastity, but the reaction of someone who, chaste till then, had already desire for another. And the dramatic consequences are even deeper still, because this is really to dismiss Artemis but retain Aphrodite. If, at the very beginning of the play, Racine's Hippolytus has already succumbed to the power of desire, has taken his garland from Artemis to Aphrodite, why should Aphrodite need to contrive a tragedy to reduce this mortal's pride?

This is the central problem, the wound which has remained open, from *Phèdre* to *Billy Budd*. The Greek tragedy has an absolute *raison d'être*. Aphrodite speaks, Artemis speaks. The necessary tragedy unfolds between. But already in Racine the tragedy has no longer this necessary character. Hippolytus and Phèdre come to death through the accident of her incestuous desire colliding with his virtuous love for his Aricie. So Billy Budd endures a miscarriage of justice through the accident of his stammer. What tragic qualities these pieces have lie in a different mental atmosphere. But the problem remains.

Racine was quite conscious of the problem. To remove the divine, transcendent element from the drama, whether because one holds the Greek religious experience to be false, or because one is enlightened and sceptical, is to move oneself towards a world of spiritual impoverishment. As a convinced Christian, Racine could never deny transcendence. So, after *Phèdre* there are no more pagan tragedies, only biblical ones. It is only after a twelve-year silence that we get *Esther*, written for a fashionable girls' convent.

Now the cardinal place in the preface to *Esther* is where Racine explains that he felt he was at last truly imitating the Greek theatre for two reasons. First, that the scenes of his subject, taken as they were from the Bible, the word of God, had been, so to speak, prepared for him by God himself. 'Je pourrais remplir toute mon action avec les seules scènes que Dieu lui-même, pour ainsi dire, a preparées.' Second, that having thus established the transcendent element, necessarily, for Christian reasons, excluded from *Phèdre*, he was able to use a chorus (excluded equally from *Phèdre*), because at last he needed it, to express just this transcendence. That he could 'comme dans les anciennes tragèdies grecques . . . employer à chanter les louanges du vrai Dieu cette partie du choeur que les païens employaient à chanter les louanges de leurs fausses divinités'.

And the truly fascinating matter is that for his chorus Racine used lyric poetry, which had to be sung. So, once the conditions were given in which the transcendent element needed to be affirmed upon the stage and within the drama, the old amalgam of poetry and music returned to power.

It has been left to our later evolutionary, technological age, whether in its optimistic or pessimistic habit, to have as much difficulty in accepting Racine's Christian poetic transcendence as Euripides' pagan. We therefore have had to base our critical values on a kind of amputation. We have needed to abstract the poetry, of, say, the *Divina Commedia* from the belief; to abstract the dramatic technique from the contents of the story. We (or most of us) cannot choose between *Phèdre* and *Esther* for reasons of faith. Or rather, to put it more carefully, if we choose between the plays, we do so for different reasons. Since we live in a world where social value is given to experiences of technics rather than of the spirit, we, whether individually convinced Christians or pagans, are not making a comparable choice to that which Racine made when he silenced himself for twelve years. All I am suggesting here is that because *Esther* demanded from Racine the dramatic experience of transcendence, where *Phèdre* did not, the poetry is different. In *Esther* there are lyric choruses, which have to be sung. But when Hippolytus gives up the ghost in *Phèdre*, he does not begin with the words 'O, divine perfumed breath', for he sees no 'soft, feathery shape' of himself the other side of death. Nor, therefore, did Racine need to tell the musicians to take up the drum, flute, and zither and play music of pipe and drum.

If we skip from Racine a hundred years to Goethe, then the scene is both changed and not changed. From the special point of view of this chapter, the most obvious change is that in those hundred years music had developed into a noble and independent art; to such a degree that the word 'music' comes to mean no longer a traditional association with the poetic element in the theatre, whether in the ritual Greek theatre or in the Christian Mass, but an art of pure sound in its own right. At that period, when Beethoven's symphonies were being created, it might be said that the conscious dramatic problem was not at all the possibility of a musical pattern within a verse drama, such as Eliot for all our sakes discusses it now, but the possibility of a dramatic pattern within a musical piece. I realize I am putting this point rather crudely; but I think that just this exaggeration can help us to feel what was new in the European art of music. For it is new; there was no art of pure music in that sense before, and I am certain that no archaeological discovery will show there ever has been. Why, and even how in any precise sense, this grace of the discovery of a new art should have descended on the European spirit over the long period from medieval organum to the so-called classical symphony is a mystery. But once it had happened and had flowered when it did flower, then the accidents of the historic period, or other rhythms of the European spirit, impinged at once upon music, as upon every one of the other arts. That is to say, that when music as an independent art flowered at the end of the eighteenth century, the European climate of opinion was already deeply involved in the swift and shattering process by which value was going over from the world of imagination to the world of technics. And the artistic consequences of the depreciation of value given to the imaginative world meant that the effort of imaginative creation began to assume, already in Beethoven's time, that superhuman quality, that desperate struggle to restore the spiritual order by increasingly transcendent and extraordinary works of art. At first, the discovery of the fascinating and fantastic dream world of the Romantic movement seemed to suggest that salvation lay in a flight from technics into fantasy. The new art of music, just because of the unrealistic nature of its medium, appeared as though designed by history to be the paragon of romantic virtue. It was the romantic art *per se*. But when the first phase of the Romantic movement passed and the spiritual disillusion returned and deepened, and later, when it seemed possible that a way forward lay in attempting to take the citadel of technics by artistic storm, then music has probably been the least successful art for this purpose, and architecture (I am thinking of the Bauhaus and Le Corbusier) may have become the most.

Is it not possible that Goethe disliked Beethoven's music not merely for reasons of his older age and of his temperament, but because he sensed deeper down that the symphonic drama, the dramatically conceived musical symphony, had no need of verse or poetry, and the prose or verse drama had no traditional place for independent music of Beethoven's kind? This has been the perennial problem for opera, and it was certainly not for such tremendous personalities as Goethe and Beethoven to become a sort of super Gilbert and Sullivan. The time was as unripe for such a union as the temperamental situation was intractable. Beethoven did not set Goethe's *Iphigenie* to music, because fundamentally there was no need of it.

Now the *Iphigenie* is the point where it *appears* as if some of the scene had not seriously changed in the hundred years since Racine. Like Racine's *Phèdre*, Goethe's *Iphigenie auf Tauris* is an adaptation from Euripides. Like Racine, Goethe dispenses with the Greek gods (in this case Athene), and like Racine thereby reduces the mythological element to the inexplicable. But not for Racine's reason. Racine, in his Christian faith, knew the Greek gods to be false. Goethe had not Racine's Christian assurance, though he certainly had assurance of transcendence in some form; but he so radically altered the dramatic quality of the Euripides story that any *deus ex machina* was otiose. Goethe makes his *Iphigenie* so naturally humane that it is impossible to think of her as ever sacrificing any human whatever because commanded by a goddess, let alone her own brother, Orestes. Not because, like the Euripidean heroine, she is capable of risking everything in a Greek trick, daring Athene to give the lie to Apollo (they were brother and sister too), but because, as conceived by Goethe, she equates the divine with the absence of all traditional sacrifice whatever. So we experience in the Goethe play less a passionate and dramatic conflict of morals or customs than a lyrical atmosphere of unshakeable goodness. This lyrical quality is practically all-pervasive, rocked to the music of the crystalline verse. There is no tragic element, no 'life enflamed by death', no 'soft, feathery shape' beyond death, no music of pipe and drum at the moment of passing, and, *a fortiori*, no room for the music of Beethoven.

What radically changes the scene in the hundred years after Goethe is a double process. Racine, as we know, turned away from the Greek myths to the Bible, to what was for him the word of God; thereby believing he had solved the problem of true transcendence within the theatre. The double process which seems to eat away Racine's solution, nearly reverse his judgement, is, on one side, that analytical temper of the mind by which the Christian tradition itself fell to pieces, towards a non-transcendental world of absolute immanence, or into a world of technics; and on the other, that anthropological, archaeological temper which made a historically imaginative sense of Greek religious transcendence once more possible.

Some of the process by which the Bible changed from the word of God, in Racine's sense, into a book of inspired literature had indeed taken place by the time Goethe wrote his *Iphigenie*. But it was very much hastened in the century that followed. We do not *expect* to find Christian transcendence, or even any transcendence at all, expressed directly in the theatre of Chekhov, Ibsen, or Shaw. We expect, rather, the expression of human relations within the appropriate social problems; or even the discussion of social problems through the relationships. Christian transcendence appears explicitly in Shaw's *St Joan*. That is to say, Joan is shown as a person who has experienced it immediately. But her personal life, her sainthood, the problems of Church and State, are all dramatized, however skilfully and passionately, with a humane tolerance worthy of a historian like Burkhardt or of a novelist like George Eliot. Shaw accepts Joan's sainthood as a fact, but he is not himself involved with Joan's God in any comparable sense to how Racine was. The nearest Shaw comes to needing music (the special music out of time and place) to express Joan's divine voices is the scene in Rheims Cathedral with the bells. But it is sentimental, not numinous. In the sense I have given to the word 'music' for the purposes of this chapter, there is no music at all in this theatre.

Now playwrights like Shaw, because it was the temper of their time, could accept the Bible as inspired literature. Anthropologists like Frazer, meanwhile, began to look at it rather as a compendium of customs and rituals, and produced the necessary apparatus of comparative research to make their point. The two attitudes inhabited the same climate of opinion. One feels a wide-reading humanist like Shaw read *The Golden Bough*, if not so certainly Frazer's *Folk-lore in the Old Testament*. But he does not seem to have been interested in the sense that anthropological or archaeological research on the Greeks might have affected his writings. The time was not ripe. The Greek scholars, like Jane Harrison, who uncovered, with a growing sense of excitement, the older, dynamic rituals behind the later Olympian façade, worked, for the most part, on the sidelines of public interests. Was this because the evolutionary, immanentist world of *Back to Methuselah*, or the materialist philosophy behind *Man and the Masses*, had no sense of, was unprepared for, even unconsciously frightened of, any transcendence that might be active? For Jane Harrison was certainly reaching through to the transcendent images of Greek mythology. And a more tremendous figure had appeared earlier—Friedrich Nietzsche.

Nietzsche was perhaps the first great European to be aware that he had, in his own person, experienced the rebirth of an ancient god—of Zarathustra. The impact of the experience was so violent that he eventually became clinically insane. But it can be shown, I think, that hidden in Zarathustra is an earlier meeting of Nietzsche with yet another god—with Dionysus, the god who came from the East into Greece to force his way like a wild storm into the measured climate of the Olympian system. (It is all described in the *Bacchae* of Euripides.) If Nietzsche in the end succumbed to the storm of the god, Jane Harrison managed to keep her head within the great wind. But she experienced enough to believe that only by examination of the Dionysiac attack on the Olympians, and of the allied cult of Orpheus, and more still, of the older rituals that lay before Homer, could any real sense be made of the how and the why of the transcendent images in Greek life and the Greek theatre. Her books have the passionate excitement of someone under an influence, of someone, despite all the scholarship, possessed. I doubt if many can read *Themis* without being affected by this sense of possession. By the time of the second edition in 1911, as she says herself, the battle had been won. The primitive ritual element in the Greek drama had been accepted for what it was, and the reality of a Greek sense of transcendence understood. If, by 1911, these things were accepted by scholars, by 1953 their range of effectiveness is vastly wider. Where Racine in his time held the Greek gods to be false, they would appear *now* to have been true, within their own sphere and period of efficacy. That is to say, if a strict Christian judges nowadays the Greek religious experience in the terms of Racine, he is the real stranger in the present world of opinion; but in Racine's century it would have been the reverse.

Now, though I began this discussion with Yeats, and the title of this section is taken from Yeats, and in Yeats's last plays the primitive, ritualistic element is clear for all to see—positively affirmed; yet T. S. Eliot is the real figure for the completion of my argument. Eliot is someone we imagine as wholly within the Christian experience, but in *The Family Reunion* he uses a Greek myth, as Racine and Goethe do, though not like them on a stage set in a scene of ancient Greece; for *The Family Reunion* is set in a scene of the present day. As if to emphasize a further difference from Racine and Goethe, Eliot does not dismiss as they did, if for different reasons, the Greek religious experience from his stage, but by a wonderful *tour de force* introduces the Eumenides into an English drawing-room. Furthermore, Eliot is more acutely aware than anyone else in this country, perhaps indeed in all Europe, of all the considerations I have been trying to set out: the general spiritual impoverishment of our life, the problem of a dismembered Christianity, the problem of the transcendent experience *per se*, the problem of poetry and belief, the special problem of the music of poetry in the theatre. I have little to contribute except the more special problem still of the music of instruments and voices in the theatre. And the possibly strange fact that I have affirmations, though not theologically Christian, which set me in some other place than optimistically or pessimistically bounded by our immanentist world of technics. So I am fairly sure that where my appreciations differ from Eliot's, any difference which is vital will spring from these affirmations. That is, I may have an affirmative reaction to experiences, which he might have to reject, like Racine before him, as theologically false. All the rest will be my lack of sensibility.

True to his acute awareness of what is involved, Eliot reconsidered *The Family Reunion* in a lecture at Harvard in 1950, reprinted in this country as *Poetry and Drama*. The words where Eliot first alludes to the two appearances of the Eumenides come within a general discussion of versification, and this is how they run:

Furthermore, I had in two passages used the device of a lyrical duet further isolated from the rest of the dialogue by being written in shorter lines with only two stresses. These passages . . . are so remote from the necessity of the action that they are hardly more than passages of poetry which might be spoken by anybody; they are too much like operatic arias. The member of the audience, if he enjoys this sort of thing, is putting up with a suspension of the action in order to enjoy a poetic fantasia.[1]

The more I reread this passage, the more it fascinates me. For I am certainly a member of the audience that enjoys this sort of thing. Is it just because I enjoy opera and operatic arias? In a sense, that is part of the reason. In opera the aria and the ensemble are generally placed where the action is halted to savour a situation; though of course there are arias and ensembles which progress from one state to another in the manner of the choruses of the *Bacchae*. To members of his audience who like opera, Eliot's rejection of his lyrically suspended moments in favour of continuous attention to the needs of the action may reduce enjoyment, not increase it. Or, to put it more generally, I can believe that when the verse drama moves thus towards opera, our whole theatre gains; especially if our contemporary opera could catch up on itself and come closer in some other ways to the verse drama. I can believe that by just such operatic tricks as lyrical suspension of the action to savour a situation, the play can be given new dimensions perhaps more naturally than by vigorous effort to make the verse play act like a prosaic one.

But if—and this is the core of the matter—if the lyrical suspension of action corresponds to a moment out of time, ineffable, when we have been made ready to see, however through a glass darkly, an image of transcendence, then suspension of action is essential. And to enhance or extend the moment, there is little to do beyond calling for the music of flute and drum, just as Yeats does at the timeless moment when Cuchulain's soul leaves the hero's strong body for 'the soft, feathery shape' of itself beyond death.

Now I know that the two appearances of the Eumenides in *The Family Reunion* were for me such timeless moments. I was in no way *conscious* of suspended action to hear an aria sung, to 'enjoy a poetic fantasia', for when they came, I trembled.

> That apprehension deeper than all sense,
> Deeper than the sense of smell, but like a smell
> In that it is undescribable, a sweet and bitter smell,
> From another world. I know it, I know it!

As Harry spoke these words, I suppose I imagined I spoke them with him. For they were in no way new, in no way strange, but expected, though unexpected. I can imagine that members of an ancient Greek audience, who enjoyed this sort of thing, found Hippolytus's words equally expected and unexpected, when he smelt the ineffable perfume of his goddess. Nor do I think it is only because I am physiologically short-sighted that I was careless of what in *The Family Reunion* the Eumenides looked like in the window embrasure; though that seems to have worried everyone else, if Eliot's own concern is general, not idiosyncratic.

---

[1] T. S. Eliot, *Poetry and Drama* (London, 1951), 28.

Having now read the printed play, I have been able to consider the musical, poetical means by which I was prepared to receive this deeper apprehension when it came. But all examination of the technique pales before the fact that such a deeper apprehension is possible at all in this immanentist world. Also I could, I think, undertake to show that Harry, in his mental and spiritual distress, is a true hero of our day—prig or not. I mean that Eliot's later judgement that Harry is an insufferable prig is, to many of us, as beside the point as to judge the Greek Hippolytus to be a prude in secret search of seduction. Furthermore, I must confess that the sense of affirmation which was most certainly gratified by the deeper apprehension of these two timeless moments in modern verse drama has not been diminished for me by any distress that I cannot analyse them down into intellectual counters; nor that I did not relate them in any way, then or since, to questions of theological truth and falsehood.

The miracle was the fact. The renewable excitement is the sense that suddenly for a time the poetry and the belief can be again one. And so my judgement is heretical in every sense: heretical perhaps from a Christian point of view, heretical in that I did not aesthetically separate the poetry from the transcendent emotion which it produced. It must wait now to see whether, after all, we are forced to relax our analytical preoccupations, and to accept our artistic miracles under the guise in which they come. I am prepared to wager that despite all the undramatic nature of Yeats's late plays, and despite all the animadversions of that kind which Eliot makes against *The Family Reunion*, these works will stand when others fall; by virtue of those lyrical suspensions of action, when we apprehend the ineffable perfume from another world, and the musicians must take up the traditional pipe and drum.

THE BIRTH OF AN OPERA

In the preface to *Three Plays for Puritans*, Bernard Shaw describes the pitiable state to which the profession of theatrical critic had brought him. 'My very bones began to perish, so that I had to get them planed and gouged by accomplished surgeons. I fell from heights and broke my limbs in pieces.' So naturally enough Shaw gave up that profession. As he says: 'I had myself carried up into a mountain where there was no theatre; and there, I began to revive. Too weak to work, I wrote books and plays.'

After five years' labour on my now finished opera, *The Midsummer Marriage*, during which time I have been sedulously secluded from public entertainments, if my bones have not perished, other vital organs seem to have. I suppose that if I could contrive to have myself carried up into a mountain, I should certainly revive. But not to begin another opera! I could imagine myself enjoying rather the novelty of a television set. One man's meat is another's poison. Shaw was broken by criticism and relaxed in creative work.

Creative work seems to have half-broken me, and I appear to seek relaxation in criticism. Criticism, that is, of my own work. For now that I have finished weaving a magic (I hope!) musical veil to clothe my strange libretto so that the final product has (I hope again!) the appearance of that indissoluble unity of drama and music that is opera, it is more than personally interesting to cast a critical eye over the devious means by which this operatic unity has been obtained. The threads which lead from inchoate beginning to substantial end are many. Of the two major ones I choose first the theatrical.

I felt (taught by Wagner in *Oper und Drama*) that the opera, however much it seems to us a mainly musical experience, is always ultimately dependent on the contemporary theatre. If we consider the main movements in the European theatre, then the various kinds of opera follow naturally. Thus, the-atrical classicism meant the operas of Gluck; romanticism meant Weber and Wagner; realism, or *verismo*, meant Puccini; fantasy, or surrealism, Debussy and Berg. (From this scheme I deliberately exclude Verdi, because his won-derful sympathy with Renaissance theatre—by which I mean not only Shakespeare but the epigonic Schiller—does not fit.) If I were to extend this list to the English theatre of my own day, then the theatrical movement could only be, as I saw it, verse drama: the theatre of Auden, Eliot, and Fry. At the precise time when I began to know that I must write an opera, Auden's plays were already out of fashion, the *première* of *The Family Reunion* had just taken place, and Fry was theatrically unborn. So Eliot had the apple (and maybe the consequences will turn out to be as distressing for me as for Paris). But while I was never sure that the verse drama plots, such as they had appeared, were suitable for modern opera, I realized that their verse technique was of itself operatic.

For both opera and verse drama use music; though the music of singers and instruments is necessarily quite different from the music of spoken verse. And in this distinction, I saw clearly, lay the difference between words for drama and words for opera. The one uses an incantation of verse in a magical fusion of sound and sense, where the other uses music proper. To recapture the the-atrical moment of Oberon's speech in *A Midsummer Night's Dream*: 'I know a bank where the wild thyme blows,' you must repeat the verses. But when the statue speaks in *Don Giovanni*, for example, no one remembers what the statue actually says, but only the sound of the accompanying trombones. So we can state a kind of rule 1: *that the verse dramatist carries out on the words themselves artis-tic operations which the composer effects by music.*

I took examples from *A Midsummer Night's Dream* and *Don Giovanni* deliber-ately, because both these traditional works make play with two worlds of apprehension. And this is the case also with the Eliot theatre, whose stage is generally a stage of 'depth'—by which I mean that we sense, especially at cer-tain designed moments, another world within or behind the world of the stage set. In *A Midsummer Night's Dream*, the supernatural world of the fairies and the natural, if fantastic, world of the mortals get entangled in such a way as to give us marvellous entertainment in this genre. The midsummer of the *Dream* is, at a far remove, the midsummer of *The Midsummer Marriage* (as it is, speaking always of a tradition, of the Bliss–Priestley *The Olympians*). Part of my entertainment is the interaction of two worlds; though the supernatural world I conjure with is not a fairy world, but another.

In *Don Giovanni*, the supernaturalism of the Statue appears only at the very end, and we have not been prepared for it. But its impact is nevertheless such that, when all the remaining characters appear for a moment afterwards in the epilogue, Leporello, who alone has witnessed the translation of the Don to hell, *is in a different range of experience from anyone else*. I have used this trick, if I may call it that, in *The Midsummer Marriage*. Some of my characters see the supernatural appearances, while some do not; at least, not all of them. Which of them do and which do not is part of the story. The same thing happens in *The Family Reunion*—that is, it happens in modern English verse drama. But it does not happen in *The Second Mrs Tanqueray*, nor in *Bohème*.

Now the word 'marriage' in my title can only mean one thing: comedy. For there is only one comic plot: the unexpected hindrances to an eventual marriage. At one period the hindrances were almost exclusively social: for example, a well-born girl marrying for love a handsome plebeian in the teeth of a furious father. Very often the handsome young man turned out, after all, to be very well-born. In any case there was no question but that the soubrette was the young lady's maid. Clearly, when fathers no longer control their daughters' marriages and ladies' maids are mostly extinct, this kind of social mechanism to the comedy is by now quite out of date, even as it was really already dating when its conventions broke Shaw's bones in 1900.

But what is the mechanism to a modern comedy? It is only when I hunt for the answer now, after the finish, that I see I instinctively decided that the mechanism of hindrance to successful marriage, or to any relationship, is our ignorance or illusion about ourselves. That is to say, it is only in the course of my plot that my characters become aware of their real selves. I took a *prim'uomo* and a *prima donna* whose illusions were, so to speak, spiritual; to match against a *second'uomo* and soubrette whose illusions were social. So the eventual marriage of the first pair became a spiritual, even supernatural, symbol, transcending the purely social and biological significance of the eventual marriage of the second pair.

And as soon as I knew my second pair were a mechanic and a pretty secretary, then at least I knew I had a new kind of soubrette.

There is up-to-date drama to be made out of the innumerable conflicts engendered by our ignorance or illusion about ourselves. So *The Midsummer Marriage* may not be singular in that only in the course of the plot do the characters become aware of their real selves. A classic instance, to my mind, is *The Family Reunion*, where Eliot conceives his hero as returning to the family precisely to discover the nature of the guilt he feels at having actually or psychologically (it seems to matter little that we never quite know which) pushed his wife overboard. In Act I he fails; and the Eumenides, when they appear, baffle him. In Act II he partially succeeds; and the Eumenides are tolerable.

Auden's *The Ascent of F6*, Eliot's *The Cocktail Party*, Fry's *A Sleep of Prisoners* (and many other plays) all use this technique. But more to my purpose is Shaw's *Getting Married*, because the hindrances to the eventual marriage of that comedy are caused, if I remember right, by the prospective couple re-examining, on the wedding morning, themselves and their intentions in the light of some book of Shavian moral doctrine. And it was with a blurred image of this situation in my mind's eye that I had my first illumination—that is, I *saw* a stage picture (as opposed to hearing a musical sound) of a wooded hilltop with a temple, where a warm and soft young man was being rebuffed by a cold and hard young woman (to my mind a very common present situation) to such a degree that the collective, magical archetypes take charge—Jung's *anima* and *animus*—the girl, inflated by the latter, rises through the stage—flies to heaven, and the man, overwhelmed by the former, descends through the stage-floor to hell. But it was clear they would soon return. For I saw the girl later descending in a costume reminiscent of the goddess Athena (who was born without father from Zeus's head) and the man ascending in one reminiscent of the god Dionysus (who, son of earth-born Semele, had a second birth from Zeus's thigh).

Even as I write now, some of the excitement of these first pictures comes back. It is the feeling a creative artist has when he knows he has become the instrument of some collective imaginative experience—or, as Wagner put it, that a myth is coming once more to life. I know that, for me, so soon as this thing starts, I am held willy-nilly and cannot turn back. But I know also that somewhere or other, in books, in pictures, in dreams, in real situations, everything is sooner or later to be found which *belongs* for all the details of the work, which is, as it were, ordained. And everything is accepted or rejected eventually according to whether it *fits* this preordained *thing*, which itself will not be fully known until it is finished.

This method of acceptance or rejection of material presented to or found by the mind is that used, of course, in fashioning any work of art. It is only when we get involved with mythological material that the game is more complicated because the material is so strange. For instance, once I had had a vision of the stage pictures I described above, it was easy to know that the temple was ancient Greek (though the young man and girl were of our time), and it seemed plausible that the myth being reborn was Greek. But, in fact, I was months, if not years, involved in the Greek experience before I could follow the thread right out of the labyrinth. So many of the loveliest and likeliest threads went elsewhere. Indeed, I can almost state a kind of rule 2: *that the more collective an artistic imaginative experience is going to be, the more the discovery of suitable material is involuntary.* The cause one searches so seriously and so long is impatience rather than clear judgement.

The matter is further complicated with an opera because the music is also at the back of one's mind, even if, for the purposes of discussion, I write as though the theatrical things all came first. For example, when I *saw* that my *prim'uomo* and *prima donna* returned to the level of the stage all armed with immediate experience of heaven and hell, I *heard* them begin to sing, one against the other, in two arias; the soprano's having coloratura, and the tenor's being rhapsodic; and this long before any words were there. That is, I sensed the musical metaphors before I searched for the verbal.

The initial stage pictures always remained the touchstone. For instance, the complementary ascent and descent is a picture of a psychological truth: that what is above is also below, just as Jehovah showed Job not only the sons of God shouting for joy, but also Behemoth and Leviathan. So I had always to consider in which direction my characters went when they left the stage, and whence they returned. And, of course, there had to be more characters than two. I gave the hero and heroine the normal operatic chorus of their fellows, and I gave the heroine her furious father, whose pretty secretary was the soubrette, whose boy-friend was the mechanic. I guessed that when the *moment* came again, the false but magical struggle between the sexes of Act I would be paralleled by a supernatural struggle of Act III between the old father and the whole young world, with the hero and heroine united. Then the temple had to be peopled with a wise priest and priestess, to whom I gave a chorus of neophytes in the shape of a group of dancers who are silent.

By that time it was obvious how near my apparatus had come to resembling *The Magic Flute*. Clearly no one now can match the innocence, tenderness, and simplicity with which that mythological experience was presented. If a comparable experience is to be presented today, our different climate of opinion will demand another approach.

I remember a young conductor in Hungary telling me how much more truly heroic Tamino is than Siegfried. That may be so. But really the judgement is a misconception. Siegfried is a tragic hero who, like many Wagner heroes, is unconscious of the collective importance of his actions. Tamino is a hero whose trials all spring from his search for consciousness and wisdom. The tradition of *The Magic Flute* is that of the quest. The incidents of the quest are traditionally extraordinary and supernatural, depicting as they do some continuous illumination of the hero. Some of the details seem unalterable, as though the mind always reverts to certain fixed images to personify certain recurring situations. At the very start of *The Magic Flute* this is so.

Tamino rushes on to the stage pursued by a snake. In mortal fear he faints. Three ladies appear and kill the snake in the nick of time. To use psychological jargon: the patient is pursued by images of negative potency (the snake) to such a degree that he gives up the conscious struggle and lets the unconscious have its way (he faints). The unconscious produces an image of salvation in the shape of the 'eternal feminine', his *anima*, his soul (the three ladies). So far all is simple and banal. The matter is more interesting when we ask: Why are the ladies exactly three?

To answer that fully would need the examination of a lot of analogous materials. I shall cite only one instance; from a story by the composer-author E. T. A. Hoffmann: *Der Goldene Topf.* At the start the hero rushes through the Black Gate of Dresden so fast that he overturns the apple basket of an old woman (fruitful Mother Nature, Eve, and her apples?). Chased off his course by the old woman's shrieks, he wanders along the river bank and then sits down and half goes to sleep under an elder tree; out of which in a little while comes a sound 'like a triad of clear crystal bells'. He looks up and sees 'three little shining green-gold female snakes'. It is the same situation and the same three.

I have taken this example from E. T. A. Hoffmann on purpose, because it allows us to sense something of the excitement with which the romantics plunged into this strange world of fantasy. (E. T. A. Hoffmann is full of it.) At the same time we can guess that it overwhelmed them just because they rarely if ever brought it into touch with everyday reality by any kind of critical or analytical judgement; while for us now, such a passive, fascinated attitude is impossible. Also I doubt if we really want again to use Wagner's method of staging an actual myth—the world of fantasy itself. It seems we must wrestle with it differently, even maybe to the extent of being conscious of why the collective mind produces traditional, unalterable images like the three. So where rule 2 ran: *that the more collective an artistic imaginative experience is going to be, the more the discovery of suitable material is involuntary*, a possible rule 3 might run: *that while the collective, mythological material is always traditional, the specific twentieth-century quality is the power to transmute such material into an immediate experience of our day.* For example, Eliot thinks that he has done this most successfully in *The Cocktail Party*. Others feel that just there he has transmuted the mythological material into commonplace, so that there is little of it left to experience.

To a certain extent the opera composer has an easier task than the verse dramatist in this respect, because there is a long tradition associating opera with the marvellous. Algarotti wrote in 1755:

At the first institution of operas, the poets imagined the heathen mythology to be the best source from which they could derive subjects for their dramas . . . From that fountain, the bard, according to his inventive pleasure, introduced on the theatre all the deities of paganism . . . And thus, by the intervention of superior beings, he gave an air of probability to most surprising and wonderful events. Every circumstance being thus elevated above the sphere of mortal existence, it necessarily followed that the singing of actors in an opera appeared a true imitation of the language made use of by the deities they represented.[2]

If we consider this tradition as legitimate and follow it through *Orfeo*, *Freischütz*, *Hänsel und Gretel*, *Le Coq d'Or*, to *The Rake's Progress* (to name one of

---

[2] *Source Readings in Music History*, selected and annotated by Oliver Strunk (New York, 1950), 658.

the possible lists), then it should be reasonable in an opera (if not imperative, according to Busoni) to have a greater percentage of the marvellous to a smaller amount of everyday. That is, of course, in an opera designed to be within the theatre of present-day verse drama, and not to be English *verismo* or English socialist realism, both successful genres. For the greater percentage of the marvellous will allow the opera composer to present the collective spiritual experience more nakedly and immediately—the music helping to suspend the critical and analytical judgement, without which happening no experience of the numinous can be immediate at all. For example, as soon as we begin to have critical doubts of the propriety, say, of the pseudo-Christian ritual of *Parsifal*, we are provoked, not enriched.

But it is clear that the composer, or his librettist, must be able to condense the necessary material easily and appropriately on to the stage, in something like the way Wagner condensed the divagatory romance of *Tristan* into three acts, where the action is minimal. Wagner thought that dramatic material which needed a lot of scene changing should be left as romance or novel. Verdi would not have agreed with him. But Verdi might have been more inclined to hold a later form of this opinion after seeing a cinematic masterpiece like *Citizen Kane*, where the cutting and the shots themselves (that is, scene changing *in excelsis*) become part of the artistic experience and put the old-fashioned scene changing of the operatic stage to shame. *Citizen Kane* is also a quest story.

Now once I had got as far as this and understood the kind of material presenting itself, and so the kind of opera I had to write, then the nagging question of what kind of music would do all that I wanted became instant.

The kinds and forms of music which appear in established operas have all somewhere sprung from the efforts of the composers to deal with their words and their theatrical situations. Composers collect together a kind of apparatus with which they can do all they want. Think for a moment of Verdi faced with the demands of a Renaissance drama like *Don Carlos*. At one point he has the Emperor Philip alone in his oratory returning again and again to the burden of his loneliness: 'But she can never lover me.' (I have paraphrased not quoted.) Verdi writes for Philip an aria in the form of a rondo (the recurring musical theme bearing the verbal burden) which fits, enhances, and enriches the situation—indeed, in a sense, *is* the situation.

But, later, Verdi must present Philip, not as the lonely old man, but as the Emperor in dispute with the Grand Inquisitor. (The conflict in Renaissance drama is often more seriously between men's passions and their duties, or even between divergent duties, than between rival desires.) For this, Verdi constructs a musical scheme out of the two deep men's voices and all the lower instruments of the orchestra. Again, the musical image *is* the situation. And it is no different when Verdi contrasts this deep dark sound with a high, clear woman's voice—the voice of young passionate love. That is to say, it is no different if Verdi, the master, creates the music that *is* the situation.

Sometimes Verdi, the tyro, fails. But it is a failure in the apparatus, not in the intention.

Wagner, at much the same period of operatic history, rejected this traditional Italian apparatus of set numbers and set situations, and constructed an apparatus which would do other things. For example, it would make Wagnerian opera out of the first words of *The Ring*, which are a stage direction: *The bottom of the Rhine.* Wagner has described how continuously he searched for the music to these words, and how it came to him in the form of a low sustained E flat, from the depths of a hallucinatory sleep, long after the text of *The Ring* was completed. The Rhine is almost a personage of *The Ring*, and the Rhine music is still sounding three operas later! This is not Verdi's apparatus, but it is Wagner's.

Of course, what has been written above is not exhaustive. I have chosen some examples of what I call operatic apparatus to exemplify the notion of apparatus. But I have chosen deliberately—and there is one other most characteristically operatic scheme which I want to add to the list before we proceed. This is the ensemble; where a situation of clear disagreement has been reached in the story, but where the characters at odds cease arguing and begin to sing altogether and at once; the peculiar flavour of this scheme being the continuing, but temporarily static, notion of *disagreement* expressed in music which *harmonizes.*

Clearly, the situation for an ensemble of this kind has to be contrived, and once the singing together begins, the music takes an accustomed course until the ensemble is over, the only really fresh thing being the issue. The ensemble must issue in the next move of the story; and if that move is to be made by one character, say, then the ensemble may leave the voice of that character eventually singing alone, high and dry, so that, without realizing why, we expect his or her decision. But there are other possible issues.

An operatic composer, then, amasses his apparatus to suit his need; either by utilizing a traditional scheme, if that will do, or inventing a new one, if nothing will do. A kind of rule 4 might run: *that in opera the musical schemes are always dictated by the situations.* Stated in this way, it is so obvious that it seems hardly worth ruling; but it is deceptive. For instance, if one character is winning and one is losing it is rarely that music can express both these characters' emotions at once. There has to be a decision as to whose? and for how long? and why?—questions which need not necessarily trouble the librettist at all. In *Don Giovanni* there is an embarrassing place where Donna Elvira has to be on the stage listening to Leporello's entertaining (but from Elvira's point of view, insufferably tactless) list of the Don's amorous conquests. As the music is all Leporello's, we do not know whether Mozart imagined Elvira as speechless with fury or proudly insensitive. No amount of stage production can ever remove the dramatically equivocal problem caused by the operatic decision in the music.

Applying rule 4 to the kind of opera I have described as being allied to modern verse drama, are the situations likely to be such that traditional operatic schemes will do, or will there be new ones? Or, to put it personally, did *The Midsummer Marriage* need new schemes? Given all that I have said to date, most of the question answers itself. That is to say, there is nothing in the marriage part of it, the comedy, which is not to be found in the schemes of *opera buffa*: recitative, aria, ensemble, and some Verdi and Puccini techniques. And there is nothing in the midsummer part of it which is not to be found in the schemes of music drama: for example, orchestral music to a natural phenomenon like a sunrise, considered as part of the drama. The only thing that is new is the same problem that worries the verse dramatists themselves—the techniques of transition.

We want to move smoothly from the everyday to the marvellous, without relying on scenic transformation during an act. For the verse dramatist the problem is the kind of verse that can sink near to contemporary speech but rise easily to incantation. For the opera composer the problem is to find a musical unity of style which will, for example, let an *opera buffa* chorus of young people of the present time sing themselves into a mantic chorus akin to that of the ancient Greek theatre. In point of fact (as the verse dramatists find), the real difficulty is in the descent to everyday—partly because it brings one dangerously near musical comedy, and generally because unsentimental simplicity is nowadays almost impossible to rescue from the banal.

The search for lyrical simplicity was therefore for me the hardest thing of all. I did not want to match the strangeness of the story with obscurity in the music. On the contrary: as the moral of *The Midsummer Marriage* is enlightenment, then the music must be lucid. The big moments seemed to take care of themselves. The little moments had to be struggled for. The transition between the world of the marvellous and the world of everyday was now gradual, now sudden. The mechanisms have all appeared before, I think, only the degree of their use is new.

In *The Magic Flute*, Tamino, the quest hero, is set down as a Japanese prince, and the priest of the temple as Egyptian. In *The Midsummer Marriage* the priest and priestess of the temple are Greek, and as the 'marvellous' couple had to have relation to present-day life, I gave them royal names, Mark and Jenifer, out of my own homeland. (For Jenifer is the Cornish variant of Guinevere.) But the everyday couple, the mechanic and the pretty secretary, I named more functionally Jack and Bella.

The two couples are tied together in the story by the fact that Jenifer's father employs the secretary and later the mechanic. Therefore I gave the father an up-to-date Americanized name, King Fisher (like Duke Ellington), but which, considered mythologically, belongs to the same Celtic world of romance as Mark and Jenifer. Jack and Bella never take part in the 'big' supernatural manifestations, which centre always on the 'marvellous' couple, Mark and Jenifer. So it is also possible to consider the couples as psychological reflections of each other. In any case, the inexplicit social function of my quest hero and heroine is an operatic liberty, which can be also, in the kind of opera to which *The Midsummer Marriage* belongs, an operatic advantage.

For *The Midsummer Marriage* is what I have called a collective imaginative experience, dealing with the interaction of two worlds, the natural and the supernatural. Therefore there are incidents, details of the story which are ambivalent if not thoroughly irrational. Such incidents (in this tradition) can be frivolous, like Titania falling in love with Bottom translated into an ass; or deadly serious, like Oedipus having begotten children from his own mother. What is clear is that such an imaginative experience is not throughout susceptible to conventional or logical analysis. Still less is it assisted by learned commentary. Did the Greek audience need a commentator to mediate between them and the tragedy of King Oedipus? Certainly not. Such rough commentary as I have made to *The Midsummer Marriage* is designed only to show that opera, just because of its music, may be the most suitable medium to hand now to renew the Greek attitude.

We can best summarize the argument by considering the effects of disregarding the four rules I have suggested. (But I shall place them in a different order.) If we forget rule 1 and allow the librettist to do already with his words things that really belong to the music, then we shall have not an opera but a play set to some music—a subtle distinction but to my mind a real one. If, however, the librettist leaves all the room necessary for the music, as agreed beforehand with the composer, but the latter forgets rule 4 and fails to produce musical schemes which *are the situations* of the libretto, then the opera is a bungle of another kind. The music may be lovely, but is irrelevant. (Rules 1 and 4 are general. Rules 2 and 3 apply only to librettists and composers wrestling with the special dramatic material that I have indicated as being allied to modern English verse drama.)

If the composer-librettist, as we may conveniently call him, forgetting rule 2, is unable to wait upon the revelation of some ageless mythological tradition, but believes himself capable of inventing all afresh, then the great danger is that the symbolical metaphor will be idiosyncratic only, and will never have the power of a collective image. If, however, the tradition is revealed and accepted but, forgetting rule 3, the traditional material is in no way worked upon so that it may speak immediately to our own day, then the result will almost certainly seem mere fantasy.

Of course, these supposed four rules are only suggestions, but they enable one to ask critical questions. And though the answers may not be precisely 'Yes' or 'No', the colloquy helps the composer-librettist to know what he is doing. Four examples:

1. By how much, and in what way, is Berg's opera *Wozzeck* more than Büchner's play?
2. Is the Auden libretto for Stravinsky's *The Rake's Progress* really a private world?

3. Is the Hofmannsthal–Strauss opera *Die Frau ohne Schatten* merely a fable?
4. Do the musical schemes to Vaughan Williams's opera *The Pilgrim's Progress* indissolubly express the situations he has taken from Bunyan's quest story?

All these questions circle around a central proposition that it is really possible to create and to recognize 'that indissoluble unity of drama and music' which we call opera—that this is more than music to a play or than choreography to an established symphony. I have really taken this proposition all the time for granted in discussing a somewhat special possibility for an opera of the present time. For I am quite sure there can be successful modern operas outside the genre I have tried to describe as that to which my own opera belongs. Indeed, I doubt if we ever *choose* to employ dramatic material of this sort. It is rather that it forces itself on us. But once this has been accepted, the modern temper, as I have said before, demands that we wrestle with it consciously to the utmost of our ability. Hence, possibly, the contemporary preoccupation with verbal—or by the same token musical and even operatic—precision and with form. For I consider the general classicizing tendency of our day less as evidence of a new classic period than as a fresh endeavour (fresh, that is to say, after the first romantics) to constrain and clarify inchoate material. We must both submit to the overwhelming experience, and clarify it into a magical unity. In the event, sometimes Dionysus wins, sometimes Apollo.

The works of art where these antagonistic functions are successfully mediated—that is, where all the struggle has been discharged into the artistic experience, and nothing is left over to our embarrassment—will constitute our ideal. Clearly that ideal will be rarely, if ever, attained. Meanwhile, it is probable that opera, whose contrived situations are fully expressed only when the music is played in the theatre, is a most natural medium for such art. I mean that its ingredients, drama and music, give us all we need to an even greater degree, perhaps, than in the verse play.

Chapter 17

THE RESONANCE OF TROY: ESSAYS AND COMMENTARIES ON *KING PRIAM*

In 1956, two continental theatrical companies came to London. One was the Berliner Ensemble with plays and productions of Bertolt Brecht. I found this visit exciting. I had read Brecht and his theories about his epic theatre, but had never seen the results on the stage. So it was a rewarding experience. The second company was that of Jean-Louis Barrault, and I saw their production of Paul Claudel's *Christophe Colombe*,[1] with music by Milhaud. This also exercised a decisive influence on me at a time when I was still searching for the right material for a second opera.

What struck me first was that the methods of the epic theatre, in their widest sense, were really independent of the *political* idea of the dramatists using them. I mean that Brecht and Claudel, one Marxist, one Catholic, both presented the epic material on the stage by scenes and commentaries, selecting or inventing those scenes out of the epic material that alone presented their view (or were appropriate to their work) *and no others*. In a certain sense this is true, too, of the historical plays of Shakespeare: so it is no alien tradition to us English.

In London Jean-Louis Barrault also read a paper on what he had learnt from his collaboration with Claudel. This taught me quite a lot about how to extract and create these decisive scenes from the whole epic. Around then, I began to lay down the form of the libretto of *King Priam* and to decide on the character of some of the music.

Secondly, a talk on the BBC Third Programme led me to a book mainly about Racine by the French Marxist critic Lucien Goldmann, *Le Dieu caché*.[2] Goldmann, through his acute analysis of tragedy in Racine's work, influenced strongly the tragic nature of *King Priam*, although Goldmann was of the opinion that tragedy in the Greek sense is not theatrically viable nowadays, in a

---

[1] Palace Theatre, London, 1956.

[2] Lucien Goldmann, *Le Dieu Caché—Étude sur la viston tragique dans les Pensées de Pascal et dans La Théâtre de Racine* (Paris, 1955). Trans. Philip Thody as *The Hidden God* (London and New York, 1964).

world which must be either Christian or Marxist. For these are both optimistic philosophies. But, being in Goldmann's strict sense neither Christian
nor Marxist, I was unrepentantly certain, from some deep intuitive source,
that tragedy was both viable and rewarding: that when audiences saw Priam's
death at the altar as Troy burned, they would feel the old pity and terror and
be uplifted by it.

Racine, as I realized from reading Goldmann, was one of the masters of
theatrical tragedy. Thus I was prompted to enter the vast epic story surrounding King Priam. But Claudel and Milhaud and, of course, Brecht
taught me how to pare away all the dross of the story, so that only the essentials—those essential scenes to *this* work—are there. Nor would I wish to leave
out Jean-Louis Barrault himself. The white sail of Columbus's ship remained
in my mind as I discussed the production of *King Priam* with its director, Sam
Wanamaker.

Modern opera is a risk. In no other field of music, perhaps, is the repertoire
so consistently of the nineteenth century. Yet it is always, at least to me, a
stimulus and a challenge. I feel that my instrumental music, nowadays, is
being fed from the operatic music. That the challenge of a new opera forces
reconsiderations of musical style, which then flows over into music for the
concert-hall. It *appears* indeed as if the changes of musical style were even the
result of extra-musical qualities of opera. I do believe that these formal
qualities must be endlessly varied and changed to meet the needs of whatever
'subject' one is dealing with. The 'subject' is perhaps the stimulus. But the
invention of the exactly necessary musical forms is certainly the challenge. (I
can remember the excitement of this challenge in my first opera *The
Midsummer Marriage*. How I was engrossed for so many years with the tremendous outpouring of lyrical music, which alone could express the 'subject'—
the quest for illumination. I can recall this excitement; but the events, in my
life, are entirely past. It was to be expected that a second opera would be quite
different. How different, I could hardly have guessed ahead.)

I have not found that when a stimulus to an opera begins to work, the
ready-made 'subject' comes immediately to hand. In fact, the stimulus seems
to begin at a point when it isn't even clear whether the eventual work will be
for the concert-hall (in the form of cantata or oratorio) or for the theatre. *A
Child of Our Time*, for example, began as a stimulus to write an opera, but
became gradually and finally an oratorio. *The Midsummer Marriage* was always
to be an opera.

The stimulus (to some large work for voices and instruments) that led eventually to *King Priam* began as a vague set of eight, somewhat unrelated scenes
that might have issued in a descriptive cantata for singers in a concert-hall, or
even in a choral ballet. A conversation with David Webster of Covent Garden
settled in my mind for me that the stimulus was really to an opera—indeed,
a tragic opera. And conversations with the producer, Peter Brook, convinced

me that for this new opera I need not invent all the story myself, as I had done in the opera *The Midsummer Marriage*; indeed, that this would now be wrong. That appropriate traditional epic material, *handled in a certain way*, would provide the tragic story, to be played out upon the stage in the actual present of an evening's performance, yet distanced by being in the past. A theatrical practice which the Greek dramatists used in their time, as Shakespeare did in his, and as Brecht and others have done in ours.

When I at last felt certain that the epic material surrounding Priam, King of Troy, would serve my purpose—or more accurately stated, serve the new opera's purpose—then arose the problems involved by the words 'handled in a certain way'. I felt that another producer, this time my admired friend Günther Rennert, could of all people best help me. In Stuttgart, in Edinburgh, in Hamburg, he worked patiently with me to clarify the inchoate urges of the initial stimulus, and by ruthless excision of all the unnecessary detail to produce a book that was both stage-worthy and precisely what this opera demanded. For the secret of dealing with epic material is to use only those incidents *and no others* which do the thing needed.

Thus, Paris and Helen were part of my story, their adulterous love, indeed, part of the mechanism of the total tragic destiny. In some other opera from the same source-book, this love might well need to be expressed in a love duet. A reasonably tempting thing to do! But in *King Priam* the real issues are the moral ones. Paris, in my opera, is quite conscious of the catastrophic public consequences that will follow from his abduction of Helen. His problem of choice issues musically, therefore, in a monologue of self-questioning, a questioning of fate and life's meaning. There is no description of the emotions of his love at all.

These monologues, which come every so often in the opera, perform the same formal tasks as do the monologues in *Hamlet*. They demanded for their musical expression something nearer declamatory arioso than lyrical aria. Consequently I have had to depart substantially from the lyrical style of most of my music in the past and find a hard, tough, declamatory style that would reflect inevitability. It did not seem appropriate to let the voices float on a web of orchestral sound, as in so many operas, but, on the contrary, to leave the vocal line free to make a kind of declamatory counterpoint to the simplest necessary instrumental accompaniment—if accompaniment is the right term at all.

The result is a sort of mosaic of musical gestures—theatrically large, if instrumentally small. These gestures recur and intertwine. Strange to the audience perhaps at the start, they become familiar by the end, when their interaction must become more intense. And when the end of the tragic drama is reached, which is Priam's death at the altar as Troy burns, there is instantly no more music (only silence) because there are no more gestures. Except the gesture of ourselves in the audience—namely, the momentary musical expression of our inward tears.

As I have said already, although the *story* is from the past, the sense of our performing this story in our own present, in a specific theatre, is consciously underlined. Because the opera is not about history—that is, how the Greeks appeared to themselves—but about eternal problems of the human heart and human destiny, which, since they are eternal, involve us now. But because we are involved, enmeshed, submerged, in the events of our own present, we need, perhaps, specially chosen stories of the past if we are to be moved in the particular way the tragic theatre demands. I am not suggesting this to be an absolute rule. It is simply a very natural one.

There remains the problem of whether tragedy, in the Greek or Shakespearean sense, is truly possible in our day. The answer, for me as a creative artist, is simply 'Yes'. I know, of course, that certain theories about modern society, and therefore of the art that is said to reflect it or alter it, hold that tragedy is impossible. That to a convinced Christian or a convinced Marxist, personal tragedy is unreal—at best sentimental. But I remain, for the present at any rate, unconvinced by these theories. I have on the contrary a positive conviction that the pity and the terror, and the exaltation strangely intermixed with these, which we feel in the theatre before the great tragic spectacles of the past, are both possible and appropriate as a spectacle of the present.

Important for *King Priam* is the Racinian conception of tragedy as being absolute. In each of the Racine tragedies there is always some point when the tragic protagonist accepts, willingly or unwillingly, his or her tragic destiny, and with it the absolute necessity of a certain conduct, which because of its uncompromising *absolute* quality, must finally end in death. And, following from this, since the *absolute* qualities of the tragic destiny and ensuing conduct are refused by the rest of us, who make up the ordinary matter-of-fact world, the tragic protagonist acting out his destiny from this absolute source is incomprehensible to those around him. No real understanding or communication is possible because *a fortiori* the sense of the tragic destiny is by its nature inexpressible. That is to say, the protagonist cannot express it, in communicative terms to his ambience. But it is expressed to *us*, in the theatre, by his or her actions. The pity and the terror and the exaltation are *ours*, not the hero's.

In *King Priam*, before the final scene of death, I allow a somewhat ironic character, Hermes, the divine messenger or go-between between gods and man—that is, between the inner world and the world of fact—to act as interpreter to us in the audience of what the final scene is to do. And this interpretation is made to us in the form of a hymn to music:

> O divine music,
> O stream of sound
> In which the states of soul
> Flow, surfacing and drowning,
> While we sit watching from the bank

The mirrored world within, for
'Mirror upon mirror mirrored is all the show.'
O divine music,
Melt our hearts.
Renew our love.

Priam was the King of Troy. But for the purposes of enjoying, receiving, experiencing the opera *King Priam*, you need know nothing exactly about the story of Troy. Because the resonances that sound in all of us when we speak of Troy arise, I think, from generations, centuries, of European concern with that immortal story. (I ask for nothing more than the accepted residue of that concern.)

Priam married Hecuba. ('What's he to Hecuba, or Hecuba to him?', as Hamlet says of the First Player.) I repeat: there are all sorts of resonances that sound in us as the role of Homeric names is quoted. In the opera Hecuba is given more flesh and blood than her verbal appearance in *Hamlet* or her non-appearance in *Troilus and Cressida*. She is the Hecuba, rather, of Euripides' *Hecuba* and *The Trojan Women* (written two or three hundred years after Homer's *Iliad*), the proud, violent, heroic, political queen.

This royal couple, Priam and Hecuba, had two sons famous in the story—Hector and Paris. Hector has always been considered the type *par excellence* of the noble warrior, husband and hero, 'guardian of chaste wives and of little children', as Homer has it. But his name has also given rise to a less noble epithet—hectoring. In dealing with his brother Paris, he certainly ranted. Both sides of his character appear in *King Priam*.

If Hector was Priam's beloved son, Paris was surely his rejected son. We are all rejected in some way or other; perhaps nowadays more than ever. I mean that nowadays, lying behind the eternal rejections of persons, are the rejections of whole races. So that the collective anguish reinforces the personal. Paris was rejected by Priam and Hecuba in the cradle—for the worthiest of reasons; rejected to a death that he escaped through the deliberate, culpable compassion of a young guard. This is the crucial first scene of the opera; the choice which Priam and Hecuba have to make as to whether this second son should live or die. And already in this first scene their characters move apart. Hecuba's decision is single: 'Then I am mother no longer to this child.' Priam's attitude is double: 'A father and a king'. He remains father to this son born to destroy him as king. Though in this first moment he can echo Hecuba and say, 'The Queen is right. Let the child be killed', some element in himself is unsatisfied. It is hardly possible to name Paris without coupling that name with Helen's. Helen became Helen of Troy through abduction. She was wife, and queen, to Menelaus of Sparta. Here, at Sparta, Paris ran off with her. This abduction appears in the *Iliad* as the prime cause of the Trojan War, and the acute disrelation between the ten years' war, with all its slaughter and eventual sack of Troy, and the cause, abduction of the Queen of Sparta, has endowed Helen with magical, supernatural qualities. She was, in fact, the daughter of Zeus the swan, 'conceived when the great wings beat above Leda'.

The opera is not concerned with the causes, real or legendary, of the Trojan War, nor with the military fortunes of the Greeks and Trojans. Much other material of the great legend has also to be rejected, however operatically tempting. In creating a fresh work of art out of traditional epic material, it is essential, in my opinion, to select exactly and precisely those incidents alone which serve, and indeed which *are*, the new work in question, and to reject absolutely all else. Thus it was tempting to include an operatic description of Paris's and Helen's inescapable, passionate, adulterous love in *King Priam*. But it did not belong to this opera. What did belong was the moral choice set before Paris, if choice there was. Knowing quite well what the consequences of the abduction would be, why did he choose to do it? Nor could he appeal for guidance to Helen. I relieve Helen of all problems of choice, in this sense. She alone, perhaps, of all the characters in the opera has a true acceptance of herself. As she says, in answer to questions, with ultimate simplicity, 'I am Helen.'

The war therefore appears in the opera as inevitable; as inescapable as Helen's and Paris's love. That is to say, it belongs to the way of life of fighting men; perhaps, finally, in some altered form, of all men always. There is no description of the war. There are just the necessary formal musical gestures. It is persons within the war that matter. Priam's efforts to unite his bickering, quarrelling sons, Hector and Paris, who, as my text says, 'once they knew they were brothers never got on'. Or, if it is the Greek camp, under the shadow of the ships, staring out across the plain at the walls of Troy, then it is the tent of Achilles, where he sits brooding, sulking with his friend Patroclus, refusing to fight. We watch how Patroclus, 'in the nick of time', restores some manhood to Achilles. And how this virile act ensures his own death.

If the men are so bound into the war that there seems no possible end to the eternal vengeance 'death for death', have the women any answers to the moral questions? Or are they only reflections of their men? Hecuba, after all, is more single, more fanatic in her pride for Troy, than even Priam. She has never doubted that the fatal Paris should have been killed in the cradle. Helen, as we know, is not a character that ever questions. She accepts herself, she accepts the war, she accepts that Paris is involved in the fighting; in fact, she thinks he should fight more than he does; but their love has an absolute quality that transcends for her all problems.

There remains Andromache, Hector's wife. Andromache echoes down the centuries as the proud, passionate, grieving widow. She indeed questions the war, and bitterly. But the solutions she offers are, as always, politically impossible.

After the men have possessed the stage for the war, I give the three women a scene to themselves. Many questions, no answers, vital and eternal differences. For the women so quickly take on the characteristics of ever recurring types: Hecuba bound up solely with all public life and the fate of the city; Andromache bound up in her home, husband, and children; Helen fatal to both the city and the home, bound up in the truth of some inescapable passion of love.

These six characters, Priam, Hector, and Paris, and their wives, Hecuba, Andromache, and Helen, are with Achilles the protagonists of the opera. Everything develops from their relations with each other.

The turning-point of the tragedy is Hector's death. If this did not unhinge Priam's mind, as Cordelia's death unhinged Lear's, it certainly faced him with a final confrontation of himself. This confrontation appears in the opera as a single huge monologue. It is a scene very characteristic of modern opera—indeed, of the modern theatre altogether—because so much of modern drama is an exploration of the inner worlds of the mind. From this confrontation Priam has only one issue—his own death as the tragic hero. Priam's death is the inevitable destined end to which the whole opera inevitably drives from the first moment of action on the stage: the parents' rejection of their second son.

Although it is clear that in an opera like *King Priam* the story has a compelling power of its own, opera is always primarily a musical experience. And because music has always a relation to itself, making a pattern of contrasted or repeated sounds, then it is commonplace enough to realize that this musical pattern must be, at some deeper level, consonant with the ethos of the story. Thus Verdi's *Otello* is not the same as Shakespeare's *Othello*. Not merely in structure, but in ethos; the emphases are differently placed. Verdi's music expresses *his* conception as exactly as Shakespeare's verse does his. Wagner's *Tristan and Isolde* is utterly different in ethos from the divagatory romances where he found the story. His *music* produces what he, Wagner, imagines. All this, as I say, is commonplace. So that it was both natural and exciting that the music for *King Priam* seemed to possess from the first notes this fundamental consonance with the purpose and ethos of the story.

If we return to the matter of Paris's and Helen's adulterous love, an important point will become immediately clear. In some other opera this love might have needed expression in a vocal duet. In *King Priam* what needs expression is Paris's problem of choice. Should he or should he not give rein to his love and abduct the Queen? And behind that, a more mysterious question: 'Why give us bodies with such power of love, if love's a crime? Is there a choice at all? Answer, Zeus, divine lover. Answer.' This musically, you see, is no lyric love aria but a probing monologue, in the temper of Hamlet's monologues in the play. There are many such monologues in *King Priam*, chiefly for Priam himself, and all are probing, questioning, struggling with the insoluble mystery of human fate. They imply a declamatory rather than a lyrical style, and I can give you one possible, not too dissimilar, example from accepted opera: Boris's monologue 'I have attained to power' from *Boris Godunov*.

Next, in order to produce sharp edges to the scenes and incidents, and even to the characters, I have abandoned the practice of letting the voice ride on a roughly homogeneous flow of orchestral sound, and in place accompanied the voice with only the minimum of orchestral gesture, if I may use that word, the barest minimum necessary to that moment in the drama. If emotions typical to a character return, then the same instrumental gesture returns, for the exact length, however short, that is demanded. And on the few occasions when conflicting emotions are given formal musical expression together, then the instrumental gestures are still, as far as is possible, retained as separable entities.

This method, perfectly proper I am sure to *King Priam, may* be disconcerting at the very start; but progressively it becomes acceptable and exciting. Because the dramatic gestures of the opera end with the death of Priam before the altar as Troy burns, the music ends with the same sharp edge as the edge of the sword that runs through Priam's body. There is a sudden silence. Then a few curious sounds that might represent *our* inward tears.

Last year I stood for the first time on the site of historical Troy. It is amazingly like what one imagines from Homer's story of the *Iliad*. I stood on a little rock hill, with Schliemann's excavations everywhere, looking out over the plain towards the sea. Only in one particular is it unlike Homer's Troy: it isn't a raised mound all round, but is a rounded spur of an escarpment.

Homer describes how dazzling Achilles sulked in his tent by the Greek ships, refusing to fight and forcing his friend Patroclus, the man he passionately loved, to stay away from the battle. Until at a crisis in the war Patroclus persuades Achilles to send him out to the battle in Achilles' armour. Patroclus was killed by the great Trojan hero Hector. Then, and then only, Achilles returns to the war, takes revenge for the death of Patroclus by killing Hector, whose body he drags round and round the walls of Troy. Achilles takes the dead body to his tent, in place of the living Patroclus, and mutilates it. Each night a goddess restores Hector's shattered body, which Achilles mutilates again. It is a horrible story, part of a rich amalgam of heroism, bodily beauty, and brutality of the Greek epics. This amalgam partly returns again in the first Elizabethan England, and there are traces of it, I think, in filmed Westerns.

I cannot remember when I first moved over from the Greek ships and tents, where I had always seemed to belong, through the walls of Troy and into the city. Once I had done so, I found there something missing from the other side, the family—namely, the royal family of Priam. (There is no family in this sense within the Greek camp.) Priam had an eldest and favourite son Hector, and a younger and despised son, Paris (the most beautiful man of his time) whom Priam ordered to be killed at birth. All three men were married; Priam to Hecuba (who lived for the city and bore only sons); Hector to Andromache (who lived for her home and whose little son was frightened of his father's huge plumed helmet); Paris to Helen ('the face that launched a thousand ships' and was a Greek king's wife). So that by going into the city, I went towards the abiding problems of personal human relationships within the family. This is the true seed-bed for all drama: namely, our efforts to re-find parents, children, siblings. Even the tragic hero who enters a world of absolutes and is somewhere mad, still, like Lear, must re-find Cordelia. (Priam had this kind of relationship to Helen.)

These three women, Hecuba, Andromache, and Helen, are each true to their identity: Hecuba to love of fatherland, Andromache to love of husband, and Helen to desire that has no obligations. The Greek goddesses Athene, Hera, and Aphrodite (whom Paris had to choose between) are their proto-types. It was a real *trouvaille* when I first realized that Paris's goddesses were also the three women in his family. His 'choice' of Helen therefore was inte-gral to him. Even at the price of war!

At the first night of *King Priam* in Covent Garden,[3] a present was brought to me, from a nurse, Sister Warren. Inside a coloured case was a conch shell from the sea-shore of Greece. When most of the guests had left the reception after the performance, we persuaded one of the orchestra's horn players to blow notes on the conch: the exact sounds that Achilles might have made as a boy! Answering a letter of thanks for the present, Sister Warren sent me a book on Schliemann's discovery of Troy. The author of the book says: 'When Schliemann went in search of Troy, he was searching for the fountainhead of Western Civilization.'[4] But it is not Troy itself, but the poet Homer who is a fountain-head. In writing *King Priam*, I certainly drank water from this foun-tain. Yet *King Priam* does not imitate Homer. There is nothing in Homer which makes Priam the central figure of the story as the opera does. One does not go to a past work of art for the past, but for the present. It becomes one's own work, to live or die on its own merits.

One of the critics of *King Priam* realized this to the full when he quoted some lines from *The Midsummer Marriage*. At the climax of that opera, in the fire dance in Act III, the moment of illumination, the He-Ancient sings

> Fate and Freedom are a paradox,
> Choose the fate but yet the God
> Speaks through whatever fate we choose.

This really is the essence of *King Priam*, and the critic was extraordinarily per-cipient, for I had these lines always at the back of my mind while composing the second opera.

It is interesting to me to look back and see how the Greek element which is in both operas has flowered so divergently. *The Midsummer Marriage* refers back to Greek comedy, not tragedy. And this Greek element was never pure and unmixed. But in *King Priam* it has flowered, as if out of Greek soil, yet in

[3] 5 June 1962.
[4] Robert Payne, *The Gold of Troy* (London and New York, 1959), 151.

England, and though I had never been to Greece. Because the great legend which has haunted European imagination for 2,500 years is as alive in English minds as anywhere else.

After the dress rehearsal in Covent Garden, David Webster told me that he had watched the stage with such intensity, drawn by its immediacy and impact, that he had been mostly unaware of the music. This was the experience of many; even in a way of myself, though I knew the music well enough as its composer! But it was the effect I had intended for *King Priam*, and it is an essential of the opera. How was it obtained?

I do not want to discuss here the effect of the music itself, or even the story, except to point out that the operatic action is very fast. Even this is a bit deceptive if looked into, but by and large it is correct. The more interesting point to me at the moment is the obvious fact that a misconceived production could easily have impaired the immediacy and impact proper to this fast-moving opera, to the same degree that the actual production at Covent Garden enhanced it. Sam Wanamaker and I had long conferences together over the exact intentions of the libretto. We also came to a rough decision as to the style of production which could best suit these intentions. We both agreed to the self-evident, but often forgotten, proposition that the *music* dictates once and for all the speed, not only of stage action, but of the characters' emotions. At Wanamaker's request, therefore, Covent Garden produced last year a tape of the piano reduction of all the music, and dubbed on to this tape the words in their correct rhythm, if not their actual pitch. Thus the producer had an absolute framework within which his theatrical imagination and skill were to operate.

When Wanamaker came to deal directly with the singers, he sometimes asked them to speak or declaim the words of their roles, especially in those places where audibility of the words was vital. He then asked them if the natural intonations they had given to these words in speech were changed by what they had to sing. The answer was practically never. This is one of the opera's sources of immediacy.

The first big aria, or monologue, of the opera is that of Priam in the second scene of the first act. Wanamaker was quite ready to freeze everyone else on the stage into immobility, allowing Priam to sing from within the stage grouping, and then by stage lighting to extract Priam's *mind*, as it were, out of the group in order to allow him a special relation to the audience. Once this special relation had been established by the stage convention used, Wanamaker then had to deal with the appearances *within Priam's mind* of the old man, the nurse, and the young guard; appearances that we in the audience have to see (and hear) as the audience sees Banquo's ghost in *Macbeth*. It was fascinating to see how natural this convention appears in modern opera, which deals so much with the inner world of man's mind.

Of the stage effects which enhanced the music, which were deliberate, though generally unnoticed, were the underlining of musical correspondences of stage placing. Thus the men's trio and prayer at the end of Act II is balanced in the score by a women's trio and prayer at the beginning of Act III. Sam Wanamaker placed the three men and the three women in very much the same positions, so that the women almost seem to step, temporarily, into the men's shoes. I found this sort of thing very exciting.

The climax of the *Iliad* is perhaps the scene where the old man Priam comes secretly to beg Hector's body from Achilles, who, in a unique moment of compassion, gives it him. The point is that nearly all the figures of Homer's epic are still half or a quarter divine. Thus Achilles had a goddess-mother, and Helen was born from the egg that resulted from the copulation of Leda with Zeus as a swan. So their whole humanity is still to find. *Achilles is totally human for this one moment.* It is what makes this scene so moving. Clearly, to make a viable opera out of such rich material, I had to pare away everything but the scenes which mattered to my point of view. Priam's attempt to have baby Paris murdered, his subsequent repenting and finding the boy, Paris as a grown man abducting Helen, and thus to the war and the senseless revenge that continues till the city is in flames and Priam himself dies at the altar. Quite as clearly, the music had to be spare, taut, heroic, and unsentimental. So that I had to set aside the earlier lyricism of *The Midsummer Marriage*, where the voices ride on a river of glowing sound, for a much more hard-hitting rhetoric, where the voices are often accompanied by a single, but essentially characteristic instrument. I found this style change immensely stimulating and exciting.

Chapter 18

DREAMS OF POWER, DREAMS OF LOVE

The question is often posed to me: with which of your operatic characters do you most identify? The assumed answer is usually Mangus, in *The Knot Garden*—the modern reincarnation of Shakespeare's Prospero as a psychiatrist. At the start of the opera, his dream is to be the 'man of power / He puts them all to rights'. The romantic notion of the creative artist as someone who can solve mankind's problems, as Shelley's 'unacknowledged legislator', dies hard. Poland once elected Paderewski, a pianist, as Prime Minister; post-Cold War Czechoslovakia has a writer, Vaclav Havel, as President; and all Greece recently mourned the loss of its most charismatic film-star politician, Melina Mercouri. Personally, though, I lean more towards the irony of Gore Vidal, whose encapsulation of the ex-B-movie star Ronald Reagan as the 'acting President' seems just about right for all such figures.

In *The Knot Garden*, Mangus is not without success in sorting out the difficulties of the six other personalities on-stage. By the end of the opera, Faber and Thea, husband and wife, previously at odds, have indeed begun to communicate. (Incidentally, an opera can achieve just that: it can take the characters through a process of transformation. In a painting we tend more to find statements of things as they are. For example, in Matisse's picture semi-ironically titled *La Conversation*, a Faber-like stripe-suited man, all straight lines, stands motionless on the left; a Thea-like figure, in black dress and green collar, all curves, sits equally still on the right: between them is a balcony overlooking the green of a garden, with a tree and flower-like blobs. Their situation remains for ever frozen. A communication seems unlikely now or in the future.) At the end of the opera, Flora also, the ward of Thea and Faber, has broken away from the confusions of adolescence, and exits 'radiant, dancing' to her brave new world. Mel, the black writer, and Denise, the tortured freedom fighter, leave together, recognizing each other as to some extent kindred spirits. But by the time of the denouement, Mangus has renounced his dreams of power:

> Prospero's a fake, we all know that,
> And perhaps the island's due to sink into the sea.

Now that I break my staff and drown my book . . .
I'm but a foolish, fond old man,
Just like the rest of you,
Whistling to keep my pecker up.

But are the successes, if that's what we dare call them, of the denouement really the product of Mangus's manipulation of the characters—in the 'magical' knot garden of Act II and in the charades of Act III? Well, partially. There is, however, another way of looking at the opera, linking it with that dramatic tradition where personal relations are considered for themselves alone, and are arranged in a kind of pattern or as a kind of dance. Chekhov's *The Cherry Orchard*, Shaw's *Heartbreak House*, Edward Albee's *Who's Afraid of Virginia Woolf?* are typical examples, studies of the games people play. Shakespeare's late comedies are the best models of all, exploring every avenue of possible forgiveness and reconciliation, amongst individuals at war with each other. Shakespeare drew partly on medieval dramatic tradition wherein the view prevailed that however extreme your misbehaviour, if you were able at the last moment, before death, to make a single act of contrition to the Christian God, you could be forgiven all. Isabella's forgiveness of Angelo in *Measure for Measure* is of this kind. Shakespeare had to cope, however, with the fact that while the act of contrition is human, the act of forgiveness is divine. In a society where the Christian religion is becoming less and less all-powerful, who does the forgiving? In *Measure for Measure*, it is a duke, who at one point in the story has masqueraded as a monk; the duke demands, by virtue of his ducal power, the act of contrition, which implies the act of forgiveness. In *The Tempest*, Prospero stands in for God: he, possessing complete magical powers, can do everything; and in the end, he can demand the act of contrition that results in forgiveness and the possibility of leaving the island to return once more to civilization. Love and forgiveness, set in opposition to power, are able to transcend the absolute nature of power. If the act of forgiveness were possible, Othello could have gone beyond the problems of love and duty, and even Wotan could have gone beyond love and power.

Interlocking with all this is another tradition that stretches from Shakespeare to the present, in which music, or poetry allied with music, acts as the agency for those special moments—acts of contrition, acts of forgiveness, submission to love—where the drama needs to be focused, clarified, intensified. In *The Tempest*, Prospero sends Ariel to sing two songs to Ferdinand. The first is a song of invitation to dancing and to love:

Come unto these yellow sands
And then take hands.

This is, as it were, the first movement, a progression towards love and life, towards the dance and communality. Quickly, however, Ariel is singing another song to Ferdinand, a song of death and rebirth, a deeper, stranger song:

> Full fathom five thy father lies;
> Of his bones are coral made;

When I myself was asked by the Old Vic Theatre in London to write incidental music for a performance of *The Tempest*, these songs were the first thing I set. Songs are indeed an outstanding element in Shakespeare's plays. We always know what their function is when they occur, whether they are light or serious. They are also very much of their period. Other Elizabethan and Jacobean songs bear a similar weight, even though they were conceived independently of any stage situation: for example, Dowland's songs or Campion's. They contain the same verbal conceits, whereby (for instance) 'to die' becomes synonymous with 'to love', 'To die, to die again' meant not only to die again but to love again, a curious conjunction of meanings.

In *The First Circle*, it is fascinating to find Solzhenitsyn using the same genre of poetic conceits, hinting at the evanescence of love. The story takes place in a technological research establishment-cum-prison called Mavrino—a converted country house in the Moscow suburbs. In a moving episode, towards the end, one of the prisoners there, a mathematician called Gleb Nerzhin, finds himself alone with a young woman, Simochka. She, actually, is free: she works at the prison, but lives outside. Gleb, however, has been in concentration camps and prisons for at least ten or fifteen years; and he is still married. Now comes the moment that seems so poignant to us— especially so, in the context of the whole novel. We realize that these two people are about to become lovers. Yet Gleb is stirred not only by love, but by a sudden access of problems which we can call duty or conscience. He suddenly tells Simochka that he is married, that he hadn't until the day before managed to catch even a glimpse of his wife for many years, and then, when they had met, found that they were really breaking apart. In order to cover up this extremity of sadness within themselves, when love has seemed so near, Gleb turns on a radio, and they hear the voice of Obukhova, a famous Russian popular singer.

But the strange thing was that as Obukhova sang, instead of feeling more and more wretched, Simochka somehow felt a little better. Ten minutes ago they had been so estranged that they had no words even to say goodbye, but now it was as though some gentle and calming presence had joined them. And it so happened that in her present mood, in a special light that fell on her, now at this very moment, Simochka looked particularly attractive. Nine out of ten men would have laughed at Gleb for giving her up voluntarily after so many years of celibacy. Who could force him to marry her later on? What prevented him from lying to her now? But Gleb was profoundly glad that he had acted as he had. It even seemed as though the decision had not been his own. Obukhova went on singing her heart-rending song:

> No joy, no comfort do I find,
> I live for him alone . . . !

No, of course, it wasn't coincidence. All songs had been the same for a thousand years, as they would be for centuries to come. Songs are about parting—there are other things to do when people meet.[1]

Solzhenitsyn's art is at its most powerful in this musical epiphany. We don't know what exactly the style of Obukhova's song might have been. Maybe it was a blues. Certainly, in the more complex entanglement of relationships at the end of Act I of *The Knot Garden*, I found nothing more apposite. One sings the blues when one's mood is 'blue', to discharge that mood by the song and so get the courage, or at least some renewal of strength, to go on again. The blues basis gives the whole ensemble a shape, a beat, slow or fast, that encompasses the whole web of love-hating personalities in one musical metaphor. It is what Mangus-Prospero later on calls

> . . . Whistling to a music
> Compounded of our groans and shrieks,
> Bitter-sweet and wry,
> Tender, yet tough: ironic
> Celebration for that trickster Eros—
> —in his masks of love.

In the attempted resolution that follows:

> . . . if for a timid moment
> We submit to love,
> Exit from the inner cage,
> Turn each to each to all

—it seemed appropriate to quote Ariel's song of invitation to dancing and love: 'Come unto these yellow sands', reinforcing it with a reference to Goethe's visionary poem *Magisches Netz*:

> We sense the magic net
> That holds us veined
> Each to each to all.

Acts of forgiveness, of reconciliation, are thus effected through the magic influence of music, not through the manifestations of Mangus's power, however well intended.

This brings us to Dov, the character in *The Knot Garden* who ultimately stands apart from the rest, who is finally left isolated, merely pitied by the impotent Mangus. For me, an identification with Dov, the singer, the musician who expresses heart-break, has always seemed close. The key scene for him in the opera comes in Act II, when he is forced by Mel to accept the breakdown of their relationship, forced to invest all in his powers as a musician. Mel tells him:

---

[1] Alexander Solzhenitsyn, *The First Circle*, trans. Michael Guybon (London, 1968), 521.

Stop howling now.
Become yourself.
Go turn your howls to music.

Dov is thus presented with his future task as singer/composer.

As the nightmare interplay of relationships in the knot garden comes to a halt, in Act II, Dov finds himself alone with Flora. She is weeping, and he goes to comfort her. How can he comfort her, but to persuade her to sing? But Flora's song (quoted from Schubert), and really a boy's song, reveals only her own innocence and immaturity. Dov proposes an alternative song. At first, in his extended aria, he sings to Flora of his childhood in the big town. But then, in the second and third stanzas, he turns away from her to sing to us in the audience. The music that crystallized tenderly the situation of Dov and Flora now evolves into an expression of something positive: Dov, though still alone and the object of Mangus's pity, at the end of the opera, can now go off into the world to create and sing songs for us all.

Following the career of Dov further, as I have attempted to do, in a composition independent of the opera, *Songs for Dov*, we can only think of him as (on the one hand) the loner and (on the other) the musician who travels the world, searching for that southern land where we hope never to grow old, but which, proving an illusion, drives us ever on towards another beckoning country; a singer, then, who sings of the *Wanderjahre*, those years of illusion and disillusion, innocence and experience, which we all pass through to reach what maturity we may; and then journeying 'full circle west', back to the 'big town' and the 'home without a garden' across the tundra of Siberia. Dov, as the grown man, the fully fledged mature creative artist, struggles with the intractable problems of 'poets in a barren age' (in Hölderlin's phrase). So, in the course of his last journey, he looks in on Dr Zhivago: and we, too, can look over Zhivago's shoulder. Pasternak, through Zhivago, suggests that one of the tasks of, shall we say, lyric poets of our period, might be just to sustain the pastoral metaphor, in its deepest sense, against the ephemera of town fashions. What Zhivago wrote was this:

Where in such a busy urban life, is pastoral simplicity in art to come from? When it is attempted, its pseudo-artlessness is a literary fraud, not inspired by the countryside but taken from academic bookshelves. The living language of our time is urban.[2]

But there are no poems by Zhivago exemplifying this supposed 'living language'. In *The Earth*, Zhivago instead comments (and Dov sings):

Then why does the horizon weep in mist
And the dung smell bitter?
Surely it is my calling
To see that the distances should not lose heart

---

[2] Boris Pasternak, *Dr Zhivago*, trans. Max Hayward and Manya Harari (London, 1958), 436.

> And that beyond the limits of the town
> The earth should not feel lonely?[3]

Yeats wrote somewhere that out of the quarrel with society, poets make rhetoric; while out of the quarrel with themselves, they make poetry. Pasternak's trope for Zhivago is all rhetoric. So we know that Dov must turn his back on it and peer into himself to find his own poetry. For the moment, he finds just two words and a hollow tap from the claves. 'Sure, baby.'

In my next opera, *The Ice Break*, the ironies for the young Yuri are much harder to resolve. He is permanently at war, with his family, with his friends. When his father, Lev, arrives at the start of the opera from years of exile in a Soviet camp, Yuri openly despises his father for having taken the line of passive resistance to violence. Yuri has grown up in a society where 'We're not pushed around. Every guy has a gun.' Yuri is no dreamer. He lives for now, and has no sympathy with the dreams of his mother, Nadia, who idealizes some aspects of the past. Accepting current racial stereotypes, Yuri finds himself at odds also with his girl-friend, Gayle, and abhors her 'fooling around' with the Blacks, like the nurse Hannah and the superstar Olympion. Yuri is the main focus for division within the opera: in particular, division between the generations, between races. He rejects his parents' dream of liberal charity and tolerance. Only after he has been badly injured in a race riot is there a hint of reconciliation: and in the final scene of Act II, when Lev and Hannah are left to comfort each other, the orchestra alone provides the musical epiphany.

Remembering Shaw's *Back to Methuselah*—whose first production in London I attended—I wanted to emulate the scene in which a huge egg is brought on the stage with a girl inside. As the egg rocks away, the girl says, 'I want to get out, I want to be let out.' The egg is broken open, and she steps out and at once behaves like an adolescent, going straight to the nearest good-looking man she can see. This image seemed to me appropriate to represent the spiritual rebirth of Yuri. In an earlier form of the libretto for the opera, I planned for Yuri to emerge from a shell. Something of this allusion was retained in the final version, when the stage instruction indicated that Yuri 'is totally (at least metaphorically) encased in plaster'. Lev even refers to the 'naked human chick', thus preserving the original image. For the musical epiphany that signals Yuri's spiritual rebirth, after the operation to remove him from the plaster cast, has been accomplished, I turn again to *The Tempest*:

> Spring, spring,
> Spring, come to you at the farthest,
> In the very end of harvest.

---

[3] Ibid. 499–500.

The young people racing through the hospital sing these lines as an anthem of hope. Goethe provided me with another reference point for the reconciliation of father and son. Goethe never knew reconciliation with his own real-life son; hence the imagined reconciliation scene between father and son in *Wilhelm Meister* has a Hardyesque pessimism. Wilhelm rescues his son, after a horse-riding accident, from the river. As a country doctor, he too must carry out an operation to bleed the young man. He looks down at the naked body of the son, lying asleep and exhausted, and says: 'Wirst du doch immer aufs neue hervorgebracht, herrlich Ebenwild Gottes! Und wirst sogleich wieder aufs neue Beschädigt, verletzt, von innern oder von aussen.' (Yet you will always be brought forth again, glorious image of God; likewise be maimed, wounded afresh from within and without.) *The Ice Break* ends with Lev quoting those words as Yuri hobbles off supported by Hannah.

For Yuri there is at least the possibility of a dream for the future. He has begun at last to grow beyond the immediate, the everyday here and now. For Donny, the young delinquent in my last opera, *New Year*, there are dreams, but little hope of their being realized. After the première in Houston in 1989, everyone asked, 'Whatever becomes of Donny?'—for his fate, his future, are left unresolved.

Others in the opera have dreams that seem likely to be realized. The protagonist, Jo Ann, a children's doctor, has to learn from her imagined lover from outer space, Pelegrin, how to sing and dance—a signal that she will indeed in the end find the strength and courage to go out into the world to practise her skills. Pelegrin and his fellow inhabitants of the utopian realm Nowhere tomorrow all disappear off into the future. Donny, injured after being made the scapegoat of the crowd's dissent during the anticipated celebration of New Year, is finally taken off into the care of his foster-mother, Nan: but not before he has handed Jo Ann a video-cassette which, he tells her, contains his dreams.

So what are Donny's dreams? Early on in Act I, he acts out a *Skarade* with his friends. Like Dov, he remembers his childhood. But his was not a golden childhood in a big city, with intimations of love:

> No golden childhood for 't orphan boy
> Only a foster-sister's love made up
> Dead parents from another land.
> So where at all do I belong?

The first question, indeed, for an orphan, is where does he belong—where does he 'check in'? He could try the Caribbean island of his roots, a potential paradise. Rejection, though, is just as possible there, as anywhere else:

> Caribo, Caribo,
> Y'sure that's where ya want to go
> And what if they don't like ya face

> Like ya face, like ya face
> What if they don't like ya face,
> O my lord, o my—

Returning to his roots in Africa is no less futile. For now, he remains the drop-out. But the songs on his video-cassette explore metaphorical alternatives—dreams, first, of power, then finally of some form of social acceptance, even perhaps love. Leaving behind the nightmare of his actual family—the father who got 'blown away in a puff of smoke' and the mother who 'ran away with another bloke'—Donny imagines situations in which he is top dog or feared predator—in the culture of today, a gang leader, drug baron, or something similar. But Jo Ann rejects such a prospect. He ought neither to aspire to the position of 'comely condor' watching 'with gimlet eye . . . the foolish prey below'; nor can he be 'the tom-cat tiger' stalking powerfully, fiercesomely alone. He has to find a family of some sort, and nature's metaphor for this might be the 'wondrous whales . . . in the waters of Nantucket bay . . . [who] boom their love songs in the deep'.

Donny's development, in actual terms, in so far as we may think of him as having a life beyond the opera, might entail some form of group therapy—rather more relevant, perhaps, than the ministrations of some Mangus figure. It is not impossible that Donny might become socially integrated, though he is bound to remain a wounded figure, an oddball, an outsider.

Chapter 19

ST AUGUSTINE AND
HIS VISIONS

My interest in St Augustine goes back a long way: I probably read his *Confessions* in my youth. What brought me back to his writings subsequently was reading an essay by Gilles Quispel, one of a series of papers presented at the Eranos meeting of 1951, devoted to the theme of 'Man and Time'.[1] (Since their inception in 1933, these meetings have been held regularly at the home of Frau Olga Fröhe-Kapteyn, on the shore of Lake Maggiore, near Ascona, in Switzerland. They were organized in an attempt to bring together a range of scientific thinkers to take stock of the world, away from the pressures of immediate, everyday situations. From the outset, the dominant figure was Jung. From the mid-thirties onwards, I read the annual proceedings, or Eranos Yearbooks, initially published in German; but the 1951 papers appeared in English translation.) In his essay Quispel sets Augustinian theology in its historical context—noting, however, that every one of Augustine's important doctrines was based on an error in the translation of the Bible! None the less, what attracted me was his account of Augustine's theory of visions, which embodies profound psychological insights. Quispel shows that Augustine's subjective notion of time and of visions as products of the memory are consistent with the rest of his thinking, all of it with a strong emphasis on inwardness.

Within myself as a composer, this set up sympathetic vibrations. I was particularly stimulated when I read the long account (quoted from the *Confessions*) of Augustine's conversation on eternal life with his mother, shortly before her death. This text became the starting-point for a new composition. To find the right musical means, however, for the communication of ecstatic, visionary states, I had to widen my investigations, taking in early Christian liturgical music and the traditional singing techniques used in expressing the transcendent.

---

[1] See Gilles Quispel, 'Time and History in Patristic Christianity', in Joseph Campbell (ed.), *Man and Time: Papers from the Eranos Yearbooks* (London, 1958), 85–107.

The music of the angels; that is, the kind of music the angels sang to the shepherds at the birth of Christ, focuses attention on the meaning of time.[2]

Faced with the procession of the seasons within the year, vital to all agrarian societies, peasants and priests alike found religious security in the certainty of recurrence. John Barleycorn had his head cut off in the summer harvest, but came to life again miraculously in the spring. Time was but an endless recurrence of seasons. This was obvious enough to a peasant or a shepherd, because it was visible. But this concept of cyclic time, as it has been called, is not obvious when extended into past and future to the recurrence of aeons or world months of 2,000 years; nor when used, as in some Hindu myths, to assume the rise, decay, and recurrence of civilizations by immutable law. Such things were unobservable, and the so-called immutable laws were of course religious and mythological.

Now although the birth of Christ falls at the winter solstice, when analogically the sun's chariot stands at midpoint in the night journey under the sea, this is not really of the essence. What is of the essence concerns the matter of eternity in relation to temporality, and the nature of God.

For once we begin to consider time not as meaningless recurrence, but as development from a beginning to an end, we give meaning at last to history. The development, the acts of history, will appear as progress or degeneration according to the meaning we give. And the meaning depends on the answers to certain questions this new idea of time inevitably poses. If temporality has a beginning and an end, what was this beginning, and what will be the end? And what is before the beginning and after the end? This is as unobservable as the immutable recurrence of aeons, and the answers are as religious and mythological as the immutable laws of cyclic time. But the myth is different.

The answer to the beginning was the once, and once only, creation by God of a temporal universe with an ordained end. The early Christian Fathers were then much exercised by the conundrums: 'What did God do before the creation?' and 'What is the nature of the eternal life of the saints when, after the resurrection of their bodies, they enter eternity—and all temporality, and the universe with it, ends?' The questions are metaphysical, and the answers therefore equally so. But the essence of the myth or belief is a conception of time as finite—that is, with beginning and end, what I have called temporality—and this finite time is then set against God's eternity. This metaphysical concept enabled the Christian philosophers—I am thinking particularly of Augustine—to see that the question 'What did God do (with his time) before the creation?' was unreal. Time only began with the creation, and will end with it. God is in eternity, not time.[3]

---

[2] I am indebted here to G. B. Chambers, *Folksong-Plainsong: A Study in Origins and Musical Relationships* (London, 1956), esp. ch. 1–3; Reinhold Hammerstein, *Die Musik der Engel* (Berne, 1962), esp. ch. 2, and a review of this book by Frederick W. Sternfeld, published (anonymously) in the *Times Literary Supplement*, 14 June 1968, p. 416.   [3] See St Augustine, *Confessions*, xi.

From this duality came the possibility of a relationship, or dialogue, between God and the world, or between eternity and time. In a sense the dialogue between God and the world is the dramatization of the metaphysical relation between eternity and time. And the music of the angels is part of the expression of this drama—as indeed the angels themselves are important actors in the drama. So that, keeping these two aspects of dialogue and relationship in mind, we can say that, in the history of God's dealings with man, the next most dramatic moment after the creation of the universe and time was the irruption of eternity into time through the birth of Christ as God and man. This inexpressible moment of the divine drama—inexpressible by man, that is—was actually expressed by the simultaneous appearance of the angels to the shepherds. What the angels then sang was the expression of a minute vision of eternity—minute in relation to the transcendent magnificence of God the Father. And this vision was a charisma—an act of God's grace—for which the shepherds, so far as we know, were not specifically prepared but for which they were predestined. The seeds of later doctrinal conflicts over predestination are all to be found in this apparently simple story.

It is the immediacy and poetry of this story, however, which kept it alive through so many Christian centuries. It forms one of the most touching scenes of the medieval mystery play cycles. Yet the philosophical concepts are never far away. In the Shepherds' Plays it was a tradition for the shepherds to compare their own rough music with the angels' music which they had just heard. The angelic music is a source of 'Wonder', because it is so much finer. As the *prima pastor* of one such play says, the angels' song

> Was wonder curiose
> With small notes emang

and points out that the melody had 'foure and twenty to a long'.[4] The shepherds 'wonder' at the vocal skill and virtuosity the angels display. The shepherds are no different, except in degree, from Augustine, who 1,000 years before had pondered on this problem and decided that the music of the angels must in some way be like the music of man but purified. Because only such purified music could express the sense of blessedness which angels enjoy as they sing eternally before the face of God. The shepherds in the plays also catch a moment of this blessedness. In another play, after the angelic *Gloria*, the *secundus pastor* says: 'For never in this world so well I was', and his friend Garth suggests they sing a jubilation.[5]

Now a jubilus, or jubilation, has a long history. St Augustine puts the facts in a nutshell. He is commenting on Psalm 32, whose last verse runs: 'Be glad

---

[4] See *The Wakefield Prima Pastorum*, vv. 306 and 414, in A. C. Cawley (ed.), *The Wakefield Pageants* (Manchester, 1958), 37 and 40.

[5] See *The Chester Shepherds' Play*, v. 441, in S. Hemingway (ed.), *English Nativity Plays* (New York, 1909), 56.

in the Lord and rejoice, ye righteous: and shout for joy, all ye that are pure in heart.' His commentary on this verse is as follows:

Notice the method of singing *and shout for joy* he (i.e. the Psalmist) gives you. Don't look for words that you may be able, as it were, to explain how God is pleased: sing a 'jubilation': What does singing a 'jubilation' mean? It is the realisation that words cannot express the inner music of the heart. For those who sing in the harvest field, or vineyard, or in work deeply occupying the attention, when they are overcome with joy at the words of the song, being filled with such exultation, the words fail to express their emotion, so, leaving the syllables of words, they drop into vowel sounds—the vowel sounds signifying that the heart is yearning to express what the tongue cannot utter.[6]

The principal notion behind this passage is the tradition, common throughout the early Christian centuries and going far back into the pagan past, that ecstasy—that is, the apprehension of the transcendent—is too huge to be expressed by words. It can only be expressed by vocalizations, shouts, orgiastic repetitions of vowels. The Greek word for this manifestation was 'glossolalia'. And glossolalia is the central technique, if I may borrow that word, which the angels use in their music.

But angelic glossolalia not only had its origins in shamanistic ecstasy; it had folk origins as well, as Augustine describes. His father was a wine-grower, and Augustine in boyhood had regularly heard this North African wordless folk-song which went by the Latin name of 'jubilus'. The peasants sang it to express well-being and joy. It was also used for calling and answering, as St Hilary, a century before Augustine, makes clear in his commentary on Psalm 65, where he writes:

And according to the custom of our language, we name the call of the peasant and agricultural worker a 'jubilus', when in solitary places, either answering or calling, the jubilation of the voice is heard through the emphasis of the long drawn out and expressive rendering.[7]

(This seems, incidentally, to suggest that the traditional Alpine singing we call yodelling is a form of 'jubilus'.)

When the angels sang to the shepherds, before they reached a 'jubilus' of vowels, they sang certain words clearly enough for the shepherds to understand. They sang: 'Gloria in excelsis Deo.' 'Glory be to God in the highest, and on earth peace and goodwill towards men.' The message of peace and goodwill was the special part of the song—the *Gloria in excelsis Deo* was, if I may put it so, the conventional or usual. For the function of angels, apart from being messengers between heaven and earth, was to enact a perpetual ritual of praise.

---

[6] Adapted from quotation in Chambers, *Folksong-Plainsong*, 4.

[7] Jacques-Paul Migne, *Patrologiae cursus completus*, Series Latina (hereafter *PL*) (221 vols., xlvii, 1844–55), 1239; see also Chambers, *Folksong-Plainsong*, 23.

This is already present in the famous vision of Isaiah, from which it can be said the whole angelic tradition stems. Isaiah described how:

In the year that King Uzziah died I saw also the Lord sitting upon a throne, high and lifted up, and his train filled the temple. Above it stood the seraphims: each one had six wings; with twain he covered his face, and with twain he covered his feet, and with twain he did fly. And one cried unto another, and said, 'Holy, holy, holy, is the Lord of hosts: the whole earth is full of his glory.'[8]

Isaiah's vision is the angels at worship—the covering of face and feet, singing 'Holy, holy, holy' before the transcendent God. The word 'praise' is implicit, not stated. In the shepherds' vision at the birth of Christ, Luke says explicitly: 'And suddenly there was with the angel a multitude of the heavenly host praising God.'[9] But it is Paul who Christianizes the Hebraic tradition finally. In the first chapter of Hebrews he tries to place God, man, and angel in a new hierarchy. He subsequently accepts the Psalmist's traditional view that man is 'a little lower than the angels',[10] who are, of course, infinitely lower than God. But Christ, God's son, has altered this older order: 'For verily he took not on him the nature of angels; but he took on him the seed of Abraham.'[11] So that through this divine incarnation the order of man is potentially above that of the angels:

For unto which of the angels said he at any time, Thou art my Son, this day have I begotten thee? And again, I will be to him a Father, and he shall be to me a Son?

And again, when he bringeth in the first begotten into the world, he saith, And let all the angels of God worship him.[12]

So the angels do not really enter the scheme of Christian redemption, their function remains what it always was, the everlasting worship and praise of God, not in time, of course, but in eternity.

The traditional Hebraic visions of Ezekiel and Isaiah and the Christianizing of Paul receive a tremendous dramatization in the splendid apocalyptic visions which John of Patmos had and which are the substance of the book of Revelation. Much of Revelation is a description of the heavenly liturgy, with direct references to Judaic temple ritual and the slowly forming Christian ritual of the Mass: the elders round the throne, like the attendant priests around the bishop's chair; the thrice spoken 'Holy' at the beginning; the opening of the sacred book; the praise for the Lamb; the final Amen.

There is however, a verse to be quoted exactly, which runs:

And the four beasts had each of them six wings about him; and they were full of eyes within: and they rest not day and night, saying, Holy, holy, holy.[13]

Three other verses run:

---

[8] Isa. 6: 1–3. [9] Luke 2: 13. [10] Heb. 2: 7; see also Ps. 8: 5.

[11] Heb. 2: 16. [12] Heb. 1: 5, 6. [13] Rev. 4: 8.

And I looked, and, lo, a Lamb stood on the mount Sion, and with him an hundred forty and four thousand, having his Father's name written in their foreheads.

And I heard a voice from heaven, as the voice of many waters, and as the voice of a great thunder: and I heard the voice of harpers harping with their harps:

And they sung as it were a new song.[14]

From these various quotations we can now draw up a list of the most constant characteristics of the music of angels, many of which were directly echoed in Christian liturgy, and deliberately. For the sacred music of the Church in the world and time is an imperfect echo of the angelic music in eternity.

From Isaiah comes the *alter ad alterum*, 'one cried unto another';[15] that is, the two choirs or voices which sing alternate verses one to another. This tradition is still present in the Decani and Cantoris of our English cathedral choirs.

From John of Patmos comes the *sine fine*, 'they have no rest day nor night':[16] that is the idea of a perpetuity of praise. This could only be echoed here on earth by the monks of certain Orders, who divided their members into twelve groups to sing hourly, day and night, in the monastery church. As Hildegard of Bingen put it: 'The members of the Order perform the duties of the angels, in that they offer up hour by hour a singing prayer.'[17]

From John of Patmos comes also the *canticum novum*, 'they sung as it were a new song';[18] which marks the new dispensation of the New Testament. And also the vast numbers 'and with him an hundred forty and four thousand';[19] signifying the gathering in of all creation. And these vast numbers sang *una voce*, as one voice; that is the tremendous tradition of unison singing, the unity of all. In the words of the Apostolic Constitutions:

This is namely the will of God, that as the heavenly powers praise God with one voice, we men on earth praise God with one voice, we men on earth praise the one true God with one mouth and one meaning.[20]

Behind it all lay the much stranger tradition of glossolalia—the expression of ecstasy in vowel sounds. This came almost to be standardized in the Alleluia. 'Alleluia' was a Hebrew expression meaning 'Praise be to Jah'—that is to Jehovah. So that the allelu- announced the praise, while -ia was used for the vocalization, the glossolalia. These alleluias were sometimes of enormous length and often extemporized. They form one of the oldest parts of the Mass.

Of course, the angels also played instruments, but here the problem is too difficult to elucidate. To put it briefly, the harps, trumpets, tubas, and cymbals the angels played are not those of any modern orchestra.

---

[14] Rev. 14: 1–3.   [15] Isa. 6: 13.   [16] Rev. 14: 11.   [17] Migne, *PL* xv. 515.
[18] Rev. 14: 3.   [19] Rev. 14: 1.
[20] F. Probst, *Liturgiae der drei ersten christlichen Jahrhunderte* (Tübingen, 1870), 180; quoted (in German) in Hammerstein, *Die Musik der Engel*, 45–6.

Because indeed it is all a metaphor. The music of the angels is the expression of eternity as against time. In Christian doctrine it is not possible to know eternity till after death and resurrection. All that God in his grace grants us is occasionally a proleptic vision, a minute foretaste of what this might be. Augustine and his mother were granted such a vision. Five days before she died, they stood together in a window embrasure of an inn at Ostia on the Tiber, looking into an inner garden. They asked each other that central question: What might the life of the saints be like in God's eternity? Augustine describes how they lost the sense of outside things to the degree that they sensed only their souls. But this was not enough. In Augustine's own words:

We went *beyond* our souls, so that we might touch that region of unending richness, where you feed Israel forever with the food of truth . . . And while we were thus talking (of eternal life) and panting for it, we touched it for a moment with the whole effort of our heart.[21]

But this moment was wordless, for he continues:

and we sighed, and left the first fruits of our spirit bound to it, and returned to the sounds of our mouth, where words begin and end.[22]

The central vision, you see, was an experience of ecstasy, which can only be expressed, in echo, by those vowel sounds he commended in his commentary on the Psalms.

I think possibly his most moving sentence is: 'O felix Alleluia in coelo, ubi templum Dei angeli sunt' (O happy Alleluia in heaven, where the angels are the temple of God).[23]

Augustine was born in AD 354 in the province of Africa on the south side of the Mediterranean. This gives him a time in history and a place. When adolescent, he crossed the Mediterranean to the north side at Rome to study rhetoric. Language became an abiding passion.

Currently, there were two languages in the Roman Empire. Latin was the spoken language of the west Mediterranean—and was to some degree universal over the entire Empire. Greek was the spoken language of the eastern Mediterranean. Augustine loved Latin and disliked Greek, but he had to learn it. It was a turbulent period for the Empire. Administratively, it was being transformed by the migrations of Goths flowing over the Rhine westwards and south. Rome itself was sacked in AD 410. Religiously, the pantheism of the pagan world was being transformed into Trinitarian Christianity. Augustine was drawn into this process decisively if, at times, reluctantly. In his twenties, he went to work first in Rome and then in Milan. Here he came close to Bishop Ambrose, who influenced him deeply, and whose beautiful

---

[21] Augustine, *Confessions*, ix. 10.   [22] Ibid.   [23] Migne, *PL* xxxviii. 1190.

hymn, 'Deus, creator omnium', he repeated to himself when overwhelmed with grief at his mother's death.

In a garden near Milan, with Alypius, his dearest friend, at 33 years of age, he had his first vision (if we may call it that, being only auditory) of a child singing 'tolle lege' (take up and read). Of course, there was no real child, as Augustine realized. Such a vision, whereby something apparently real appears to someone in an extreme mental state, is relatively common. In Augustine's case, it led to his final admission into Christianity and to the extreme asceticism that was regarded as necessary in that period.

Some months later he decided to return with his mother to Africa. They travelled overland to Ostia, the port of Rome, and rested there before the sea voyage. Here, five days before Monica's death, Augustine had a second vision, which Monica shared—of eternity. This experience, known to mystics, is much rarer.

Augustine described his two visions in the *Confessions*. Vision I concerns the stubbornness of his will and the dispersal of his emotional energies in dissipation of the senses. Vision II concerns the dispersal of his mind upon the evanescence of things, and came to him through his prolonged inner struggle as to the meaning of time. There is no present—because it is instantly past. We cannot in this temporal existence experience a true present. In fact, we know time only through the mind, which is constantly shifting from the immediacy of sight (*contuitus*) towards the future (*expectatio*) or the past (*memoria*) with such rapidity that the soul is for ever distended (*distentio*) in all directions without a centre. To have any inkling of such a centre, the contrary is necessary—namely, concentration (*intentio*).

Vision I, therefore, gives a centre for his affections by submission to his God's will. Vision II gives a centre to his soul. This vision is, however, an act, in Augustine's terminology, of divine grace, and a crowning mercy in his life. For he now knew the reality of this eternal *ante* (before all time) through experience. But as a moral creature within the temporality of our life on earth, he can only experience eternity momentarily and involuntarily. If—and in Augustine's words this 'if' grows into a tremendous rhetoric—we could indeed prolong this vision (his vision II), then that, he believes, would be the 'eternal life of the saints' which he and Monica discussed as they stood in the window embrasure.

For all his rhetoric, Augustine was a priest, not a poet. He should be compared with Dante, who in *The Divine Comedy* pursued finally the same vision. The composer setting Augustine's text is in this sense a poet. But not really a poet, so much as a master of words. In the *Confessions*, Augustine describes the vision of eternity as completely silent and wordless. A composer sympathetic to Augustine's preoccupation with the nature of time, wishing to describe this silent wordless experience through the sound of singing and instrumental playing, might use some of the techniques discussed above—as indeed I did during the period of composing the piece. Additionally, much of the extended

instrumental coda to the second part of the work was suggested by the persistence of the athletic metaphor in Augustine—running to get away from
time, running away from things as they were, running towards things as they
will be.

Further, I chose to amplify the text with other Latin quotations from the
Confessions and from the Latin Bible. Augustine, in his reflections on time and
in his account of his vision at Ostia, repeatedly echoes St Paul (in his Epistle
to the Philippians[24]): 'forgetting those things which are behind, and reaching
forth unto those things which are before, I press toward the mark for the prize
of the high calling.' Like Augustine, I felt it important to remember also what
immediately precedes these words in the epistle: 'I count not myself to have
apprehended.' This concludes the work, being spoken by the chorus in Greek
and then in the language of the locality where it is being performed: by such
means, in my own way, I signalled that we have to come away from the vision,
out of the concert-hall into the street.

The style of the work is not the contemplative kind, as in oratorio or
Passion, but declamatory, even at times ecstatic: hence the role of the baritone soloist. In performance, despite the tripartite division of the score, *The
Vision of St Augustine* should be given single and entire. Its overall genre is
perhaps impossible to pin-point: rather, it is in a tradition of individual
works—for example, Holst's *The Hymn of Jesus* or Charles Ives's Fourth
Symphony—where the constituent elements and methods may be disparate,
but their essence is one of distillation.

[24] Phil. 3: 13–14.

Chapter 20

ASPECTS OF BELIEF

Although I speak now as an individual person hoping to convey to you what *I* believe, and though I must indeed speak with my own particular voice recognizably different from all the other fifty million or so voices of my countrymen; yet it is obvious that I am only a person whose individual characteristics and beliefs are embedded in a tremendous background of given racial and cultural traditions, of special aptitudes and disabilities I share with all the thousands of my musical colleagues, and of particular ways of thinking and feeling forced on me by my psychological type.

I remember remarking, when I first read Evelyn Underhill's celebrated book, *Mysticism*,[1] how the way to the central experiences was inevitably conditioned by the type; whether, for example, the desire was a passion to know or a passion to love. Underhill admits—indeed stresses—the various ways due to differing temperaments (though these are limited and come again and again) to what are probably for all types the same fundamental experiences of the mystic state; but the examples she gives of great mystics are all Christian. She makes no study of Islamic mysticism—to travel a little east from Europe. Because of her eventual full acceptance of Christian dogma, she is unwilling, perhaps even debarred from considering whether the mysticism that can feed Christianity is the same mysticism that can feed other great faiths. And if so, what this may imply.

I know something was made clear for *me* by a statement of T. S. Eliot's, where he remarks in a discussion of the necessity for religious faith: 'and for us, religion is Christianity'.[2] I know I speak for many beyond myself when I say the question that I at once have to ask is: if religion means for *us* Christianity, who are *they*, and what shall be appropriate to *them*? And if the Christian God demands as an article of faith that they and their religion are to be treated to eternity as inferior, without any rational or sympathetic examination, then one can find oneself, as C. G. Jung expresses it, in the intolerable position of being more rational and more humane than one's God.

Now I believe that this dilemma is deeply significant for the new one world in which London is calling Asia, or Delhi, Europe. It is possible that the

[1] Evelyn Underhill, *Mysticism* (London, 1911).
[2] T. S. Eliot, 'The Humanism of Irving Babbitt' (1924), in *Selected Essays*, 3rd edn., 480.

problem seems simpler to a Hindu because of the traditional tolerance of that religion. But that is deceptive. After all, it is not the humane, tolerant men anywhere that take part in religious riots. Yet the greatest Indian of them all, Gandhi, was a tragic sacrifice to Hindu intolerance and fanaticism. I believe that Gandhi endured, as no one more, in body and spirit, the dilemma of how a religious man shall behave in our modern world. Gandhi is one of the men by whom I have been most deeply influenced.

I don't think the West has produced in this period a religious leader of such power. Our seminal figures are the great scientists, like Einstein or Freud; men who examine sensations, outside and inside, with a discipline of impartiality such as the world has never seen before. These men speak with the tongues of millions, because of the universality of the things they discover in the name of science. Atomic fission is the same process in any continent. So, perhaps, is the Oedipus complex. Freud may appear superficially nihilistic, but there is a creative side to his techniques. He clears away much cant and prejudice to lay bare the essentially human. Aseptic maybe, amoral even, his work is a powerful catalyst in the experience of adjusting to our new world.

For my part I am moved more by Jung than Freud. Without in any way belittling Freud, I know that I cannot abide entirely in his therapeutic examination of the collective primitive in us; I need to balance such a terrifying therapy with an equal examination of the collective non-primitive. All the mass of inherited lore and tradition, of spiritual wisdom and revelatory myth. Jung has found a way to bring this collective non-primitive into relation again with our excessively rationalistic, empirical modern minds. And this way is forced on us by the terrible psychic unbalance caused by our excessive materialism. Not all neuroses will give way to Freudian therapy. Some of us are driven by other agonies to a deeper analysis, until we meet on the labyrinthine paths of the collective unconscious those events, age-old predilections of the mind, which Jung calls the archetypes (of which, more later).

But Jung's discoveries cannot escape—that means help *us* to escape—the dilemma I spoke of before as significant for our new one world. Christians have asked Jung if he was prepared to direct his patients to personify the archetype of the saviour by Christ rather than Buddha. Jung said he could not. For him, as for me and for many many others, the dilemma must be lived with; as a penance or a privilege, with sorrow or with joy. I believe further that this particular dilemma stands as example for many other such problems which we cannot as yet solve but must suffer—and indeed as deeply as we have strength for, if we are to respond to the needs of the time; if we are to be on the side of the angels in the struggle to give aid to what shall be. It is because I know that I am fully committed to these polarities, these dilemmas, these uncertainties, that I cannot find satisfaction in the security of a traditional faith.

I spoke at the start about the special aptitudes and disabilities of being a musician. I am unsure how much these musical characteristics colour one's beliefs. Probably very little. But being a composer among musicians is more radical; because one is thereby a member of a further class—one is an artistic creator. I have deliberately said 'artistic creator' rather than 'creative artist' (though that is the more usual), because the English language permits one to throw the accent thus first on one term, then on the other—on the artist, or on the creator. If I were wanting you to give your attention more to the artist, then I would be asking you to consider the importance of fantasy and imagination, and the mystery in our sense of the beautiful. And I know that Plato held our desire to enjoy and possess the Beautiful to be the most immediate proof of a metaphysical reality. But I want you to give your mind rather to the artistic man as creator; to imagine what it feels like to be driven, whether we will or no, to spend our life fashioning ever new images; to consider how that must colour our beliefs—to have this dominating and imperative faculty within one. The drive to create has been so constant through the ages, and is so intense in its operation, that it is difficult for those submitting to it not to feel it as evidence of things beyond the individually personal. So that maybe Jung is right when he says that, if once the artistic creator, leaving personal idiosyncrasies aside, gives expression to the archetypes of the collective unconscious, then he also speaks with the tongues of millions—as Einstein, or Jung himself, or Gandhi.

I have found this experience, in so far as I have known it, to be the most absolute and positive I know. I have an untarnishable sense of certainty with regard to it. I have faith in its ultimate benevolence, even while I know that the coming to birth of archetypal images is inevitably disquieting and bewildering, before the world achieves a beneficial relation to what is happening. And it is clear that this is something not quite what Plato meant by our desire to enjoy beauty. It is nearer to the creation of the mysterious mythological tragedies, like *Oedipus Rex*. I believe that the faculty the artist may sometimes have to create images through which these mysterious depths of our being speak to us is a true fundamental. I believe it is part of what we mean by having knowledge of God.

Here I am in England. In England I live, and was born; half Celt, half Anglo-Saxon. In England are my bodily roots, and in England is my daily present. If I think of Germany, where I have often been—or of France or of Italy—I feel indeed no barriers, but feel kinship, both racial and cultural. This racial kinship is of the past, not of the present. But I find that the cultural kinship with Europe, with all other lands indeed, tends also to recede into the past. I see English Alcuin at the court of Charlemagne; I see the Irish monks at St Gall, or the sixteenth-century English lutanist, Dowland, home from Nuremberg from his travels in Germany and Italy. Just as a German might see Bach's youngest son in the London of Dr Johnson. For this sense of our cultural communion as chiefly in the past is probably common to all of us. It is never like the sense of our daily present, which is something quite other.

I am in England here and now—but in France or Germany too, because of the cultural kinship. This began perhaps when my Celtic ancestors had their homeland in Bronze Age Bavaria, and becomes ever more defined and conscious as I imagine the years of history passing over from then till now. Or perhaps not quite till now. The first German I ever spoke was the German of Goethe. Of his time I think I am more conscious than of any other in Germany.

I am thinking too of Hölderlin. Not so much of the young Hölderlin of the nostalgically Greek *Hyperion*, but the Hölderlin of the late poems, when he became prophetic of the European madness into which we have since fallen. Sometimes Hölderlin feels that the older pre-Christian gods are about to have a glorious reawakening. But more clearly he senses that, if indeed the many gods of our pasts are coming to life again, it is not yet for our mental health.

The gay gods of Greece were those he chiefly loved.

> Aber Freund! Wir kommen zu spät. Zwar leben die Goetter,
> Aber über dem Haupt droben in anderer Welt.
> Endlos wirken sie da und scheinen wenig zu achten,
> Ob wir leben, so sehr schonen die Himmlischen uns,
> Denn nicht immer vermag ein schwaches Gefäss sie zu fassen.

(But friend, we come too late. Truly the gods are alive, but up there in another world. They are endlessly active there and seem to mind little that we live, so well do they protect us, for a weak vessel cannot always contain them.)

But to be thus unable to sustain the gods when they came, and to know them so only 'in another world', was deeply and prophetically bitter to him.

> Zudessen dünket mir ofters besser zu schlafen, wie so ohne Genossen zu
>   seyn,
> So zu harren und was zu thun indess und zu sagen,
> Weiss ich nicht, und wozu Dichter in dürftiger Zeit.

(Meantime I often think it better to sleep, being so without comrades, to have to wait so, and what to do and to say meanwhile I don't know, and what poets are for in a barren time.)

When I have pondered on the actuality of Hölderlin's 'und wozu Dichter in dürftiger Zeit', I am struck ever anew by the tremendous vitality and drive of the image-making faculty in man, which has since Hölderlin sustained, or rather forced, so many poets, painters, composers, to create in *immer dürftigerer Zeit!*—'in an ever more barren time'. Naturally enough, indeed, I wonder at it, for I suffer this drive, within my limits, myself.

But let us think for the moment of Nietzsche, who certainly suffered both from the clear consciousness of the disintegration of our spiritual sensibility within an insatiable materialism and from an inescapable creative drive; suffered, yet further, possession by a god. Jung wrote just before the war a monograph suggesting that Nietzsche was possessed not in fact by

Zarathustra, but by Wotan. If this is so, then perhaps it means that we can never dare to know consciously that God possesses us. I may, like Hölderlin, love the gay Greek gods (though I must tremble before their dark and terrible natures), yet at the moment of intense creation, when music, if it is to live, must be searched for in those depths of the psyche where the god- and devil-images also hibernate; then how am I so sure, as I am, that I shall take no harm and the music be sane?

The answers are both personal and impersonal. Speaking impersonally first, I should answer that through Jung one can come to a viable, and partly even voluntary, relation with those psychic events, age-old predilections of the mind, which he calls the archetypes of the collective unconscious. Jung shows that there is as a psychological fact a *central*, or centralizing, predilection of the mind, an archetype of integration, of the union of opposites, of deity maybe, taking often the image of a human figure, the incarnation of a god or saviour, of Christ or Buddha. This archetype he finds endlessly active in the human psyche, even in periods like the present, when the overt public values are entirely those of scientific materialism. So beyond mere hope, I believe there is now reasonable knowledge that our desperate need and longing, as the tension of the opposites grows greater, will force a re-animation of the archetype of the god as saviour.

But Jung is quite clear that the longing for a more spiritually balanced life is still, for the vast mass of our people, pressed down into the unconscious by the dizzying social value given everywhere to the wonders of technics, and that this repressed longing, starved of the life-giving food of our attention and value, breeds violence and discontent. For we are still at the stage when to the individual alone, or shall we say, to certain individuals alone, comes at this time the inescapable duty to make conscious the repressed longing locked up in the inner violence and psychic disarray. But it follows, I am afraid, that any person driven along the path of integration, will by that in itself come into a polarity between his new values and the present overt values of our mass societies. Let him remember Hölderlin's 'weak vessel' and the price of Nietzsche's pride—and be humble.

Speaking now personally, I should answer that I cannot experience the archetype of integration in the direct way many others have done, because the creative artist is physically conditioned by the activities of the image-making drive which will not be gainsaid. My experience indeed is that most of the seemingly non-creative things an artist does—whether to take up teaching, to enter politics, to undertake Jungian analysis—are really phases of the inner creative life, and directed therefore to the ends of the art he practises. These non-creative activities are only secondary. I can never prosecute them for their own sake, even though for a time I feel sure I do, and only come to see the *real* and creative reason later on. Although, therefore, I may never know the fullness of personal integration, so that I may give an example in my daily life of one willing and able to sustain the polarity between his new, private values and the public old, I can yet know that the sympathies of my art lie with these possibilities; and, more important still, know that my art might form a tiny fragment of the great mirror in which we see our unconscious longings reflected as images that have power to change us whither we must go. Goethe wrote somewhere:

> Und umzuschaffen das Geschaffene
> Dass sich's nicht zum Starren waffne
> Wirkt ewiges lebendiges Thun.
>
> And refashioning the fashioned,
> Lest it stiffen into iron,
> Is work of an endless vital activity.

Think what an extraordinary piece of the mirror this process led to in *Faust, Part Two*! Is not the creator almost already mad to search for poetry in such depths? But is not the work of art inexhaustible and, if strange, magically sane? As Yeats put the matter differently, in a letter: 'I can entirely understand the excitement a God feels on getting into a statue.'

In August 1978 I took part in the Tanglewood Music Festival. Between rehearsals I was taken to visit the Hancock Shaker village which is preserved a few miles from Pittsfield, Massachussetts. In a public room of one of the buildings there were three or more pictures, painted by Shaker women, intended originally for private viewing only. One of these pictures I found so striking that I was driven towards reconsideration of a perennial problem—namely, what, if any at all, are to be the religious icons of our period. I made the following notes:

I believe in a reality of the physical world outside, experienced through the senses and formulated generally by the scientific intelligence.

I believe also in a reality of the spiritual world within, experienced, in my own case, by some intuitive, introspective apprehension of a kind which, in the past, was formulated generally by dogmatic, revelatory, received religions.

Since I seem to accept present-day cosmology, geology, biology, and so forth as scientists propound these matters, and this acceptance is something I share with almost everyone else (other than certain fundamentalists), then the first belief (in an outside reality) seems to join us all together.

The second belief, superficially, is divisive. I suppose I am here using 'believe', already, in a different sense.

I may believe in a spiritual reality, but I don't believe (in the usual sense) that Christ was the Son of God, or that Allah dictated the Koran word for word to Muhammad, or that the miraculous life of the Buddha is historical fact. I have always thus to try and disentangle some apprehension of spiritual treasure (which I would want to hold on to) from the elaborate costumes and dogmas associated with 'belief'.

Here it is, surely, that we all join together again. For traditional believers, with various degrees of awareness, are engaged in the same paradox; be they Pope or Dalai Lama. (The fundamentalist is again outside all this.) For it is not possible to believe in a cosmology of incomprehensible, infinite space, of geological time running into billions, and evolutionary time running into millions of years, *and* to believe in the costumes and the dogmas of the great male-dominated authoritarian religions of the past, without a tension in the psyche that is manifest or repressed.

I knew this most vividly in Jerusalem. To enter the breath-takingly beautiful Dome of the Rock mosque and peer down at the stone from which Muhammad began the night journey to heaven and back; to visit the church of the Holy Sepulchre and stare at the tomb from which Christ rose from the dead to appear to Mary Magdalene in the garden; to watch Jews of today weeping at the Wailing Wall for the loss of a temple nearly 1,400 years ago: for me to do all these things was to find myself temporarily both wonderingly close to the believers around and strikingly apart. On the other hand, to meet Muslim, Christian, or Jew in a bar or a coffee-house, later, when we might well have discussed those extraordinary phenomena known in scientific jargon as DNA, black holes, or silicon chips, meant that we could be quite together again. It is not that the 'religious' agnostic is in any better intellectual fettle. He may be more conscious of the general irrelevance, in our time, of the iconographic and ritual aspects of the old faiths. Having no fixed iconographic or ritual reference point himself, maybe he is equally irrelevant—certainly, he is equally impotent. So then, is nothing to be said or done? Not quite.

To return to the Shaker picture. At my first sight of it, before I had time to rationalize, I thought it might be a Tibetan mandala. I was deeply moved. Here, indeed, there seemed to be an icon of the numinous—sexless, spaceless, timeless. So it seems plausible to imagine a more public iconography from a collection of such pictures: Jung appeared to imply this. It must, however, be an iconography that is detached from established religious ritual: for in effect, it needs a new ritual, in which we are all there, fully defined in terms of sex, space, and time. My intuition is that such a ritual (which might lack a liturgy or dogma) would come, if not *from*, certainly *through* the theatre—using theatre in its widest and most universal sense. For truly, 'the question is no longer one of reconciling Orpheus and Christ, but one of a world vision that makes the sacred possible at all'.[3]

Balzac, in a curious novel, *Séraphita*, created from his imagination a supernatural figure called Séraphitus-Séraphita: seen as male or female according to the needs of the petitioner or seeker. In *The Ice Break*, I found I had to discard Astron-Astra and be content with an androgynous Astron. Not only because the former seemed so distressingly uncouth a name, but also because

---

[3] Walter A. Strauss, *Descent and Return: The Orphic Theme in Modern Literature* (Cambridge, Mass., 1971), 12.

only thus can this figure of the 'chorus-in-imagination' be a legitimately anthropomorphic 'angel'—the messenger, not the God. As Astron himself says, somewhat vulgarly (what else?):

> Saviour?! Hero?! Me!!
> You must be joking.[4]

It is left for Yuri, the 'fractured' man, miraculously healed in body and perhaps temporarily in soul, to say of more mundane but yet more vital matters:

> Chastened, together,
> We try once more.[5]

A few years back, I received a copy of the latest issue of *Index* magazine containing all sorts of literature that had been censored. There was in this a set of short poems by a young Polish poet which had been censored in this way, but were now translated and made available. Amongst them was one tiny poem which was concerned with what the poem could do as a tiny voice in this great world. It was addressed to me, to you, to himself, to God.

One of the lines which went right inside me was: 'Cherish the man, but do not choose the nation.' That's me, too. It gives me courage, for it seemed to me a signal. I suggest that if he heard *A Child of Our Time*, he, too, would get a signal. But I'm sure that if he and I tried to get together and form a party or collective or even an epistemology, we should merely deceive ourselves.

---

[4] Michael Tippett, *The Ice Break*, Act III, sc. 5.   [5] Ibid., Act III, sc. 9.

Chapter 21

THE MASK OF TIME

Many artists have felt impelled, towards the end of their lives, to give expression to the transcendental in some aspect or other. We can find this in Blake, in Yeats's last poems, in a painting like Gauguin's *Who are We? Where do we come from? Where are we going?* In *The Mask of Time*, I tried to crystallize some of my own mature responses to the most fundamental matters bearing upon man, his relationship with time, his place in the world as we know it and in the mysterious universe at large. The gestation period for such a work was, of course, a long one, dating back to the early 1970s—almost a decade before I actually put down any notes.

It became evident during this period that I could not emulate Haydn and write another *Creation*, accepting the biblical version of Genesis. Nor could I envisage a powerfully dramatic, intensely personal treatment of the Catholic Mass after the manner of Beethoven's *Missa Solemnis*. Our century has acquired such vastly extended notions of space and time that I felt it would have been an error to rely on past conceptions of the ontological and the transcendental. This meant also avoiding the alternative late Romantic solutions of the sort we find in Delius's *A Mass of Life*, which, by setting Nietzsche, flew in the face of the Christian orthodoxy favoured by oratorio composers, or Mahler's Eighth Symphony, which juxtaposed a grandiose realization of the Latin hymn 'Veni, creator spiritus' with a setting of the last scene of Goethe's *Faust*. Admirable and moving as all these compositions are, they only provided me with the negatives (so to speak) against which I could determine my own direction and goals.

I could not disregard the recent cosmological discoveries. On the contrary, they became a stimulus to my sense of wonder and mystery—though my ironic side prevented me from becoming (literally or metaphorically) starry-eyed. I once heard an astronomer, for instance, say on television that with the possibility of placing one of the newest telescopes on a satellite outside the earth's atmosphere, 'We can see beyond the "edge" of the universe.' What happens, I asked myself, when we reach the 'edge' of the universe? Do we fall over it, as in the days when the earth was thought to be flat? Do we meet God? Or what? At the time, I could identify it only as dream territory, and echo the scientist Loren Eiseley: 'But I dream, and because I dream, I severally condemn, fear, and salute the future. It is the salute of a gladiator ringed by the indifference of the watching stars.'[1] That quotation heads *The Mask of Time* as a kind of motto, and there are hints of it in the text. (In actuality, when I visited Jodrell Bank some years later, I was able to hear the sound of a star rotating millions of light-years away *in the past*—a genuine cosmological sound!) Ultimately, *The Mask of Time* evaded the metaphysical questions: as in the past, I could not come down on the side of one God or another, or associate myself with any specific ideology or clear intellectual stance. I had instead to accommodate a plurality of co-existing viewpoints.

My composition at best offered fragments, or scenes, from a possible 'epiphany' for today: hence the heterogeneity of the musical conception, which is written 'for voices and instruments'. It is a pageant of sorts: hence the 'Mask' of the title, used in the tradition of the Renaissance masque, which was a theatrical form with a great diversity of ingredients, a mixture of formality and flexibility, and an ultimately lofty message; by using the alternative spelling 'Mask', I deliberately suggested a contemporary ironic ambiguity. The piece had to take this form, if we remember that time can be thought of not only as stretching backwards and forwards, but as an eternally changing *now*; and my own tool for understanding and expressing something of all this was that of metaphor. As a creative artist, indeed, I can *only* depict everything through metaphor. Such a position is not far removed from that of the scientist. Indeed, Eiseley's highly theatrical metaphors struck a chord within me:

The cosmos itself gives evidence, on an infinitely greater scale [than the stage theatre does], of being just such a trick factory, a set of lights forever changing, and the actors themselves shape shifters, elongated shadows of something above or without. Perhaps in the sense men use the word natural, there is really nothing at all natural in the universe or, at best, that the world is natural only in being unnatural, like some variegated, color-shifting chameleon.[2]

The text for *The Mask of Time* is thus compounded of metaphors drawn from many sources. These are swallowed up within the music, so the libretto should not be read as 'literature'; but there are certain pervasive themes worth identifying. One is the notion of the *fixed*, the unchanging in nature; and related to this, the plight or status of the individual in a universe which, on one level, is thought to be ever expanding, and on another, contains fixed and recurrent elements. Arising from this is our present need for a new basis for affirmation—what *can* we now praise, what can we affirm? Throughout the work, also, we are confronted in varying degrees with the polarity between knowledge of the kind obtained through intellectual processes (the knowledge of scientists) and that obtained from deep inner sensibilities (the knowledge of creative artists). Sometimes in their divinations of the future, these different sources of knowledge coincide and complement each other.

---

[1] Loren Eiseley, *The Invisible Pyramid* (New York, 1970), 2.   [2] Ibid. 119.

The idea of *reversal* has many overtones and connotations within the work. (Over a period of years, I encountered it in the *I-Ching*; in Heraclitus's notion of the 'identity of opposites'; in Jung, who preferred the Greek-derived *enantiodromia*, meaning 'to run to the opposite'; in modern physics, for example, the mechanics of the pendulum; and in so-called reversal psychology.)

The most personally significant of these references relates to the satellite that reverses its course—Halley's comet. Like Eiseley, I was taken from my bed as a child by my father (in 1910) to see the comet; only my poor eyesight prevented me from seeing it with full clarity and understanding when it returned in 1985. My text quotes Eiseley:

MEZZO.   'Remember', he whispered in my ear, 'it will come back.'
BARITONE.   . . . speeding on its homeward journey toward the sun'.[3]

Early during the gestation of *The Mask of Time*, I was deeply impressed by Jacob Bronowski's TV series *The Ascent of Man*, and in due course I also read the book version. By his very reversal of the title of one of Darwin's books, *The Descent of Man*, Bronowski signalled an affirmation of faith in science which was as much a challenge to me as, say, that of a religious faith from the past; possibly even more so. For Bronowski's affirmation was not the blasé acceptance of a *status quo*. It expressed the hard-won faith of someone who had lost many members of his family at Auschwitz. Indeed, for me, the most moving episode in the entire series occurred when, standing at the pool of that horrendous prison camp, he confronted the perverted use of scientific achievement:

This is where people were turned into numbers. Into this pond were flushed the ashes of some four million people. And that was not done by gas. It was done by arrogance. It was done by dogma. It was done by ignorance. When people believe that they have absolute knowledge, with no test in reality, this is how they behave. This is what men do when they aspire to the knowledge of gods.

. . . Every judgement in science stands on the edge of error, and is personal. Science is a tribute to what we can know although we are fallible. In the end the words were said by Oliver Cromwell: 'I beseech you, in the bowels of Christ, think it possible you may be mistaken.'[4]

In some respects, the general conception of my work, and some of its detailed contents, owed something to Bronowski, but its thrust was rather different, reflecting my own sceptical, if not pessimistic, appreciation of what science can mean to us now. Planned as a work that would occupy an entire concert (roughly about 95 minutes), *The Mask of Time* was laid out in two parts, separated by an interval in performance, each part comprising five movements (some linked together or divided into smaller units). Part I followed Bronowski in depicting the creation of the cosmos and the emergence of human civilization and an earthly paradise (or at least the basis for one in

---

[3] Ibid. 7–8.   [4] Jacob Bronowski, *The Ascent of Man* (London, 1973), 374.

settled human societies). But already I felt it necessary to preface this with a movement, which I called 'Presence': this established at the outset a basic polarity—between a cosmos stretching backwards into infinity, forwards into infinity, and the individual in the immediate place and time of the concert platform, here and now. My principal metaphor as a musician is that of sound. To depict the cosmos metaphorically, I was impelled actually to use the word 'sound' at the start of the text; and for the chorus this meant elongating and altering the vowel *sou*-nd.

> Sound
> where no airs blow.

Sound, by definition, means a movement in air: there can be no sound 'where no airs blow'—this contradiction suggests how (musically) the cosmos comes into existence.

   Against this, the tenor soloist cries out:

> All metaphor, Malachi, stilts and all . . .
> Malachi, Malachi, all metaphor.

In Yeats's poem 'High Talk' (which I have adapted), the whiffler stalking about on stilts in front of the circus parade is a perfect analogy for the human being trying to remain unswamped by the mêlée of experience, trying to assert an identity; it struck me also as a marvellous image of the artist, trying to put his message across.

   Yeats would sit up all night in his tower and meditate on the world. He would hear:

> A barnacle goose
> Far up in the stretches of night;

this I used to reinforce my opening polarity. And I was able to use Yeats's image of dawn—'night splits and the dawn breaks loose'—as a reference point throughout the work. Thus, at the outset, I established a basic technique of pitting soloist(s) (representing the individual human stance) against the chorus (functioning in many capacities). My own text continued to mingle with lines from Yeats:

CHORUS.   Exploring
           Exploding
           Into time
           Into space

TENOR.   I, through the terrible novelty of light,
           stalk on, stalk on.

After the echoing and re-echoing of sonic effects in 'Presence', there follows, without a break, an extended instrumental 'sound picture' of dispersal (consequent upon some supposed explosion 'in the beginning' to one of stability (as of the galactic universe, the stars, and the sun). Here, the tradition of Purcell and Haydn seemed relevant: music can create order in the cosmos.

At the appropriate moment in the progression to stability, the four solo voices counterpoint different mythological concepts of creation. They evoke Shiva—a threefold deity associated with creation, stability, and destruction—recurrently through this work. Shiva here creates the world through dance; later on, Shiva is seen as a destructive force. The soloists also evoke Orpheus, the mythological musician who was able to use music to influence what went on in the natural world. Thus music itself remains the central metaphor: 'music is of itself divine.' (In Western thinking, that notion has been central to the aesthetic of many philosophers and artists, from Schopenhauer to Stravinsky.) The concise sequence of lines that follow polarize the alternative bases for affirmation. The scientific affirmation, based on actual knowledge, is asserted in Yeats's line 'Measurement began our might', and its absolutes are tersely expressed—'But I know.'

On the other hand, the artist's intuitive mode of creating order is exemplified in:

> Shall we . . . ?
> Dream backwards to the ancient time;

again in: 'My ear rehearses river noises' (evoking the 'man in black space' brooding upon 'river noises' in Wallace Stevens's poem *Metaphor as Degeneration*); and also: 'Steadying the mirror's echo of the mirror's light' (which recalls the resonances of an inner vision recounted at his death by King Priam, in my eponymous opera).

The actual vision of Halley's comet is balanced by the traditional religious vision of

> A flight of angels through the sky
> singing, singing:

(which of course, like the images of Orpheus singing, of river noises, etc., stresses the primacy of the sound metaphor).

The final rhetorical effusion for the four soloists here is thus no less ardent than in the chorus from part II of Haydn's *Creation*, from which I 'stole' the line 'Achieved is the glorious work.' The chronological evolution of the world continues with a depiction of the world of the jungle—with those fixed elements in creation which have preceded any human being, by millions, perhaps billions, of years. Much of this (third) movement is indebted to my reading of Annie Dillard's *Pilgrim at Tinker Creek*.[5] Dillard writes of the wild and aggressive nature encountered in America (characteristic of Australia and other countries, also, but not of England). She concentrates on the horrors that seem to be normal and ineluctable in nature. She is dis-

---

[5] Annie Dillard, *Pilgrim at Tinker Creek* (London, 1973).

turbed by its many cruelties (as all humans must surely see them) and particularly by the recurrent fertility processes which are often synonymous with destruction. Her text had an allusive character that appealed to me, so (with permission) I quoted it extensively. It included a horrific account of a giant water-bug poisoning from the inside and then eating a frog; equally incredible, the lacewing laying her eggs, then eating them up, then laying more and eating them up, and so on. Against this, I set a question by the supposed Creator:

MEZZO. Allah asks:
TENOR. The heaven and the earth and all in between: thinkest thou I made them in jest?[6]

The tenor breaks into the description of the lacewing, asking Jehovah for an explanation:

> What's it all about?
> . . . And do you know, he couldn't . . .

In the face of this lack of an answer from on high, only the negatives can be understood as a basis for affirmation: the mezzo sings: 'The fleeing shreds I see, the back parts are a gift, an abundance.' Dillard searched for a redeeming vision:

> Look
> . . . the mountains part.
> The tree with the lights in it appears . . .
> Sound . . .
> . . . The mocking bird falls
> Look
> . . . and time unfurls across space like an oriflamme.[7]

The soloists in all this manifestly belong to the here and now. On the other hand, the chorus provides a background of jungle sounds—bird-calls and animal cries, not transcribed exactly, but 'anthropomorphized'—built out of verbal tags which are distributed in and around the wild, panic scream of *Merde!* It took me some time to work out how to produce this choral background. I asked various people for suggestions as to motifs and rhythms and so forth. Then one day, a repeated bird-call outside the house caused a 'tag' to surface in the memory: 'I can't sing cuckoo, I can't sing cuckoo . . . !' Much earlier, my friend Evelyn Maude had told me another: 'A little bit of bread and *no* cheese!' Thus I created my own texture of onomatopeia:

> Clatter-chatter, clatter-chatter, Monkee
> Pad, pad, the huge cats prowl . . .

---

[6] Annie Dillard, *Pilgrim at Tinker Creek* (London, 1973) 19–20.   [7] Ibid. 182.

These choral cries come forward or recede in counterpoint with the soloists' words: I used a similar technique in *The Vision of St Augustine* to produce the effect of a door opening and shutting through the sky into heaven.

Man's emergence in history, his nomadic wanderings at the mercy of the elements, after the ice-cap in the Northern hemisphere had moved south, then north, over thousands of years, forms the content of the next 'scene'. The music tracks downwards into the cave where man inside the ice-cap had some contact with the transcendent:

> Touch the sacred with our hand?
> Images of bison running.

The music tracks upward again, with the ice-cap moving back to the north and the gradual establishment of settled societies. Following Bronowski, I have attributed this to the genetic accident of a particular kind of wheat grain which could be cultivated. It is also the beginning of a communion between man and nature:

Suddenly, man and the plant have come together, man has a wheat that he lives by, but the wheat also thinks that man was made for him because only so can it be propagated. For the bread wheats can only multiply with help; man must harvest the ears and scatter the seeds; and the life of each, man and the plant, depends on the other.[8]

Instead of images of transcendent experience deriving from rituals of hunting, now human sacrifices are necessary to propitiate the gods in the sky responsible for good weather and the harvest. Lines from Eliot's *The Waste Land* served my purpose—

> Then spoke the thunder
> DA.

—along with an evocation of the violent rituals of the past, still a memory encapsulated in the pyramids and temples at places like Chichen Itza and Uxmal (with its famous echoing courtyard) in Mexico, which I visited around the time of composing the work.

The communion of man, nature, the animals, and the deities are of the essence in the next movement, 'Dream of the Paradise Garden'. A garden has to have walls, because there is a threat of invasion from outside predators and pillagers, using horsepower, as Bronowski pointed out[9]—hence my line 'A thief, a Centaur jumped the wall'.

This movement dramatizes some of the situations in Milton's *Paradise Lost*, beginning with a kind of Renaissance madrigal for semi-chorus and an instrumental transition (dominated by flutes and harp)—in the form of a saraband. The four soloists are now individualized. I could have used the names Adam and Eve, like Haydn, but Man and Woman seemed less restrictive. The deity

---

[8] Bronowski, *Ascent of Man*, 68.   [9] Ibid. 80–6.

was more of a problem, and I settled for Ancestor, as an indication of the most ancient and primal of god-like manifestations. The choice of animal was more interesting. I chose the dragon because it had such splendour of form, not least wings: later, when the perfection of paradise breaks apart, the dragon was demoted to a snake, hostile and threatening, crawling away to its hole, no longer glorious. The crux of the movement is, indeed, this reversal from a state of perfect communion into separation. The Ancestor, asked for assistance, becomes a 'pure inviolate deity' who ascends into the sky, unable to offer an explanation: its impotent advice is 'but you can pray to me'.

My treatment of the exclusion of Man and Woman from Paradise was not, however, Miltonic. I stressed instead the loneliness of those cast out, forced apart from communion with nature and the deity; there is only a note of sadness and nostalgia for 'the everlasting place of dream'.

Part II of *The Mask of Time* departs from the chronological progress previously maintained, to focus on the individual in history: man not as a mythological figure in a remote age long past, but the actual human being on this earth now. Reading Shelley's last and unfinished poem, 'The Triumph of Life', I was struck by an analogy with Yeats' in his tower. Thus, as at the beginning of part I, the tenor solo stands for the poet. But this time his role is far more developed.

Shelley, at the time of writing the poem, was in Lerici, in Tuscany. He depicts himself spending the night on top of a hill, an insomniac poet meditating upon the world. At dawn, in a dream-like state, he looks seawards to the west. Behind him is the chariot of the sun going across the sky. He turns this into a great tragic image of the chariot rolling on, carrying a mass of humans, some of whom get thrown off; it is as gruesome and as grim as any of the scenes of animal behaviour depicted in Dillard's book. (The inexorably onward rolling and jerking of the chariot are represented in the music by a repeated ground bass, its two components separated by a sudden hiatus.) The scene is described first by Shelley himself, then through the eyes of Rousseau (who is Virgil to Shelley's Dante). Just as St Augustine could stand in an actual place and have a vision of eternity, so Shelley now can ask himself in an actual moment and place: 'What do I see of the absolute?' The answer that emerges is a transformation from the chariot scene to the portrayal of Shelley's own death (for which I was indebted to Richard Holmes's biography[10]). Chasing the sun in his boat, Shelley encounters a storm and drowns. So, over the course of the whole movement, we have progressed from dawn to midday and back to night. When Shelley's body was recovered, it had (for legal reasons) to be burnt; but legend has it that the heart would not burn: hence the coda to the movement.

To depict the rise of science, the theme of knowledge obtained by intellectual activity, I felt the emphasis must now be on instrumental music, with

---

[10] Richard Holmes, *Shelley: The Pursuit* (London, 1974), esp. 712–30.

choral links: hence the sequence of three chorale preludes on the plainsong 'Veni, creator spiritus'. These pin-point three historic movements in the triumphal progress towards a climax of 'measurement' and 'might'. With Pythagoras on Samos, the independence of physics from metaphysics is only a hint: but his graphics of measurement began a process which reached a significant stage in the alchemists' defiance of Church dogma in researching the possible mutation of elements. This crucial quest for power over the elements and the ability to transform them gave the movement its title (for which I am indebted to Peter Maxwell Davies), 'Mirror of Whitening Light', referring to the alchemical purification, or 'whitening' process, by which a base metal may be transformed into gold and, by extension, to the purification of the human soul. It also refers to the spirit Mercurius, or quicksilver, the agent or generator of this transformation process:

> O rose-red cinnabar, you sombre metal
> hell-heated
> hotter, hotter!
> radiant
> look, look!
> a silver and liquid pearl of mercury.
> For fire is alchemy.

With the splitting of the atom, the social ambivalence of the technology that has resulted is as blindingly clear as the moment of Hiroshima itself. Shiva is summoned once more to evoke a dance of destruction, and the brass music of the coda explicitly symbolizes the explosion. In the sequence of episodes in the eighth movement, we thus have Fire and Arithmetic, then *Fire and Arithmetic*.

I could not have written a work of these dimensions without including some kind of threnody for those individuals who have lost their lives in a brutal world. At first I considered Wilfred Owen's poetry, but was then introduced to that of Akhmatova. Her 'Poem without a Hero' and 'Requiem' took me away from the First World War and into a wider domain. Her experiences are those of all Russia. The Russian experience can probably stand for all that is comparable in time of war or revolution. Through translation into other languages, and perhaps through translation into music, it has indeed become a world experience. So here it is the keening voice of the solo soprano, in an act of remembrance and mourning, that dominates, against a background initially of humming male voice choir.

The ending of the work was problematic. I could not produce a Mahlerian peroration. I cannot, after all, produce 'answers'—answers to the ontological dilemma, answers to the apparently eternal eruptions of violence and brutality in the world as we have known it. I could focus only on the individual, on the courage and imagination that have enabled individuals to survive.

I chose thus to portray three individuals in a group of three songs, drawing various strands together from the entire work and looking towards the future. The first song, 'A Severed Head', presents scenes from the mythological life of Orpheus, not merely that part of the myth which so obsessed the European imagination from the sixteenth century onwards, that dealing with the death of Eurydice and Orpheus's failure to bring her back from Hades, but also Orpheus's death at the hands of the Furies, the Thracian Women who tore his body to pieces and threw his head into the river, where it floated down to the sea, still singing. A trio evokes Orpheus, returning alone from hell, 'stalking on' (in Yeats's phrase, used earlier) into the daylight. The baritone soloist sings a setting of four lines from one of Rilke's 'Sonnets to Orpheus'. The Rilke message is similar to that of Annie Dillard's book: only a person who has been in the dark can praise; Orpheus visited Hades, therefore experienced this darkness. The trio then depicts the Furies and Orpheus's death; and the baritone soloist (representing the singing head) enunciates the triumph of Orpheus's song, its eternal potential:

> Order the screamers, O singing God!
> That they may wake flowing,
> bearing on the river-race the head and the lyre.

The second song, 'The Beleaguered Friends', presents an explicit situation involving actual people. A group of anti-Nazis in Peking in 1944 awaits the end of the Second World War. While waiting, they listen to a series of lectures on the *I-Ching* by Helmut Wilhelm[11] (son of Richard Wilhelm, its renowned translator). The *I-Ching*, the oldest book in the world, is essentially a book of prophecy and divination. Leibniz who for some time had been trying to validate spiritual truths in mathematical terms, thus making them, as he thought, irrefutable, reacted enthusiastically when the *I-Ching* reached him through the agency of Jesuit missionaries. He recognized in it a system that ran parallel to his own binary, or dyadic, numeral system: and in retrospect, it suggests a fascinating convergence of Eastern and Western thinking. My own text refers to the *I-Ching* twice. The first time occurred previously in the fifth movement, where it signals the loss of paradise.

Now, in this song, I have mentioned the two methods of using it: sorting yarrow stalks and the throwing of coins. The Emperor's diviner 'juggling yarrow' and the blind flautist using coins are no longer in existence. Yet we can make use of the book if we wish. In Wilhelm's last lecture, he gave a demonstration at the request of his audience, of the yarrow stalks method of using the book's divinatory powers. The resulting hexagram was Deliverance. Good fortune can come, provided we act properly.

As earlier, in setting Akhmatova's poetry, I have widened the metaphor to stand for a more universal matter of morale in our violent and turbulent times; a metaphor for endurance, in short.

---

[11] Helmut Wilhelm, *Change: Eight Lectures on the I-Ching* (London, 1975).

Lastly, in 'The Young Actor Steps Out', I came back to the tenor solo, standing for the poet, the lone individual at the start of both parts of the work. Here he is the young actor, wearing a mask—as we all do, if Shakespeare's 'All the world's a stage' is to be believed. The idea for this came from Mary Renault's novel of classical Greece, *The Mask of Apollo*.[12] One scene in it impressed me deeply: it is where the young actor, on holiday in Olympia and sightseeing, goes inside the temple of Zeus. He peers at the great statue of the god. As his eye travels up, he meets the 'face of power', which utters these words:

> O man, make peace with your mortality,
> for this too is God.

To cap this, I needed to make the sound 'where no airs blow' (which is the metaphor in this piece for the transcendent) momentarily all-powerful, present, and immediate. After much searching, a poem by Siegfried Sassoon, 'Everybody sang', gave the clue—endless singing, wordless, involving both soloists and chorus. Sassoon's poem was a signal from the battlefield, a lone voice from Flanders; but his vision of survival—'The singing will never be done'—is, like Akhmatova's, a world experience, as such essential to my pageant. At the end, the transcendent celebration is abruptly cut off. We come out of the concert-hall into the street.

[12] Mary Renault, *The Mask of Apollo* (London, 1966), 20.

Part IV

THE ART OF PERFORMANCE

Chapter 22

THE SCORE

If you look at a printed copy of one of my large-scale works, such as one of the symphonies, you are likely to regard it as a finished entity. It has many pages; it has many thousands of notes. Now those notes have been invented by me as a series of instructions to enable people with the requisite skills to perform the work. I have, in principle, nothing to do with the performance: my concern is simply with *invention*. The instructions must of course be accurate, precise to the last possible detail—though on reflection that last detail is not totally realizable. There are limits to which music can be considered an exact science; there are many pitfalls in the intermediary processes between invention and realization. Far more so than the context and manner in which a painter's canvas is exhibited—size of room, companion pictures (if any), methods of lighting, and so forth—music enters a somewhat indefinite region when it is performed. Many factors will remain outside the composer's control: the acoustics of the hall, the extent of the performers' accomplishment and commitment to the highest ideals, and so on. In theory, the matter could be solved partially by a series of legal injunctions, supervised by the composer and publisher while still alive, and by appointed trustees during a designated period after his or her death. Some have taken that course. But what an atmosphere it creates! The guide-lines I am offering here are meant not to restrict but to stimulate: to give some background information that facilitates an informed approach to the scores and helps illuminate certain matters of style.

The composer who must at all costs have the most absolute and unyielding accuracy in every rendition of his work is better off in an electronic studio. In recent decades some have gone that way. But while doing so, they still came up against the matter of public presentation: audiences always felt odd, sitting in rows as at a string quartet concert, but listening instead to sounds emitted from loudspeakers. Does one applaud at the end, and *who* does one applaud? The composer (if he is still alive to take a bow)? The machine-operator, who pressed the right switches at the right time (or maybe didn't!)? Such questions have lately been bypassed by the new technologies that have returned electro-acoustic music to the domain of live performance. And even if they cost an arm and a leg in the initial stages, they are now increasingly (thanks partly to the example of rock music) available to creative music-makers of all sorts.

Late in life, I availed myself twice of these new wizardries—notably the ubiquitous techniques of music 'sampling'. For the opera *New Year*, certain special effects were needed, some of which might (had I been living in an earlier century) have been created by standard orchestral means—flight music for a spaceship, singing fountain, groaning lake. I felt, however, that electro-acoustic realization would enhance the distinction between the two worlds of the opera, 'Somewhere Today' and 'Nowhere Tomorrow'. (Belatedly, I was intrigued to learn that when in 1921, a (silent) film was made of Aleksei Tolstoy's post-revolutionary novel *Aelita*,[1] a similar contrast of musical support was envisaged: the music accompanying the everyday Soviet scenes was standard salon chamber music, whereas the music for the spaceship and utopia had utilized a Theremin, probably the first electronic instrument of note.) Even so, modified versions of some of the effects for *New Year* had to be produced—especially the ascent and descent of the spaceship—so as to accommodate the varying speeds at which the staging of the episodes in question could be accomplished and also the specific dramatic context. The end result, above all, had to be integrated with the rest of the score and, in acoustic terms, appear to come from the stage, sometimes enveloping the auditorium in sound, rather than obtruding separately from the standard public-address system; the effects had, in short, to be part of the magic of the presentation and certainly part of the 'performance'. Whilst integrated thus into the score, such effects were never remotely conceived as a contribution to the repertoire of electro-acoustic music. Their purpose was sharply circumscribed.

Approaching closer to the character of music, and certainly needing to be integrated fully, were the final set of 'breathing' effects created for my Symphony No. 4. Originally, rather hastily, indeed carelessly, I simply specified 'Wind machine' in the score. Naturally, at the earliest performances in Chicago, conducted by Sir Georg Solti, my specification was observed literally. But the sound was entirely wrong. Various solutions were tried out after that. One most favoured was the amplified breathing of an actual singer. The drawbacks were that conductors and singers always imagined the sounds differently. Given the number of notes to be got right in the piece, the breathing sounds tended always to be left till last, when there was little time for proper rehearsal. Another solution was to have a tape made in the BBC Radiophonic Workshop, which would be replayed at performance. This was inflexible, and I quickly came to realize that the sounds were not what I really intended. Ultimately, the problem I faced was to go back to the beginning and try to remember what it was I had intended—to dream myself back into the world of composing the symphony, after nearly twenty years and several large-scale compositions. In the end, the amazing new techniques of

---

[1] Aleksei Nikolaevich Tolstoy, *Aelita* (Berlin, 1923).

'sampling' gave me the scope to experiment at little cost. The outcome was a 'definitive version' consisting of a set of sound samples on floppy discs for reproduction and performance on a midi-piano. One of the 'breathing effects' in the score (between rehearsal figs. 90 and 95), which had never previously either been audible or the right kind of sound, was now achieved as a violent storm simulation, audible above the orchestra playing at fortissimo level. But the main advantage, which I could not have dreamt of when I wrote the work, is that the breathing effects are performable flexibly in relation to the varying tempi adopted by different conductors.

Musical executants often make allegiance to the composer's score a matter of faith. However, the question always to be asked at the outset is: Which score? This is quite germane, in my own case. Unlike many, I have had just one publisher for fifty out of the sixty or so years of my composing career. Luck, indeed! At the same time, that has meant an awful succession of different editors, of printing styles, and of methods: and it is already there, even before the performers have become involved, that the interpretive processes begin.

Right up until the 1970s, it was a characteristic feature of Schott house style that all the instructions in the score should be in Italian. But the Italian musical jargon of previous centuries is inadequate and imprecise in relation to the needs of almost any composer today. *Tempo ordinario* meant something in Handel's day (though scholars will dispute exactly what); so did allegro, adagio, and so on; but such terminology is unrelated to contemporary needs. To be constantly translating expressive indications into Italian for me made little sense. So, for many years, with Schott's agreement, I have given all such instructions in English.

I am not, it goes always without saying, the first composer to fall foul of the metronome. In earlier times, I attempted to decide metronome markings myself. This was a mistake. Those in all my early scores are unreliable. At a later period, from about the mid-sixties, I decided on metronome indications by having an accomplished repetiteur-pianist (most often, the incredibly versatile John Constable) come and play through scores at the piano, enabling me to listen to the music, as it were, from the outside. This has proved safer. Even so, the metronome is no god. Performers and conductors (including composers interpreting their own works) have always followed their instincts—and, let us hope, always will—achieving satisfactory interpretations at tempi which are at variance with the printed metronome marks.

There are certain stylistic traits that are not easy to pin-point in exact language, let alone ensnare with a metronome figure. One such is encapsulated in the word 'lilt'—untranslatable, probably, in any other language. It sums up neatly the airy lightness and grace which probably stem from an awareness of inherent dance-like properties. In my *Divertimento on Sellinger's Round*, the opening string melody (see Ex. 22.1), derived from an Orlando Gibbons fantasia,

Ex. 22.1 *Divertimento on Sellinger's Round*

phrased in three's against a duple beat, needs above all 'lilt'. When I elaborated this into a divagatory episode in Symphony No. 4, involving all the
strings in phrasing in three's against a duple beat, that 'lilt' was much harder
to achieve: it entails everyone placing little accents on the first note of each
phrase, but then lightening the tone considerably for the succeeding notes (fig.
119 *et seq.*) Lilt disappears from the music if the tone is strongly sustained
throughout.

The two pairs of string lines, doubled at the octave, at the start of String
Quartet No. 2, need to spring forward from an emphatic appoggiatura (see
Ex. 22.2). The same is true of the opening gestures of Symphonies Nos. 2 and
3. With the former, the Vivaldi-inspired dance rhythm in the cellos and basses
is launched by a strong opening downbeat (see Ex. 22.3).

Ex. 22.2 *String Quartet No. 2*

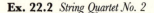

The contrasts between the two sorts of musical material in the first movement of Symphony No. 3, a polarity I have dubbed 'arrest' and 'movement'
are all too easily undermined. The important point here is that the initial
sense of 'arrest', of gearing up for an explosion of energy, can only be
achieved by holding back at the start, sitting firmly on the first dotted
crotchet, then releasing it with a succession of staccato chords.

Likewise, the horns in the first bar of Symphony No. 4 (and wherever the

Ex. 22.3 *Symphony No. 2*

motif is repeated) have to project a sense of a real triplet figure, with a strong first note and a lighter second note growing through the rest of the phrase (see Ex. 22.4). In all too many performances, the horns simply play heavy single accented notes, with no feeling for the line.

All the matters just mentioned derive from the influence right the way through my scores of pre-classical music, above all the prevailing linearity of their conception. The implications of this for my orchestral writing are

Ex. 22.4 *Symphony No. 4*

considerable. Firstly, there is the question of my use of so-called additive rhythm. I have already suggested how the opening send-off gesture of a piece can influence the ability of a performance to project its linear momentum forward. A further point is the need for performers to imagine, if possible, that the barlines have disappeared. This is implied in the clash of lines at the start of *Concerto for Double String Orchestra* (see Ex. 22.5). The norm for execution of these lines entails ensuring that final notes tied across the barlines actually grow across the barlines.

Ex. 22.5 *Concerto for Double String Orchestra*

Also disclosed are larger conceptions of phrasing than might at first appear to be the case: for example, the opening of the slow movement of this work should be thought of as one long phrase, building up to the bluesy (or madrigalian) clash of major and minor in the fifteenth bar.

My immersion in early music, on the one hand, and my affinity with jazz, on the other, have nurtured a temperamental dislike for romantic ritenuti, those pull-ups that so often destroy the kind of lengthy phrasing I have just illustrated. Right away in the First Piano Sonata, I have cultivated throw-away final gestures (e.g. at the end of the finale) instead of big perorations: and even where the music unwinds slowly to a close, as in the slow movement of the Double Concerto, that does not imply a big pull-up. For the last ten years or so, I have avoided terms like *rit.* and *rall.* and written 'ease' or 'ease a little'.

Some of my scores are replete with references to so-called early music styles and idioms, and when these are not perceived, the result is usually a distortion. The *Fantasia Concertante on a Theme of Corelli* has suffered particularly in this regard. For the record, I would make the following points.

1. The dynamics at the outset are specifically marked to ensure that the cellos in the concertino and *concerto grosso* groupings are in the foreground.

2. Fig. 4: In the opening repeated chord motif of the Vivace there should be a real upbeat and downbeat (up-bow and down-bow are specified), not two equally strong chords. This applies right through to the end.

3. Figs. 10–13: This is a reference to the so-called goat's trill found in the vocal writing of Monteverdi and his contemporaries.

4. Figs. 22–39: concertino group—a dance-like Vivaldian virtuosity is apt here.

5. Figs. 39–46: The fluctuations of tempo are written into the score, but are not a cue for exaggeration. The cello melody should have a Puccini-like intensity.

6. Fig. 46: The three components in the fugue are defined by bowing styles: on the string for the violas 2 playing the (Corelli) subject; off the string for violas 1 playing (my invented) countersubject; and *louré* for the cellos playing (Bach's) countersubject. The dancing lilt of my countersubject (in violas 1) indicates the basic tempo: and this should be maintained right through the climax in swirling triplets for high violins, even if it means straining the players to their limits! Again, the unwinding of the fugue into the pastorale that follows is not a cue for exaggeration. Even though it reaches a climax with the *sffp* in the third bar of fig. 76, the momentum of the playing should not yield; and the indication *largamente ma quasi in tempo* at fig. 77 also suggests a gentle relaxation of tempo, not a signal to put on the brakes.

7. Fig. 78, 2nd bar onwards: this is not a slow movement to send everyone to sleep, but a typical Corelli-style pastorale in characteristic *siciliano* rhythm, with a rocking lilt in the rhythmic figure.
The grandest sonority of all is at fig. 84.

Many of the details whose interpretation I have sought to clarify in relation to the *Corelli Fantasia* can be found elsewhere in my works. For example, the preparatory music for each of the ritual dances in *The Midsummer Marriage* reaches a climax with two repeated chords (like those mentioned in point 2 above). The temptation is to articulate them as two equally strong chords, with the result that the first becomes more than a demisemiquaver long. This should be avoided: as I have suggested above, the first is clearly an upbeat to the second.

In some respects the mosaic style adopted in scores from *King Priam* onwards is easier to handle, since linearity becomes more incidental. A general principle is that tempi and character enunciated in the exposition of the main thematic blocks should be retained whenever they return. Piano Sonata No. 2 and *Concerto for Orchestra* are the key examples of this, offering little, if any, room for departure from the exact lengths and kinds of articulation specified. The discipline this imposes is considerable. In the opening movement of the concerto, the return of each of the nine thematic ideas should always involve a return to the original tempo and articulation, no matter how much they are lengthened, abbreviated, or affected by new contexts of juxtaposition and superimposition.

My dramatic vocal style crystallized and widened in scope after I had encountered and studied the music of Purcell in the 1940s. But the seeds of all this existed beforehand, in *A Child of Our Time*. From my experience of conducting this work and assisting at rehearsals, I have found that if the purely musical things are all right, then the most helpful thing I can do is to get the singers to tell the story in part II as clearly and directly as they can. The spirituals then take their proper place and style. For instance, 'Nobody knows'—the crux of the boy's profound distress—is stressed thus:

> *N*obody knows the trouble I see
> *N*obody knows but Jesus.

Their cries of help:

> O *brothers*, pray for me,
> O *mothers* pray for me
> and help me *not* to commit the crime.

To blur all this is to disturb the sense of the boy himself—his story.

The next number follows naturally: 'The boy becomes *desperate* in his agony.' He does commit the crime.

The 'terrible vengeance' that is the consequence really does need to be driven; for no choir likes to portray ferocity and brutality—all of them want to be gentle! I've found it best to concentrate on the explosive B's of *B*urn, *B*eat, *b*reak—as though spitting. (Incidentally, earlier, in the 'chorus of the self-righteous', the strings can strengthen the chorus with ruthless emphasis on the first note of the quaver duplets on each beat. In the most recent editions of the score, this is marked accordingly, as separate bows for each duplet.)

At the end of the boy's story comes the only spiritual for a woman's voice. (I shall always remember Jessye Norman in Colin Davis's recording singing 'Bye and Bye' with a kind of diaphanous floating of the high voice; very tender and gentle, no hurry.)

If the story of part II is presented thus, the preparation for the story (in part I) seems almost easy. Part III, after the story, is, I suppose, a bit more complicated, because we are invited to consider the story's implications. But the *serenity* of the instrumental trio for flutes and cor anglais turns us at last round the corner: we can sing of hope, and joy, and to spring. The very last chord should be done something like 'Lor—d' (accent over the *o* and diminuendo down to pp) as though bending the knee.

As it has long been my practice to plan pieces some time in advance, and only begin writing down the notes when I am confident that the basic planning has been done, I have rarely revised works after completion, even less so after publication. In my very early days, some post-composition revisions were occasionally necessary. I cut part of the first movement of Piano Sonata No. 1; in 1944 I replaced the original two opening movements of String Quartet No. 1 with a new single one. The finale of String Quartet No. 3 has never seemed to me to fulfil the level of expectation aroused by the preceding four movements. At one time, William Glock urged me to rewrite it; but the then Professor of Music at Edinburgh University, composer Hans Gál, concurred with my view that this would be a mistake. Better to leave it and concentrate on new pieces. In the event, though, after some experimentation, I thought it would enhance its effect if it were linked to the fourth movement and thus evolved naturally out of it. This modification has been made in later editions of the score and parts.

Beyond these examples, I have tended to change only small details after a score has been published. Most often Schott have been able to print a final score in advance, or at least in time for the première, confident that there would not be any drastic revisions. The only incidental calamity I can recall was when *The Vision of St Augustine* was rushed into print in time for its première in a public concert by the BBC, and the blue of the cover of the vocal score came off on the choir ladies' dresses! Schott proof-reading is probably more thorough than it used to be, especially given the support and guidance of Michael Tillett and Meirion Bowen, experienced collaborators and amanuenses of many years' standing. The wrong notes that tended to proliferate in early editions are gradually being eliminated in new editions.

Working with performers on a composition can sometimes be helpful. Certainly, in the case of *The Blue Guitar*, I learnt a lot from Julian Bream, who in due course helped edit the piece for publication. On the other hand, Julian felt that the order of the second and third movements should be changed, so that it ended with some degree of technical display. I accepted his suggestion at the time, though subsequently, after hearing it played by various other guitarists, came to the conclusion that my original order was preferable— fireworks in the middle, slow reflective movement to end.

Discussions with Paul Crossley assisted a lot in the composition of my Third and Fourth Piano Sonatas—particularly the latter, which took account of his demonstrations of the possibilities of the third pedal. Working with the Lindsay Quartet and Michael Tillett on my String Quartet No. 5, I decided to extend the final section of the second movement by several bars; I also changed around the instrumentation of the episode in the first movement from fig. 30 to fig. 35, and again from fig. 90 to the end, so that the cello had the repeated-note assertions and the viola played crotchet double-stopped chords along with the violins; by that method, the 'ringing' effect I wanted could be better achieved. When I first began writing for the electric guitar, in *The Knot Garden* and *Songs for Dov*, I knew relatively little about the potential of the instrument. It was also a bit of a gamble, since there were few executants with the essential combination of abilities: fluency, accuracy in reading music, and experience in following a conductor. In that opera and song cycle, an electric harpsichord was thus specified. No longer: since meeting Steve Smith, one of a new generation of versatile young performers, at home in many genres of music-making, all my electric guitar writing has been scrutinized and reinforced with Steve's special technical know-how.

Composition for the theatre can easily run into bigger problems, requiring drastic rewriting or cutting of the existing score. Generally speaking, since I have made it a point of principle that the conductor and director should not merely know of the character and dimensions of an opera years in advance, but should have the finished score nine to twelve months ahead of the pre- mière, I have not encountered too many such difficulties. Like many others writing for choreography, I found I had written too much music for the ritual dances in *The Midsummer Marriage*, and at John Cranko's request cut many of the repetitions of particular sequences. As it happened, this seemed to tighten up the structure considerably, and the same applied when the ritual dances were played as a concert piece. The cut version thus remains my final one, and I do not sanction reinstating the omissions.

Chapter 23

THE STAGE

My first direct experience of professional opera was when I was a student in the 1920s and took part as an extra in a performance of *Die Meistersinger* at Covent Garden. Standing there amongst an immense chorus, I was impressed first of all by the sheer size and depth of the stage. What also became imprinted on my memory was the image of the man in the prompt-box—only visible to us performers—continuously conducting and mouthing words. The dimensions of the Covent Garden stage affected my thinking when, decades later, I embarked on *The Midsummer Marriage*. Maybe I tended too much then to discount the possibilities of those smaller theatres where, as it has turned out, all my operas have since been presented with some success: though, to be fair, regional opera companies in Britain had not acquired the stature they have now.

When a composer's dramaturgical thinking differs from that of, say, Puccini or Bizet, introducing concepts from the living theatre of today (and I include in that cinema and television), some element of risk is involved. Audiences now at big houses like the New York Metropolitan Opera or Covent Garden, anticipating familiar star turns and stage routines, are likely to feel uneasy. Given that the texts of my operas disclose many symbolic over-tones, it is often in the smaller houses, attracting an audience that is sympa-thetic to innovation, that they make their best impact. The alternative version of *The Knot Garden*, with an accompanying ensemble of twenty-two players instead of full orchestra, has already enabled the piece to gain wide currency. *The Midsummer Marriage* and *King Priam* have been toured in smallish theatres without a substantial reduction of the orchestral requirement.

Like many other composers, I thought initially that I could describe in detail what should happen in an operatic presentation. The libretto for *The Midsummer Marriage* thus specifies a great deal: for example, '[Bella] rings a hanging bell. After a moment's expectation, the doors of the temple slowly open, and the Ancients come gravely through them and on to the upper stage. King Fisher goes down stage right and keeps his back to the Ancients.'

For the choreography of the dances in Acts II and III, I also wrote para-graphs of fanciful description. In retrospect, this was a mistake. All theatre stages differ, so all productions must vary. Opera is a collaborative art-form,

in which the composer, director, choreographer, and designer have all mutu-
ally to respect the different expertise they bring to bear. All productions—
unless they are to ossify into the form Gilbert & Sullivan took while copyright
was still held by Doyle Carte—must balance the composer's intentions
against the desire to bring the piece to life in the first instance, and to renew
and revitalize it thereafter with new interpretations. The elaborate descrip-
tions of stage picture and action in the libretto for *The Midsummer Marriage* may
be considered a starting-point for fresh thinking. But no one should try to
observe them with mechanical literalness. With my four subsequent operas I
have confined myself to general information as to the intended style and character of the presentation, and have kept details to a minimum. The directions
in these libretti are perhaps more apposite.

King Priam, using a story, characters, and situations out of Homer and an
explicitly clear, Brechtian manner in both text and presentation, is undoubtedly the least problematic of my five operas. The others invite a greater variety of interpretation. With all of them, though, I do basically prefer
productions that tell the story. While welcoming an attention to symbolism, I
do not feel this should be allowed to obscure the main thread of the action.

In the wake of the half-dozen or so productions of *The Midsummer Marriage*
since its première in 1955, I have often regretted not including in the list of
dramatis personae the Sun! Sunlight, indeed, is essential, not merely as an
embellishment for the action, but as one of the main agencies whereby we
experience the passing of the hours on that unreal Midsummer Day, beginning at dawn and returning finally for another dawn. Bright sunlight, of the
kind that turns concrete into water, is often impossible in stage sets that dis-
pense with a cyclorama and substitute a black box.

The place of the action here is a magic wood; and however that is conceived, it should be a real place which at times becomes surreal. This magic,
that surreality, are essential in a kind of dramaturgy that entails action not
only within, but above, beyond, and below the set. Linked with this is another
basic premiss: the distinction between the mortals in the wood and the
immortals (or Ancients) inhabiting the temple. A distinction already represented in the division between singing and dancing chorus, it should nevertheless not be obscured, as it provides the basis for dramatic tension
throughout. That tension in Act I is an agon or contest between the sexes, and
I have used the standard operatic tradition of the singing contest to bring it
to a climax. The contest has no resolution: however, the re-entry of Jenifer
and Mark into the realm of the immortals at the end would make it logical for
their two arias here to be choreographed. In Act III, the contest is between
Age and Youth—and Youth wins; Jenifer and Mark reappear explicitly in the
context of the fourth ritual dance, thus counterbalancing the choreography
added to the contest arias in Act I.

Another distinction that should be apparent is that between the two pairs
of lovers, one royal, one ordinary: there are no 'elective affinities' here to mix

them up, as in *Così fan tutte* or (for that matter) *A Midsummer Night's Dream.* King Fisher can easily get caricatured as the melodramatic villain. He has two aspects: first, the successful businessman—we should know that the moment he appears on stage; second, the Fisher King, or symbolic king of the Waste Land whose death is necessary for its renewal—hence his role in Act III. Lastly, there is Sosostris, a human figure, but one who enters into a trance-like state. She is a mysterious figure in every way—certainly not a housewife fortune-teller.

The length of *The Midsummer Marriage* makes it a considerable undertaking for any company in terms of rehearsal time, and has often led to requests for substantial cuts in the work. Many of the proposed excisions have been crude, and have ignored the elements of balance and proportion that make a number of musical repetitions essential to its structure. In general, if some pruning is deemed essential, I would tend to sanction it more when it is applied to Act III than Act I, where the style, characterization, and formal outline of the work are established. Ever since its première, there has been a desire to make the fourth ritual dance the conclusion of the work, and reduce the existing final scene to a brief coda. This I have opposed, as the new dawn at this stage is essential to the action, and at the very end we should feel that we are about to come out of the illusory world of the theatre into the street.

Undoubtedly the most preposterous cut to which I was once asked to agree in relation to a presentation of *King Priam* was that the opera should end after the scene where Priam succeeds in begging back the body of his son Hector from Achilles, the two of them then going off together into the sunset! Naturally, I gave it short shrift. It would have sabotaged completely the unfolding of a story dominated by Fate: Priam's death at the hands of his younger son Paris is clearly his destiny, and a romanticized outcome is both foreign and irrelevant. All the action in a production of this opera ought to be depicted as part of the operations of Fate. That is the main discipline its style imposes. The characterization here should offer few difficulties. But since the key to the opera, musically, lies with its monologues, it would appear to me unwise to diminish the scale of Priam's climactic monologue in Act III.

As with *The Midsummer Marriage*, the remaining three operas either specify or imply a choreographic element. In *The Knot Garden*, dance is one of the main metaphors, and some of the scenes are explicit song-and-dance routines. The services of a dancer or choreographer as assistant to the director would appear worthwhile; likewise in *The Ice Break*. In *New Year*, the choreographer and director are as far as possible equal in status, their common objective being to integrate dance into the action as much as possible and elide the distinction between singing and dancing chorus.

The dramaturgy of both *The Knot Garden* and *The Ice Break* derive a lot from the methods of cinema and television. The scenes dissolve into each other at great speed (and, incidentally, the two operas are in consequence uncuttable). This is a big challenge not only to the designer, but to the seven characters in

The Knot Garden, some of whom have double roles, themselves today and their prototypes in *The Tempest*. It is worthwhile to think of a good deal of the action as a series of games. Mangus, the psychiatrist, who assumes control early on, at one point takes Flora off with him to get more costumes for the games. The costumes (which can of course include masks) are indeed an important element. The dressing up, the game-playing, is halted temporarily with the appearance of Denise, the tortured freedom fighter, whose problems are political and social rather than psychological. Act II might be thought of as the undressing of the characters, as they lay bare their problems. The dressing up begins again with the charades of Act III. There are many ways of realizing the knot garden itself: lighting and film can certainly be brought into play where resources allow, even though there have been productions that have relied entirely on the intensity of the singing and acting. One thing I do look for, however, is that moment towards the end of Act II where the hostile labyrinth briefly becomes a 'fabulous rose-garden': it affords an intimation of the forgiveness, the reconciliation, the 'timid moments' of love that are on the horizon.

With both *The Knot Garden* and *The Ice Break*, there is a temptation to site the action in the 1960s, the era of flower power, permissiveness, racial riots in America, and so on. That was never my intention. The period, or documentary, element in both is minimal, and should not be stressed. This is particularly the case with *The Ice Break*, the least performed of all the operas. Here my original introductory note on the role of the chorus seems apposite:

The chorus is always anonymous, whatever group it represents. It must be masked in some form, not only to enforce anonymity, but so that the stage representation is unrelated to the singers' real body, in the sense that, for example, the traditional black-and-white minstrels might be played by Chinese. The masking is also necessary to show that stereotypes altogether are in question, rather than any presently exacerbated example, e.g. 'black and white' . . . however much the dramatic action seems to move at time towards verisimilitude, [the] stage 'reality' is constantly splintered by a complementary 'surrealism'.

The slang element in the libretti of my operas, inevitably a product of the different periods in which I wrote them, may mislead directors into too readily linking the action with those periods. Already, however, with *The Midsummer Marriage* we have moved a long way since the era when lovers went 'down the roadway courting', or when the conventional roles of married couples are summarized thus:

BELLA.   While you're at work I'll mind the place
                  And wash the clothes and cook the food.
JACK.   And I'll work overtime in case
                  We need more money in the purse.

Even the argot of *The Ice Break* sounds dated:

OLYMPION. Wow! this chick wants balling?

But that is all to the good. I dare prophesy that, provided the piece is still played, these elements will not stick out at all in fifty years' time; they will simply be part of the overall ambience in which the more general contents are to the fore.

With *New Year*, I approached as far as I dared the character of a musical, and I thus favour the use of all the stage techniques deployed within that genre. This includes amplification of voices. In the case of the presenter—originally conceived as a television-style voice-over—it is absolutely essential. At times, it may be necessary for other of the solo singers—for example, Donny and Regan in their 'rap-style' confrontation in Act II. For the chorus it may also at times be advisable. I am not at all amongst those who regard the amplification of voices as a distortion of their true character. It is simply a matter of technique. Broadway and the West End theatres of London abound in singers who have learnt to use microphones with ease and naturalness. The technology now exists, also, to achieve the best possible results. It is simply that the training of opera singers has yet to catch up! The miking of voices in *New Year* should ultimately be regarded as part of a sonic canvas that includes specially created electro-acoustic effects (as I have mentioned above), and, if properly realized, should simply fall into place as part of the magic of the piece.

The role of the Presenter in this opera was a bit of a gamble. So far, the view has been taken that it is difficult to present an unseen voice-over figure in the live theatre; on television, yes. Maybe one day a method will be found—but I am not dogmatic on the subject. Conversely, in any case, the Presenter's lines, introducing the penultimate scene in Act III, were found problematic for a television presentation:

> Time must stand still
> While the spool is rewound
> Assembling, full speed,
> All the bits that we need
> Till the moment of flash-back
> is finally found.

I allowed this to be cut.

The oddest figures in all my operas are the messengers, go-betweens linking the contrary realms of mortals and Ancients or deities, the inhabitants of 'Somewhere Today' and 'Nowhere Tomorrow'. Madam Sosostris is the most mysterious, Hermes the most effective in encapsulating the workings of Fate, Astron-Astra the most daringly ironic, the Presenter the most affectingly human, ultimately articulating the cry of all mankind:

> One humanity
> One justice.

The least worthwhile avenue for any director, however, is to make these figures the corner-stone of a didactic conception. Form my operas to survive,
they must withstand all the risks of theatrical presentation, indeed bask in its
excitement; and notwithstanding all the guide-lines I have given here, the
director who takes that standpoint and makes the audience laugh and weep,
feel chastened or elated, has my full backing.

Part V

AFTERWORDS

Chapter 24

A COMPOSER AND HIS PUBLIC

It is an act of faith to address an invisible audience. Is that faith anything to do with the much deeper faith, the faith in the ultimate virtue of the creative act, which a composer must have to write music at all in this time? What, in this matter of the composer and his public, has been there always and what is new?

We have been for centuries used to receiving letters through the post, sheets of lines and blobs on paper, which when taken out of the envelope tell us things, and often in such a tone that we can imagine the loved (or hated) voice speaking out of the ink. This is the primeval miracle of any communication at a distance. So living a thing indeed is a letter that when Nora's husband in *A Doll's House* tears up the letter that should have reached his wife, we feel that something has been done much more destructive than any burning of waste paper, for the letter is a symbol of communication, and to prevent it from reaching its destination is to do the two people concerned an injury.

Or, to be more up to date, we can think of Menotti's operetta *The Telephone*, where a young man in a hurry has difficulty in proposing to his girl because she is so constantly interrupted by telephone conversations. The young man only succeeds when he has the sense to go out to the nearest call-box and put his proposal by telephone. The satire turns all upon the possibility that in modern society we value communication at a distance too much. But to be more up to date still, and to consider the techniques of communication by radio, is to be forced to admit the extraordinary immediacy of the method, particularly of television. There is a dash of the fabulous about communicating instantly as though the space between Broadcasting House and one's home were annihilated. In so far as communication is part of art, surely the new conditions of communicating will affect to some extent all the various arts. Particularly, perhaps, the art of music, because music depends only on the immediate perception of sound, and not, as in literature, on sight, or the reading of words (as though we had been sent a very long letter).

I used to think, before radio came, that the song recital was tending to die out as a means of making music before a public; that it had had its day, and that with the decline of the recital would come the death of the song (as a musical form). But radio suits the genius of the song recital very well, and the sound in our home can be intimate and delightful. Remembering what I once thought, I am gratified now to realize that I have since written works for voice and piano, and hope to write more. We respond to the new means to hand.

Again, a young composer must have always wondered just where his public was to be found. But in our day, when there seems a kind of law that the more seriously a composer applies himself to his art, the less public he can have at all, the serious young composer may come to feel he cannot start anywhere; that his public must remain for ever non-existent. Yet the truth of the matter may be that his public is just of ones and twos, those few folk really interested in new things; and here it is that through the radio, if his music can once be played, his public of ones and twos can be assembled, so to speak, without assembling. This is in fact what does happen. Most new music begins its real public life on the radio.

Nevertheless, radio has not changed our musical social life so radically that we go no more to concerts, because radio cannot reproduce all the real thing. I remember in the old Queen's Hall the young Furtwängler conducting the Beethoven Ninth, his back properly turned to the packed audience, but this same back receiving all the while those invisible waves of absorption and attention which a great public gives to great music. Psychological conditions of performance were then magically made which are virtually impossible in a studio. These are still the dream conditions of the composer, I think. This is his public in the flesh. This is where he wants to be played and understood. This still means more to him than radio. As Joyce Cary has said, this public is classless; or, perhaps, it is the class of all the lovers of music. It is never all the human race, but only some. And despite our new methods of communication by radio and television, the big public that wants to hear music in concert-halls and see opera in theatres is still our idea of the musical public.

If, then, I as a composer want to have a living relation with this big public which goes to concerts and operas, I must consider how to get round, or mitigate the incidence of, that law which seems to say that the more serious a modern composer is, the less able he is to speak to anything beyond a coterie. Obviously I cannot alone, by myself, remove the wide and enduring disrelation between all new art and the big public. That there is such a disrelation now cannot be denied.

Let us now call the composer and the public the producer and the consumer, because that is the relation between artist and public; but this relation is not so immediate, and therefore so obvious, in the arts as in commerce. If it were so, there would be the same demand for the latest music as there is for the latest house furnishing or for television. But, as we all know, the popular demand for television is part of the general preoccupation of our society with gadgets, and with speed, and with mechanical progress; with a gay time; and not really a popular demand for art communicated through television. The huge public for radio or films or sport or whatever holds the demand of the consumer to be paramount; and in so far as this public is our government and state, then the modern bureaucratic machines also hold to this 100 per cent consumer point of view. Seen from this point of view, the composer is only a servant of the big public, whose taste he must accept or starve.

Put bluntly in this way, it does sound rather excessive. We all know that the big public is extremely conservative and is willing to ring the changes on a few beloved works till the end of time, and that our concert life, through the taste of this public, suffers from a kind of inertia of sensibility, that seems to want no musical experience whatever beyond what it already knows. When this taste is indeed the national taste, the art of the nation certainly dies. But the creative artist is passionately determined that it shall not die. In fact, totalitarian societies which are pathetically conformist and afraid of the new have had to stamp him out. They are afraid—even of the struggling composer with his tiny public; afraid of his passion, of his violence, of his unaccountability. For it is a fact of musical history (and this goes for the other arts as well) that during the last half-century, or even earlier, every major composer has at the outset found the taste of the big public and its consumer point of view unacceptable. And in counterblast there has never been a period where so many manifestos have been issued demanding the absolute freedom of the artist to create what he likes, so many proclamations of a 100 per cent producer point of view.

I think of Bartók, who was certainly a victim of this division. To the end of his life he had relations only with those small, select groups which side with the artists against the big public. He died in poverty. It does not matter whether his extreme works are banned in his homeland—that is, in Hungary—or only seldom played over here. The issue is the same. He stands a terrifying example of the maximum disrelation between a great creative energy and the mass public.

This brings us to my next point, which arises out of the fact that while patronage might have kept Bartók from undernourishment (he received in fact a great deal of patronage during his life), no amount of patronage could bring his extreme producer point of view into relation with the extreme consumer point of view of the big public. The big public and the critics who spoke for it could hardly deny his creative integrity, but they absolutely rejected his music. No doubt Bartók, for all his courage, was hurt and haunted by this rejection. The last works, which seem so much less dissonant, may have sprung from a deep desire to issue from the profound dilemma of the time by moving somewhat back from his extreme point of view, back towards the conservative public. Or these last works may be the result of a fatigue and loneliness. In no sense can the dilemma be resolved by sneering at the difficult composer on behalf of the big public, or by despising the big public in an attempt to take up cudgels on behalf of the new composer. The dilemma is not a conspiracy but a fact.

Why won't the big public ever come any way to meet artistic integrity when it takes extreme forms of expression? How can a great composer (like Bartók) go forward at all in what looks like a voluntary cul-de-sac? Surely the matter is that the very big public masses together in a kind of dead passion of mediocrity, and that this blanket of mediocrity, whether Communist or capitalist, is deeply offended by any living passion of the unusual, the rare, the rich, the exuberant, the heroic, and the aristocratic in art—the art of a poet like Yeats. While it is clear from Yeats's life and writings that in this very passion of defiance an artist can find both material for his art and vigour for his despised activity, we know from other examples that he may starve.

Because, given our present disrelation between artist and public, it is obvious that patronage from one side, from the public, and directed to satisfy the official taste, cannot for that reason be used honestly to satisfy the creative urges of the great artist. In truth it is an illusion to think it really ever has been. When Haydn lived at Esterházy under the direct patronage of his Prince, he composed music that satisfied the energies of his creative life (that is, of himself as producer) as well as satisfying the needs of the musical entertainment for the court (that is, of the consumers). Principally, he could do this because his public was not in any sense a mass public, but a select public of cultivated people as interested in the newest music as in the newest house furnishings. There was then no dilemma.

But in the case of Bach, whose patrons were the municipality and the Lutheran Church authorities, there was a dilemma. Bach was accused of being difficult and obscure, as well as of being somewhat old-fashioned. His creative gifts were not fully absorbed by the consumers who were his public and his patrons. The modern composer's dilemma is only Bach's dilemma writ large. His hope is that his works will nevertheless survive, as Bach's have survived, whether they can be absorbed by the musical consumer of his time or not. In the end, the question of value and survival seems independent of whether the conditions of production are like Haydn's or like Bach's. What alone has immortality, if there is to be such in any period, is the work of art born from just this living passion of creation. The dead passion of mediocrity may kill the living artist and the nation's art; but it cannot project its own deadness beyond its own death.

Having, then, outlined the general conditions as I see them, where do I stand myself? I must now affirm simply that I know of no other absolute in this matter than the power of such creative energies as I possess; that I look, therefore, at public and patronage through the eyes of a dedicated person, who must do what he has to do, whether the issue is acceptable or not; that my passion is to project into our mean world music which is rich and generous; that I hope I reject mediocrity as intensely as it rejects me. But these violent words spring from the vigour and passion of my artistic life, not from any violence in my person.

Indeed, when the creative energies are not fully used up in bringing to expression what I need most deeply to say, then I have enjoyed doing works for specific commissions—works like the orchestral suite for Prince Charles's birthday. This is relatively simple and unambiguous. I have been less sure when a patron has wanted a work of art. I doubt if this can be done at all except in the sense that the composer is given some financial assistance to his life while he writes such a work of art as he may; or simply, that the consumer agrees to consume, or to try to consume, exactly what the producer produces. If the patron (whether an individual or a festival or the radio) has not understood clearly the reality of this situation, the matter can easily be a cause for distress rather than relief. Patronage by the community at large of creative artists can be easy and unambiguous only in a society where all the artefacts (the gadgets, if you like), the furnishings, the clothes, the songs, the poetry, the images, are lovely and full of power and grace and of a fine and generous tradition. Such a society cannot be found in metropolitan Europe today—or in Moscow, or in New York. The beautiful things are rare. And state patronage is too much the mirror of the commonplace culture of our day to be able to alter this situation except occasionally and by accident, as when Le Corbusier builds a whole new city in India.

A contemporary composer realizes all this fairly clearly. Sometimes he offers his talents for commercial gain, sometimes he patronizes himself by obtaining money elsewhere, sometimes he receives public financial help for the work of art he wants to compose. He must accept the last in fear and trembling. There is absolutely no guarantee that, in this present period of cultural anarchy, his patron's taste will agree with his. He must hope it will be reasonably so. But the much deeper hope is a product only of his vigour as an artist, the hope that his work of art will belong in the great tradition.

And what is the great tradition? I would prefer, like Yeats, to call it activation of the Great Memory: that immense reservoir of the human psyche where images age-old and new boil together in some demoniac cauldron; images of the past, shapes of the future; images of vigour for a decadent period, images of calm for one too violent; images of reconciliation for worlds torn by division; images of abounding, generous, exuberant beauty in an age of fear, mediocrity, and horror comics.

Chapter 25

THE COMPOSER AND PACIFISM

People come to pacifism for many reasons. My own conviction is based on the incompatibility of the acts of modern war with the concept I hold of what a man is at all. That good men do these acts, I am well aware. But I hold their actions to spring from an inability or unwillingness to face the fact that modern wars debase our moral coinage to a greater degree than could be counterbalanced by political gains; so that the necessity to find other means of political struggle is absolute. That was certainly my conviction during the Second World War. My refusal to take part was thus for me inescapable, and my punishment with a relatively light term of imprisonment logical.

Nuclear warfare has only reinforced this sense of incompatibility between acts of war and our idea of man. It has also forced many fresh minds to wrestle with the problem. Submission of oneself to this moral dilemma no longer seems perverse or ill-timed. The necessity to do so is manifest to all, even if for the majority the moral dilemma is easily swamped by the concern for survival. Such a concern may also affect artistic creation in a sharper way than any concern for the morality of nuclear war could do. Young artists are bound to feel a more extreme sense of insecurity than my generation did. Clearly, though, no creation is possible unless the continuity of life in time is postulated.

Even so, the reconciliation of the primary function of the artist—to create—with the urgent necessities of a wartime situation is not achieved without difficulty. It implies an intricate backcloth of intellectual debate—a debate that has deep roots.

A disciple, on one occasion, asks Confucius what he would consider the most important thing if he were entrusted with the government of a state, and he answers: 'The rectification of the names.' For Confucius, names are not mere abstractions; they signify something ideally co-ordinated with actuality. To each object, the name comes as the designation of its being. And if an object is correctly named, something essential is contained in the name regarding the nature of this object. 'If the judgments are not clear, the works are not accomplished. If the works are not accomplished, then rites and music do not flourish. If rites and music do not flourish, punishments are not equitable.'[1]

If an object is incorrectly named, then we tend to put the value we attach to the name on to the object, which will become thereby incorrectly valued. From this springs every sort of muddle. Nothing is more desirable in our day than this rectification of the names: we must constantly begin again at the beginning. There have, for instance, been attempts to prove that living beings are only machines. Pavlov's experiments demonstrated that by habitually associating the sound of a bell with the eating of food, the mouths of dogs will water at the sound only. That physiological process can be thus reduced to apparent mechanism is meant to convince us of the mechanical nature of life. Life thereby acquires the lower value of the machine, and the machine the higher value of life. But in the end 'life' and 'machine' are different names for different things. Rectification first enables us to speak of them correctly. And to speak of them correctly will enable us to act correctly with regard to them—and so on.

Now, when value passes to the machine as against life, it also passes to science as against poetry. Basil Willey, in *The Seventeenth Century Background*, deals exhaustively with the artistic consequences of the division of sensibility into areas of 'true' statement (science), and 'fiction' (poetry).[2] The value, as a society, which we attribute to art is not only affected by this division into 'fact' and 'fiction', but is also conditioned by our notions of morality. Thus the Greeks felt the concepts of the Beautiful and the Good to be so close together that they used one word to do duty for both. It took centuries of Christian teaching to break them apart and to arrive at a position where, with Puritanism, the beautiful was felt to be bad. But the Greek position seems to express something equally fundamental in us—hence the strength of the humanist revival when it eventually came. 'Exuberance is beauty', said Blake. The Protestant viewpoint, however, by its nature inimical to art, still forced him to equate exuberance with Satan. Art goes its own way, and cannot be brought within the Church.

I do not believe that the gains of Christian morality can be merely thrown overboard, though I believe with Blake that exuberance is beauty, and with the Greeks that beauty is good. In like manner, I find the world of imagination to be as 'real' in its own right as the world of empirically observed 'facts'. I can but suffer the tension of these contradictory concepts in the joyful faith that something desirable will spring from the struggle.

These endless dualisms, of spirit–matter, imagination–fact, even down to that of class, have led to a position psychologically where modern man is already born into division, and his capacity for a balanced life is seriously weakened. Total war on the scale of that endured in the early 1940s was possible only because everyone seemed able in entire unconsciousness to project

---

[1] Helmut Wilhelm, *Confucius & Confucianism* (London, 1934), 51.

[2] Basil Willey, *The Seventeenth Century Background* (London, 1945).

his inferior side on to the enemy. (We must be grateful that, more lately, the imprecations of ex-President Reagan about the 'evil empire in the East' did not produce a comparable conflagration.) A lot of modern art attempts to find expression for the anguish of these divisions. But in the long run this divided state is fatal to art. The only concept we can set against the fact of divided man is the idea of the whole man. The outward sign of such an inner health will be an abundance of creation, whether of values or works, in a world of destruction. This is why a pacifist artist can be so positive. He sustains that abundance.

Burkhardt began his 1870 lectures: 'Our theme is the State, Religion and Culture in their mutual bearings.'[3] He showed how, in the great state emerging at that time, a moribund Church was becoming practically of no account, or was being suppressed without unduly shaking society, while culture and the State begin what approximates to a struggle for mastery.

First and foremost, however, what the [modern] nation desires, implicitly or explicitly, is power . . . [The individual's] one desire is to participate in a great entity, and this clearly betrays power as the primary and culture as a very secondary goal at best. More specifically, the idea is to make the general will of the nation felt abroad, in defiance of other nations.

Hence, firstly, the hopelessness of any attempt at decentralization, of any voluntary restriction of power in favour of local and civilized life. The central will can never be too strong.

Now power is of its nature evil, whoever wields it. It is not stability, but a lust and *ipso facto* insatiable . . .

Inevitably in its pursuit, peoples fall into the hands . . . of the forces which have the furtherance of culture least at heart.[4]

Hence the basic confusion in trying to use total war, the most destructive exemplar of power, as a means to defend cultural values. These values have their roots in *local* civilized life—in a context where individuals flourish and where communities act from a standpoint of consensus. Total war, fought for whatever reason, accentuates aggregation and centralization to extremes, destroying not only local life, the family, but all forms of collective social harmony.

In general, 'men are no longer willing to leave the most vital matters to society, because they want the impossible, and imagine that it can only be secured under compulsion from the state.' Hence the State is expected to supply 'culture' and entertainment, as it supplies employment, social security benefits, or the police. But while the State can supply the motions of culture in abundance, it cannot produce the values. In fact, the bureaucratic mind becomes instinctively hostile to all culture it 'does not understand'. The State may even suppress certain art as antisocial, or feel it to be at best mere self-

---

[3] Jakob Burkhardt, *Reflections on History* (London, 1943), ch. 2, p. 33.   [4] Ibid. 85–6.

indulgence: as such, it takes over Protestant ideas of morality, wherein creative exuberance is dangerous.

Further, the deification of mass brings in its train the worship of numbers and size. A piece of music is valued according to the position its recording has reached in the sales charts. It is by no means unknown for the artist himself, petted if he is popular, neglected if he is 'difficult', to cease to be stimulated except by these conditions. Well may we echo Burkhardt's question: 'What classes and strata of society will now become the real representatives of culture, will give us our scholars, artists and poets, our creative personalities?' Or is everything, but everything, to turn into big business?

In our mass society, the State may have the means to provide culture on a mass basis. This is not synonymous with abundance of art. I remember meeting in prison the notion that anyone who had a gift such as music should be exempted from conscription. Behind this feeling lay the idea that the whole province of art was outside the disillusionment of war and politics, an area of feeling where the good and the beautiful for ever abide together. Behind the mass demand for entertainment lies somewhere the desire for the true abundance: to drink at the perennial fountain of proportion and exuberance.

Marcus Aurelius defined the 'seminal ideas' of Stoicism as 'certain germs of future existences, endowed with productive capacities of realization, change and phenomenal succession'. The rise of Christianity is an example of a 'seminal idea' of tremendous power. Marxism felt itself to be such an idea, though the promised 'withering away' of the State never happened, and its assertions have lately been denied. Pacifism too hopes to be an attitude which corresponds to a general latent desire, born out of the force of contemporary circumstances. Therefore our principal job is to search ever more deeply for the true 'nuclei' of potential change, so that we come nearer to reality, and in doing so widen and deepen our message correspondingly. This is likewise a part of the activity of the artist.

The search for such values is not essentially a matter of book learning. Confucius, for example, taught in simple concrete parables; Mozart composed with tones of limpid clarity. Nor is it a matter of will in the narrow sense. It is rather a kind of waiting upon understanding, of letting the values we really want live through us. Yet it is also the exact opposite. For 'truth cannot make men great, but men can make truth great. It is not truth which regulates the world, but man must take the place of truth; then the world will be regulated.'[5]

The first movement is a withdrawal to find our bearings. As Eliot put it:

> We must be still and still moving
> into another intensity
> For a further union, a deeper communion.[6]

[5] Wilhelm, *Confucius*, 85–6.   [6] T. S. Eliot, 'East Coker'.

Thus we make a contract with abundance of the spirit. The second movement is to return with joy, bringing our sheaves with us. Thus we make a contract with the abundance of material possibilities.

In practice we, the pacifists, shall have to work in groups deliberately small
enough to be personal. My own experience is that ordinary people always
respond to genuine values if one is not too frightened to offer them and the
circumstances are sufficiently personal, so that the dead weight of mass opinion is relieved; as long, also, as one does not confuse oneself with the values,
remaining before *them* equally an ordinary person. It may even be possible
occasionally to take the big audience by storm. But, in fact, methods will follow naturally once we have rectified the names.

There is, in short, a choice: between confusion and further debasement of
public life, and clarity, the revival of standards. That clarity makes possible a
prodigality which the composer, and artists in general, can positively assert as
the very foundation of a civilized existence. The confusions that result in a
mad, destructive war cannot be reconciled with the clarity that nurtures the
values of a constructive 'peaceable kingdom'. In identifying with the pacifist
cause, the composer is taking the only stand compatible with a belief in creativity.

Chapter 26

THE ARTIST'S MANDATE

Hölderlin is a moving example of the Socratic madness which I speak of in this chapter. For he enjoyed the divine madness of poetic creation, yet suffered long periods of alienation into a clinical madness. If I am right in suggesting, in a previous chapter, that the artist's job as such carries with it the constant, though for most of us mild, danger of impairing the sense of reality, then Hölderlin's real madness was in some way connected with his divine madness. But how, we do not know.

Is the word 'madness' the key word which induces us to think that Freud or Jung can help us understand better how artistic imagination functions? Jung seems to suggest that the artist with certain sensibilities is driven to explore deep levels of collective unconsciousness in order to bring forth images which by their fascination and power will compel us against every intellectual objection to reorder our lives. I state it in this deliberately crude way so that Jung's therapeutic preoccupations are clear. There is great danger in Freud's or Jung's theories of art of losing sight of the aesthetic in its own right. Greek tragedy is a perhaps too happy hunting-ground for depth psychology. One cannot see, however, what either Freud or Jung contributes to understanding the emotion we feel before old Chinese vases.

Again, stated in the way I did, Jung's theory seems to throw the accent all upon the future. Yet part of the aesthetic emotion is an immediacy of appreciation, of the ineffable moment exactly present now. We can be struck by the beauty of a Wren church in the middle of ugly London, by something momentarily there, yet eternal, neither past nor future. Or by Mozart reaching us on disc or radio through an open window. I am unsure whether modern art does this for us in the same degree. 'Here the men of today and the men of yesterday must part company. Anyone whose ears do not burn, whose eyes do not cloud over at the thought of the concentration camps, the crematoriums, the atomic explosions which make up our reality—at the dissonances of the music, the broken tattered forms of our painting, the lament of Dr Faustus—is free to crawl into the shelter of the safe old methods and rot.'[1] With sensibilities tuned to such a temper, what sort of art shall we get?

[1] Erich Neumann, 'Art and Time', in Campbell (ed.), *Man and Time*, 29–30.

'We must acknowledge the evil, the blackness, the disintegration which cry to us so desperately from the art of our time, and whose presence it so desperately affirms.'[2] The ineffable moments will be harder won.

That the artist, whether composer, poet, or painter, has a special gift, no one ever denies. But how valuable we think this gift is to society and what its real function is there; these are matters not of fact but of opinion. A chess-playing genius has a special gift; or to take an example of more bodily endowment, a world-record-breaking athlete has a gift. Are these special faculties of the same kind as the image-making faculty of the artist? And again, even if we take them to be somehow of the same kind, do we hold them of the same value?

I have no idea how old in history is the chess-playing gift, but it is difficult to see how it existed before the invention of chess; so here is a truly remarkable, and quite unpredictable, gift which appears out of the blue, but directed specifically to the game of chess—to a limited social accomplishment, useless of course in a society which has never heard of chess. I suppose that in these non-chess-playing societies other specifically directed social gifts appear. Whatever they are, they will hardly be more mysterious than the birth of a chess genius.

Now while we agree that a gift for chess playing cannot be older than societies which play chess, and have played chess presumably for centuries, we might suppose that transcendent athletics—that is, the combination of a fine physique with a certain mental temperament—had always existed. But it is not quite so simple as that. There are many old societies of folk of remarkable physique, especially in Africa, which would appear to have had no social interest in athletics as we understand it. We call the world festival of athletics an Olympic Games, and that is the only true name, because athletics, in this sense, is of Greek origin, dating from the four-yearly festivals at Olympia. These festivals were intensely social, and indeed, at least initially, religious. The games were held in honour of Olympian Zeus, and began and ended with ritual. During the period of the games, all wars in Greece temporarily stopped. Is part of our present tremendous social interest in athletics and the Olympic Games because we respond to anything which begins with individual virtue yet lifts us right out of our single selves to some other plane? The Greeks made statues of their Olympic winners, and set them up in the precincts of Zeus's temple. In a sense we are doing the same.

So I am quite clear that athletics, even if we have lost the Greek tradition of human beauty which was mixed with it, is a very intense social interest indeed—potentially an ennobling one—perhaps even an aesthetic one. Or rather, to keep to matters of fact, athletics in its origin was not only well-being

---

[2] Erich Neumann, 'Art and Time', in Campbell (ed.), *Man and Time*, 30.

and bodily discipline, but a part of worship, and worthy of music, poetry, and sculpture.

There were older societies which did not develop this amalgam of fine physique and bodily beauty to honour the gods; but it is clear that the gift of creating images, the special gift of the artist, is as old as man himself. The pre-historic cave-paintings which go back before the last ice-age are astonishing, not just because our prehistoric ancestors drew recognizable bison in the dark depths of their caves, but because, in face of these drawings and paintings, we have the same fundamental artistic emotions as before any art of historical times. Not that we can ever explain or define what these artistic emotions are; the point is that we know them when we feel them (even if they may be felt in a very simple and primitive way, in the pleasure of just *looking* at a streamlined car), and we feel them in an extremely powerful form before the art of the cavemen.

To return to the Greeks: they discussed eagerly the nature of these aesthetic emotions. They hoped to tabulate and rationalize them, but they admitted too that there were irrational elements in the process of artistic creation which could not be explained. As the Greeks said of themselves, it depended whether you were under the influence of the god Apollo or the god Dionysus. In a dialogue of Plato, Phaedrus asks Socrates, as they lie in the shade talking by the little stream of Ilyssus, how he thinks artists gain a true sense of their art. And Socrates answers:

If you mean how can one become a finished artist, then probably—indeed I may say undoubtedly—it is the same as with anything else: if you have an innate gift for art, you will become a famous artist, provided you also acquire knowledge and practise; but if you lack any of these three you will be correspondingly unfinished.

Is not that a splendidly up-to-date and lucid answer? It is Socrates speak-ing under the influence of Apollo. But it might also be any modern rational-izing psychologist. We sort out the basic elements and name them as innate gift, knowledge, and practice. In so far as we understand what they are, gift, knowledge, and practice are basic. They remain unchanging characteristics and necessities of artistic production for all time.

Yet Socrates was well aware that innate gift is a question-begging term. Looked at from another point of view, it begs the very question we want to ask: What is the nature of the 'innate gift' upon which *art* builds, by know-ledge and practice? And Socrates gives a very famous, but also much debated, answer.

He considers first whether what we call madness might not really be of two kinds. One kind is clearly a disease—the rational mind being disordered and unamenable to the will—and even if we picture it as though the sufferer's per-sonality has been possessed by some other and alien personality, yet this pos-session is unhealthy and often markedly antisocial. But the other kind might be a madness, where the invading personality, though unaccountable and irrational, is yet beneficent and creative; possession not by a devil, but by a god.

Socrates thinks there are four common examples of divine madness. The first is that of the prophet, such as the oracle at Delphi. The second is the madness or frenzy which expiates inherited guilt. (This is peculiarly Greek, and hardly touches us in those terms—though Eliot's *The Family Reunion* is a modern play about it.) The fourth is the madness of the lover—especially divine when the passion of love leads to love of beauty and wisdom of the beloved person. And creative art is the third. As Socrates tells Phaedrus:

There is a third form of possession or madness, of which the Muses are the source. This seizes a tender, virgin soul and stimulates it to rapt passionate expression, especially in lyric poetry . . . But if any man come to the gates of poetry without the madness of the Muses, persuaded that skill alone will make him a good poet, then shall he and his works of sanity with him be brought to naught by the poetry of madness and see their place is nowhere to be found.

I find that a splendid admission of the irrational, unaccountable elements in creative art. It is Socrates speaking under the influence of Dionysus. But it is also strangely similar to the findings and views of modern depth psychology. Refashion the language a bit, and it would be up to date.

But even if we can make Plato sound up to date, we cannot do away with all the twenty-three centuries in between as though they had not happened. Plato's account of artistic inspiration did in fact remain more or less unchallenged—and we all recognize it in a well-worn passage of Shakespeare. But after Shakespeare, in the following century, the dynamic and direction of social interest underwent a change. Art and interest in art continued, but a new element began increasingly to gather to itself the energy of social interest; that element was science. It is such a well-known story that I need not repeat it here. All we have to consider now is what this increasing social interest in science and technics, this fascination which scientific technics exercised, what it did to the social idea of art, not to the process of art itself. And it did a great deal. For as the social interest went over increasingly to technics, to all those reasonable and predictable things which science discovers for us, so the society at large lost interest, and in the end lost understanding of that irrational and unpredictable element in the works of artists, without which, as Socrates put it 'their place is nowhere to be found'.

I may make this clear by considering some personalities of our own century; and first Einstein. Einstein, by a process extraordinarily like artistic creation, produced theories about the universe we live in, which turned topsy-turvy the scientific picture established in the main by Leibniz and Newton, in the century after Shakespeare. And Einstein's picture of the universe is, furthermore, so strange and difficult, few of the rest of us know what it is at all. Even the scientists disagree. If men go in rockets to stars at incredible speeds, will they grow as old as if they had stayed on earth? Or, to put it in more neutral terms, will the clocks on board the rocket really go slower, or only appear to? Perhaps the trouble starts with what we mean by the word 'appear'. But my immediate point here is that Einstein's world picture is very difficult, if not impossible, for laymen to understand; yet no one has any doubt of his greatness and of his social value. We are more ready to put up a statue of him in the precincts of Zeus's temple, than of Gordon Pirie or Zatopek.

But now let me turn to a figure on the borders of science, to Freud, the inventor of psychoanalysis. Here was someone who also turned our picture of things—or rather, our picture of ourselves—topsy-turvy. And the results, for which Freud certainly claimed scientific justification, have been perhaps more devastating. But it is clear that we are much less ready to consider him great, in the way we conceded greatness to Einstein. For with Freud, however scientific he felt himself to be, we come close to irrational and incalculable forces; indeed, to the most irrational and powerful of them all; the emotion, drive, instinct, we call sex. However much sex is neutralized, tabulated, rationalized—de-sexed in fact—in order to bring it within the boundaries of our divine science, yet in *ourselves*, in persons and living societies, it is an incalculable power that stems from a very different god than the god of science. As the Greeks put it, even all-powerful Zeus succumbed at times to the power of the gods of sex, Eros and Aphrodite.

Freud speaks with the voice of millions because he speaks of our inner drives. But we do not like it; we may even be afraid. And fear, especially unconscious fear, turns easily to anger and to hate. To use Freud's language, we project upon him, or his ideas, our fury at being made aware of the inevitable violence and irrationality of the sexual forces within the body of our private life. The unwished awareness was all the more resented because it came to a society not open like that of the Greeks, but self-restricting, as was European society in the Victorian age of Freud's youth.

And now let me name two of the giants in creative art of our time: Stravinsky and Picasso. What social value does mass society accord to them? The answer is inescapable: none. They, or rather their works, live only on the fringe of the mass society proper. Their names and their reputations may be perhaps widely known, but not their works.

Now just as sex, though hopelessly refractory to our scientific attitude, cannot be suppressed or charmed away, so it is true of the desire for art. But if real social value is not in fact given to art, because given to science, then the sensibilities and faculties we employ when we give rein to our desires for art are not those with which we design and make our precision instruments, but our more primitive and untrained ones—occasionally, even some of our debased ones. And from this amalgam of instinctive desire for art with untrained and unformed sensibilities arises that phenomenon which we are all familiar with—mass-based entertainment. All the mass-based entertainment in the world cannot add up to a half-pennyworth of great art.

What happens, then, to the creators of great art, if such there be, in a time when the real social value is given to science and mass entertainment?

To return first to the point about reputation and works. A friend of mine, a Swiss conductor, who with his wife has long been a generous patron of individual artists, put the matter to me rather well, when we were talking this summer. He said: 'An artist at the present moment is never really being paid for his creative work, but only for his publicity value.' He did not mean this cynically. He was just stating a fact—and in his opinion a welcome fact. The creative artist can, and does, put up a semblance of living within the values of the mass society of our day. He can do this, and thereby get a livelihood with greater or lesser success, it seems, in either Communist or capitalist society; that is, in such industrialized societies as exist. But this only makes all the more mysterious what he is doing in relation to society when he creates. So back we are where we began.

I suggested before that Socrates' description of the irrational and incalculable element in creative art was close to the findings of modern depth psychology. I was thinking of Jung rather than Freud. Jung has made an exhaustive study of the image-making faculty of the psyche, not because he has great aesthetic interest in modern art, but because he finds that that part of this faculty, especially when the images come free, in dreams and visions, is supremely beneficial to us, if we are in psychological trouble. These spontaneous images which arise from within present often a complementary, or even opposed, view of things to that of our rational, or conventional, conscious mind; and during the process of living with and studying these images as they appear, the inner attitude changes, in such a way that it becomes more attuned to reality than before. Naturally enough, this therapeutic view of spontaneous dreams and visions has led Jung rather to the study of religious psychology than of art. But he shows too how the artist *also* speaks with the voice of millions when the images he plays with come from the depths of the collective psyche. And yet this voice of millions may be only a voice to come; because the collective images may as yet be only complementary, or downright opposed, to the prevailing conscious values of the time. The new images that break first upon the world through this or that great artist will only slowly be accepted, as the general attitude changes in their direction. And though the public may entirely reject the new images at their appearance, the art will nevertheless stay, because of the power it has from expressing the sensibilities which will appear. It is not easy to make all this crystal clear, without difficulties and even mystifications. But that description is at least of something dynamic, not static. And the confusions and mystifications come chiefly from the extreme difficulty of dealing in static terms with a dynamic process.

Of course, confusion is not confined to artistic matters. Economics would provide another example; especially the economics of any dynamic society, or the economics of the accumulation of capital in the present, in order to have much more of something in years to come. Now a creative artist is doing exactly that. He is accumulating our artistic capital, the results of which will last for long after his own death. And to accumulate this kind of capital is his unwritten mandate. There is no question in our day of the artist receiving a true mandate from *society* to create. The mandate of society is to entertain, and that mandate is clear and uncomplicated. But the mandate of the artist's own nature, of his special and innate gift, is to reach down into the depths of the human psyche and bring forth the tremendous images of things to come. These images are not yet art. It takes a lifetime's work to mould them into works of art. For this the artist can have no reward but the joy of doing it. He creates, because without art, in this deep and serious sense, the nation dies. His mandate is inescapable.

Chapter 27

TOO MANY CHOICES

The precise beginning for the essay, the moment when my mind became aware of a seemingly new way in, was a half-sentence by the painter Kokoschka. Kokoschka wrote a kind of manifesto at the end of the last war, which he entitled 'A Petition from a Foreign Artist to the Righteous People of Gt Britain for a Secure and Present Peace'. It is a considerable petition, and quite early on appears the half-sentence, printed in bold type: '. . . **a fallacy is blurring the clear distinction between what is in and what is out of the mind**.' I am puzzled by the word 'fallacy', but on enquiry, Kokoschka sent me a message that it is what he meant; there is no question of mistranslation, for he wrote his petition in English. If we discard the word 'fallacy' and think again of those names in the last chapter, Einstein and Freud, we can sense that whether we turn our eye into space or into the psyche, we are confronted with ambiguity and relativity. Surely this is part of what is 'blurring the clear distinction between what is in and what is out of the mind'?

Or, to take an example from politics, the Iron Curtain is both an external fact of electrically wired fences and minefields and an internal attitude. The attitude engenders the dividing frontier and the Curtain; the Curtain then reinforces the attitude. The impasse becomes exceedingly difficult and dangerous to remove, and induces violence of all kinds. How can we avoid this inevitable violence unless we have first disentangled the attitude from the gestures? I doubt if we have the means at all yet to distinguish between an external fact like human pigmentation and the inner attitude of a colour bar. Or to locate exactly that part of oneself which is Christian, if one confesses that faith, in converse with a Muslim or a Hindu, seeing that the Muslim or the Hindu is equally confused by the 'blurring of the clear distinction between what is in and what is out of the mind'.

Yet, this fascinating aphorism of Kokoschka does not appear in the essay following, because I found it too stimulating, too exhaustive. It belongs to the same class of ideas as the Confucian rectification of the names. Neither Kokoschka nor I are true philosophers, so we are not equipped or gifted to rectify the names, or to unblur the clear distinctions between what is in and what is out of the mind in all the endless ways the blurring operates in modern life. I imagine, indeed, that the blurring is a perennial problem in times of confusion and transition; as, indeed, China has known already more than one period when the Confucian rectifications were appropriate. But Einstein and Freud, in the sense I spoke of them in the last chapter, have accentuated our feeling of relativity, and perhaps thereby of insecurity, in a way which seems new to us as we suffer it.

I tried to limit the scope and range of themes, and achieved only partial success. I began with the ideas of East and West, only of course to find that these are as blurred as anything else of their kind. They are geographical entities, yet also historical, political attitudes. (What in the ideas is outside the mind and what in?) But they served as an entry, because it is possible to ask ourselves questions with these blurred counters which can help us towards the feel of our own time by comparison with an earlier time. Thus I ask what East and West meant to Columbus and mean to us. I then contrast the view of our one world as seen from an artificial satellite in orbit, which might be called the view outside the mind, with the view a Hindu can have of a Muslim, or a Christian of a Muslim, which might be called part of the view inside the mind.

Inevitably, I have eventually to reduce the 'we' of my discourse from mankind in general through the endless divisions to the class of men of which I have a specialist knowledge—creative artists. I then consider how much they need to be aware of the manifest complexities of our time. How they fare if they are convinced Christians, or if they are agnostic. How they sustain themselves without and within against the tremendous social interest in technology. How they are to act if the technologically interested society in which they may be caught by the blurring fact of an Iron Curtain or a colour bar is absolutely inimical to any spontaneity that has power. In all this I speak of the creative artist in his prime and maturity. I am not really considering Jimmy Porter.

Then there is the problem of time. This seems to me so strange that I do not discuss it properly in the chapter at all. I merely evasively state it. If there is only one meaning of time—historical time in a straight line—then it is an anguished matter if one's society is like Poland, continuously and absolutely in the path of history as we have known it so far, or like England, where our island fortress has for centuries not suffered the armies of the invader. Can Poland never be free? The Polish intellectual often despairs, as he does now. But I can imagine that the Polish peasant may survive with his dumb vitality unimpaired, because his sense of time is not of this historical kind, but of an eternal renewal in which every spring is the miraculously pristine sprouting of the new corn. If, through our deepening sense of relativity and insecurity within and our nuclear armaments without, we all, English and Polish alike, stand equally in the path of history, what then? Shall we, like the peasant, find time as a straight line inadequate, because too frightening, and will the other sense of time, of an eternal return, sustain us better? Or are these two senses of time really complementary and in some unexplained way both necessary, even though superficially and intellectually they seem contradictory? Buried within this problem, at any rate for me, is the further sense of moments which are out of time altogether.

Lastly, by a rather abrupt transition, I move from the two senses of time to the two ways of art: abstraction and humanism. I do not suggest these dualities are analogies, for we do not experience them as such. But I think that the deep relationship between all dualities is a problem of abiding fascination for me. I return to it again and again. I find it reflected in such seemingly contradictory figures as D. H. Lawrence and Blake. I may not experience the division and the copulation in Laurentian or Blakeian terms—I am neither a novelist nor a mystic; but I cannot escape the special impact of any art which seems to be the product of a marriage. Lines of a Rilke sonnet haunt my mind:

> Nur wer die Leier schon hob
> auch unter Schatten
> darf das unendliche Lob
> ahnend erstatten.

(Only he who raised his lyre also under shadows, may with divining tongue sound the infinite praise.)

Recently I have been thinking again about two Renaissance figures: Columbus and Galileo. The Columbus who first occupied my attention was the *Christophe Colombe* of Claudel, through the stimulus of the visit of the Jean-Louis Barrault Company. But, of course, Claudel's way of responding to the Columbus story soon gave place in my mind to a response more consistent with my own interests and predilections—which may be only a way of saying with my prejudices.

Like Claudel, I nearly always find it impossible to remain for long responding to a past historical period without my present interests bit by bit demanding attention, until they soon occupy once more the whole mental field. So the past, which has stimulated the train of thought, becomes only a means to illumine the present. Not of course as pure history, because I am emphatically no historian; nor as politics or economics; nor as anthropology or archaeology, and so on: but as sensibility.

Columbus sailed off to the west to reach the East. But, as we all know, he never found the East by going west. He found a continent in between—a new west, the New World. From my present point of view, it is the fact of this New World, and not the fact that the earth was soon proved to be round, not flat, which matters; because though the first ship to sail right round the world and back into port was an image which forced men to see the earth in an absolutely new form, the very fact of a New World to the west, where men might begin again in communities free from tyranny and prejudice and tradition, gave reality to dreams and impulses, which deepened into a whole continent of new experience. And we can now take up in mental hands and finger this American amalgam of flight from tyranny and tradition, dream of communal innocence and good, stimulus of adventure, and hard struggle to push a frontier ever back to the west and finally into the sea. After that, there is no more frontier.

Very well then, there is no more frontier; but is that a final fact? In Russia now, is the adventure and hard struggle to push the frontier back to the east, over the Siberian tundra, part of the same human experience as the wild American West? I do not think so. For there is no place in the Russian amalgam, that I know of, for flights from political tyranny and traditionalism or dreams of simple innocence and good. The centre of the experience seems to be the overwhelming social stimulus of the industrialization of a peasant people, flowing to the eastern seaboard in a vast wave of economic expansion following upon planned and deliberate surveys. Against this overwhelming social experience, the horrors of the Siberian labour camps, where those at odds with Soviet society are certainly not free as folk were free on the American frontier—against this overwhelming social experience, the horrors seem . . . ? That is a question which must come up again later.

In England now, the overriding dynamic of mechanization (the new factories, new industrial techniques) is not so socially universal, although, in my opinion, just as fundamental. We compartmentalize our social life more easily. We can, as academics, for example, or as artists, inhabit smaller worlds where the social primacy of technological advance can appear as a monstrous philistinism. But that too is a matter which must come later.

Englishmen who are directly responsive to the stimulus of technocracy, on the other hand, and who may be exported to the dark continent of Africa, find no true frontier there, but, like their Russian colleagues in Siberia, find the inexhaustible appetite for industrialization. Oil, diamonds, hydroelectric power, uranium—these seem to be the value-words, and engineer the honorific title.

This will hardly seem strange in so primitive a country as Africa. It can be made to seem strange, at any rate more complicated, in land with centuries of civilization to their history, like India or China. Yet there it is for all to see. And there the circle completes itself. The industries of China flow north to meet the industries of Siberia, or east to face Japan. Japan looks across the Pacific to the one-time American frontier. That is exactly the view that sputnik has, encircling the globe so many times in the day. Sputnik tells us that now at last the world is round. With its mechanized voice, it is an image of a scarcely credible scientific age. It is the frothy bauble of the unappeasable urge to industrialize the world. It is on its dark side the herald of ever more limitless weapons of warfare, youngest brain-children of our unappeasable death-wish.

Sputnik, then, with the superficial vision of its technological eye, saw that the world is one. But emotionally one—that we certainly are not. For instance, sputniks go far too fast to observe locality. But for all the free or forced migrations of our time, 99 per cent of mankind still live in a locality.

And localities have cultural traditions so old, they flow in the bloodstream. Consider the ending of that rich, unforgettable attempt to stretch the sensibility to cover East and West—I mean the novel *A Passage to India*; the last meeting of the Indian and the Englishman, the falling back from friendship, each man marrying back into his own race:

Fielding mocked again. And Aziz in an awful rage danced this way and that, not knowing what to do, and cried: 'Down with the English, anyhow. That's certain. Clear out, you fellows, double quick, I say. We may hate one another, but we hate you most. If I don't make you go, Ahmed will, Karim will, if it's fifty-five-hundred years we shall get rid of you; yes, we shall drive every blasted Englishman into the sea, and then'—he rode against him furiously—'and then,' he concluded, half kissing him, 'you and I shall be friends.'

'Why can't we be friends now?' said the other, holding him affectionately. 'It's what I want. It's what you want.'

But the horses didn't want it—they swerved apart; the earth didn't want it, sending up rocks through which the riders must pass single file; the temples, the tank, the jail, the palace, the birds, the carrion, the Guest House, that came into view as they issued from the gap and saw Mau beneath: they didn't want it, they said in their hundred voices, 'No, not yet,' and the sky said, 'No, not there.'[1]

But change the horses to motors, and change the characters appropriately; deaden the sensibility, and repress religious feeling; then newer and other voices will say, 'Yes, yes, now,' and the aeroplanes in the sky will say, 'Yes, yes, here'.

Yet we cannot all deaden the sensibility or repress religious feeling. And what happens to us, then, in our one world? I want to quote now from an essay by T. S. Eliot called 'What is a Classic?' For in this essay Eliot considers this question within the strictest limits of locality, as referring exclusively to Europe, to Rome, to Virgil. Yet all is discussed as applicable to ourselves now. And it is in this sense one must appreciate this half-sentence: 'The Roman Empire and the Latin language were not any Empire and any language, but an Empire and a language with a unique destiny in relation to ourselves.'[2]

If we look at this statement carefully, we soon see that it is only provocative at its end. That is to say, we understand the words 'the Roman Empire and the Latin language' in a reasonably conventional and agreed sense, even though we know now that the Roman Empire seems quite different in the history books of Arabs or Turks. (Is not the European heritage of the Empire and the language being rejected now in Algeria?) But with the words 'a unique destiny in relation to ourselves', we can be provoked into a sharper awareness of their import.

The sense of a 'unique destiny' allies itself in my mind with the notion of Christianity's beginning at a single and unique moment in time, and with the

---

[1] E. M. Forster, *Passage to India* (London, 1924), ch. 37, p. 316.

[2] T. S. Eliot, 'What is a Classic?' (1945), in *On Poetry and Poets* (London, 1957), 68.

peculiar sense of history, even perhaps Marxian history, that this Christian sensibility engenders. But certainly the Hindu has no such sense of a unique destiny. Nor has the Buddhist. So we are forced back on the strict limitations to the last word in Eliot's half-sentence, the word 'ourselves'. And this 'ourselves' is the same as in an earlier Eliot essay, where he is discussing the spiritual vacuum caused by lack of a religion, and in which he says: 'And for us religion means the Christian religion.'[3]

Clearly, then, Eliot's 'us' is not always Forster's 'us', even though their blood is the same. And we cannot escape the question as to whether Forster's imaginative experience, which forced him to stretch his sensibility from us to them, over the divisions of the blood, is to be more commended in our one world, just for this reason, than that part of Eliot's imaginative experience which forces him to accept all the limits of the locality and to glory in its unique tradition. Like the climax of Auden's 'Hymn to St Cecilia': 'O wear your tribulation like a rose.'[4]

For there is a splendid arrogance, perhaps even prophetic arrogance, in a later sentence of Eliot's essay on 'What is a Classic?' which begins: 'We need to remind ourselves that . . . Europe is . . . still, in its progressive mutilation and disfigurement, the organism out of which any great world harmony must develop.'[5]

'Europe is still . . .'. That is the rose. But further on again, I get an inkling of the tribulation. There is a sentence which runs: 'So we may think of Roman literature: at first sight a literature of limited scope, with a poor muster of great names, yet universal as no other literature can be; a literature unconsciously sacrificing, in compliance to its destiny in Europe, the opulence and variety of later tongues, to produce, for us, the classic.'[6]

'Unconsciously sacrificing' . . . 'for us'; that is the tribulation. And behind this 'unconscious sacrifice', in the literary and cultural sense, lies another sacrifice; that which has half-turned any poet anywhere, every creative artist, into an outsider. But to discuss this, I must return to Galileo.

My original stimulus to think about Galileo came from Brecht's last play, *Leben des Galilei*, which I have read but not seen. Brecht's own stimulus to write the play was the news of the splitting of the atom. He uses the life of Galileo to dramatize the political and social problems of modern science. He shows us Galileo, after the torture by the Inquisition, publicly confessing to untruth, in the confident knowledge that truth once published must prevail, because truth is independent of all conscientious questions, such as his own personal behaviour before the Inquisition. Brecht's Galileo, as he no doubt intended, is an equivocal hero. And to us who read the play now, knowing

---

[3] T. S. Eliot, 'The Humanism of Irving Babbitt' (1928), in *Selected Essays*, 3rd edn. (London, 1951), 480.

[4] W. H. Auden, 'Anthem for St Cecilia's Day' (1942), in *Collected Shorter Poems* (London, 1966), 173–5.

[5] Eliot, 'What is a Classic?', 69.   [6] Ibid. 70.

that Brecht wrote it before the war, there is an added irony, because Galileo's personal behaviour (the private lie as public confession) is so humanly similar to the sorry spectacle of the many degrading confessions under totalitarian communism, as Brecht might himself have experienced bodily, had his exile from Nazi Germany been in Russia and not in the United States.

Yet Galileo's science, as Brecht clearly saw, had an objective truth that was indeed to prevail if—and that is the important proviso—it was upheld by social pressure. I do not mean 'social' in only a narrow, Marxist sense. I mean social also in the sense of an emotional dynamic which rises from generation to generation from the collective psyche, until one social constellation—say, in this case, medieval Christianity, with its symbols of heaven and hell, Trinity and Virgin—goes slowly over into an opposed constellation, say, then into rationalistic Enlightenment, with its god of science and devil of superstition, its atom and ray and quantum.

It seems to me a desperate waste of energy not to face the fact that changes of social constellation in this sense effect temporarily quite absolute changes of social status. Yet, while within the community as a whole the status thus changes, the person is, just as before, born with an undeniable and individual gift and faculty. If, under one constellation of society, men with scientific interests and faculties are socially negligible until with the rising tide they become dangerous, and Giordano Bruno is sent from the Inquisition to the stake; then, under another constellation of society, men with religious and poetic faculties, desirable to themselves personally, become absolutely negligible socially. Under the strain they have committed suicide—many have gone mad.

I have, of course, deliberately over-simplified the argument so that I could dramatize it—just as I dramatized the problems of local tradition within a technologically round world in the persons of Eliot and Forster—and just as I began to dramatize the political problems of an overwhelming social need to industrialize one's backward country by reference to the Soviet labour camps in Siberia.

I think everyone chooses and everyone sacrifices. In the first instance the choices and sacrifices are involuntary. We are born into such-and-such a society, which has a particular set of dominant values to which it gives absolute status. And we are born with such-and-such gifts and faculties. Most people's faculties allow them to grow up in sympathy with the rising or reigning social dynamic. If that be named their choice, then their sacrifice is simply of those values which the reigning social dynamic suppresses. The sacrifice, like the choice, is unconscious. They only become aware of the matter through contact with those whose gifts do not permit them to grow up in sympathy with the conventional scale of values. Or they begin themselves to be temporarily unbalanced by the force of the repressed values rising unbidden from within.

If they examined these repressed values seriously, then of course they would at once realize their dangerous contradiction to the conventional modes of the time. Therefore, the usual course is to consult a psychiatrist as to methods of restoring the sense of social fitness. And where the psychiatrist is able to do this, then he receives as much social status as the doctor.

But for the negligible minority, born like everyone else into the society of their time but whose individual fate it is, through the accident of their special gift or the persistence of their psychic unbalance, to become increasingly aware of those values which their time has refused and of the repressed violence within the society that has sacrificed too much—for this negligible minority, the problems of which choice and what sacrifice, or which stimulus and what response, are intricate and complex. For in our one world of no more frontiers there are too many choices offered for any one person to accept them all. And so the person who becomes aware of the matter has ever to take stock of his position to see how he is to behave satisfactorily in society at all.

To repeat: even if a majority do make easily and naturally the socially adapted response within their community, they are in fact the prisoners of the choice (between one social constellation and another) which the community as a whole has made, or is making. But to be thus prisoners within a dominant social attitude is to make a sacrifice inside the individual psyche; the sacrifice of those sensibilities and apprehensions which have virtually no social status—none, at least, when pitted against the terrific overwhelming power of the socially conventional. And further, that just so fast as a man is made aware of this personal sacrifice, whether by natural temperament or by the complementary power of psychic disturbance, just so fast is he moving away from the prisoner's base of the socially adapted, towards the no-man's-land of the socially questionable. If the psychiatrist leads him safely back to prisoners' base, then all is well. If he does not get back to prisoners' base, he becomes a member of the negligible minority at odds with their society. And that is a different matter.

It is another matter again, though allied, when we are born with interests and faculties which can be socially fulfilled only in opposition to the dominant attitude. As Yeats put it, in his incomparable and personal imagery:

> Conduct and work grow coarse, and coarse the soul,
> What matter? Those that Rocky Face holds dear,
> Lovers of horses and of women, shall,
> From marble of a broken sepulchre,
> Or dark betwixt the polecat and the owl,
> Or any rich, dark nothing disinter
> The workman, noble and saint, and all things run
> On that unfashionable gyre again.[7]

[7] W. B. Yeats, 'The Gyres', *Last Poems* (London, 1939).

To many members of Yeats's profession, this sort of thing has seemed like whistling in the dark to keep the courage up. I would myself say that if fine poetry is to be made out of the artist's present predicament, then Yeats is a master in this manner. (It is more difficult, I think, to discern how this general problem affects music and painting.) And if fine poetry is read and enjoyed, then the predicament of the negligible minority seems by that to have meaning also for the majority. But that would probably be a rash conclusion. It argues, I think, in too logical a manner.

By calling on Yeats to speak, I have narrowed the negligible minority down to that handful of men and women whose fate it is to be gifted with spontaneous artistic vision. Yet, at the risk of repetition, I must make it clear I know, too, that the experimental scientist is also burdened with a creative gift. The point I am stressing is that in a scientific age like ours, the scientist feels his gift to have 100 per cent social value, while the artist knows that his gift, according to his nation, has 0.5 to 2 per cent value. (These figures are dramatic, not scientific!)

Viewed from sputnik, our world is round and much the same all over. Sputnik has a superbly technological soul. I am sure his proper pride is really in this technology, and not in the political accident that the first of his race was Russian. The round world of science, whether Communist or capitalist, is confident. It will go on inventing everything, however risky, because it is upheld by unimpeachable status. The social pressure which sustains this status is still incomparably more powerful than that which gives us qualms in the stomach about total destruction.

This being so, it would seem that the predicament of the creative artist in relation to such society is the same the world over. From the lofty view of sputnik this is so; but on the ground of the locality it is less so. In a community like modern Russia or modern China, where the drive to industrialize a backward country has so overwhelming a social pressure behind it, many humane values can, indeed perhaps must, be neglected. I am sure all Russian women in cities want, with part of their femininity, to dress like the women of Paris. But with another part of themselves they submit willingly to the absolute social priorities which the drive to industrialization demands. In the same way, I doubt if the Russians, as a nation, are so very much more harsh than the rest of us; so if and when they are able to turn their social eyes from the five-year plans, they may abolish the labour camps altogether.

As for the creative artist, to return to him again, he may be also, by his very function perhaps, a humane value which can, indeed perhaps must, be neglected. We all know that the artist-entertainer in Russia, as in the West, has tremendous position. He is like the psychiatrist who guides the temporarily astray back to prisoners' base. So, too, the creative artist, who can give expression to the necessity of industrialization: he is like the pep-talk purveyor, the comrade in the party pulpit. But the creative artist whose fate it is to be like the analytical psychologist in face of spontaneously generated individuation—he is lost. He is silent and dead.

People like myself, the permitted if negligible minority of the West, can never be properly balanced in this matter, unless we keep trust and feel sympathy with the men and women who are born into such totally driven societies—born with God-given apprehensions and faculties that are technologically unwanted. What happens to them, I do not know. Within the triumphs of their community, theirs is a personally tragic destiny. God, or nature, has chosen them in the first place, and they grow up to fulfil that choice. Then there comes the socially inevitable sacrifice. They are, indeed, 'as though they had never been born'.

I must admit that I can never get these silent colleagues quite out of my mind. I find them to be, for me at any rate, a kind of absolute. They are born with a gift to respond to a certain challenge, and they try to make that response. Their society lives under pressure from a different challenge, and demands certain other responses. This predicament then becomes, to the man who suffers it, a kind of challenge—and I dread to think what kind of personal response it sometimes demands.

But such sympathy as one may feel also sets a problem. For it seems to me unrealistic not to make with one side of ourselves a generous response to the grand historical spectacle of huge nations dragging themselves up industrially by their boot-strings. Yet, if one's choice is to live by certain neglected humane values, one may have to sacrifice that kind of response, because one needs to be true to one's nature, whether East or West. If one chooses and sacrifices in this way, then one does, without invalidating by that choice or that sacrifice (even the tragic sacrifice of one's death) the accepted values of one's society. The more open we become to stimulus, the more drastic, personally, may have to be the response; because the stimulus is contradictory and complex. There is no more frontier.

Returning to an earlier matter, we know that however stubborn the local traditions remain, the varieties of culture from all over the round world impinge on us more and more. So there is a kind of choice to be made here too—as between one tradition and another; or as between local and global? I do not want to repeat what has been mentioned above through the voices of Eliot and Forster. I should like to add only that maybe the important challenge is to awareness. Even if a writer writes of English experiences in the English of England, his language is bound to be related now to the English of America, or of Black Africa, or even of India. He maybe personally committed or uncommitted, but his spoken language is alive and sensitive to an increasingly single world.

It may be more difficult to discern how these general problems are reflected in music or painting. I think music is a somewhat special case, because the polyphonic and harmonic music of the West is unlike anything that the rest of the world has ever heard before. It is so powerful and splendid a medium that all the rest of the world is learning it. If Europe exports musicians to other lands, they go to found academies and orchestras and opera-houses, modelled on those of Europe. The jazz musicians go first (if only on discs) and the straight players eventually follow. There is a deceptive easiness about it, because the language of music (like the language of painting and sculpture) is without racial frontiers. But the danger to music is that this easiness of travel, combined with the lack of any rival musical tradition of equal power, can leave us Europeans distressingly complacent, stupidly unaware of the possibly parochial content of our art. We are apt to regard it as a merit in ourselves, when we restrict our view to, say, Salzburg or Bayreuth, for the past—or when we withdraw into the fortresses of coterie, for the present. To my mind, such unawareness means a challenge evaded. This is not a choice and a sacrifice that I can commend to myself. I do not know what the objective consequences are to music, but I feel we have to live in the tension which awareness brings. Otherwise I am lacking in a certain quality of humanity.

It is much the same if we consider time rather than place. An endlessly increasing past demands from us an ever varying response. Malraux has gathered together into the acceptable image of the imaginary museum all this stimulus to contemporary artists in face of the accumulation of artefacts from bygone ages. I think the importance may be less in the practical possibility that individual artists can pick and choose their next style from the museum, if that is the way they work, than in the altered sense of history as a whole. If prototypes of one's pictures are preserved there in those caves from the ice-age, then one's values are inescapably altered. Once again I feel that the apparent unaffectedness of music in this respect, owing to the impermanence of sound as a medium and our extreme preoccupation with the late-invented polyphony, is a deception. 'Drum, Pipe, and Zither' (to use Yeats's title) have a history, one suspects, as old as paint. That men danced in the caves, the very footprints will show us. But the rhythm and melodies to which they moved faded on the air at the instant. Yet with imagination, returning into the past through the music of living primitives, we can feel these rhythms in our blood, on our pulses now. And though that is not so sharp an experience as to see the picture preserved on the cave wall, it is of the same kind.

For myself, I ally this sense of the past with those Indian religious myths of creation which, unlike the story of a unique creation in Genesis, are designed to enforce the idea that creations and aeons have already been, and will be yet, innumerable. There is no rational means of bringing these contradictory apprehensions of time into unity, though they can both be savoured in the mind. There is a sense of time as unique, from Genesis to world's end. And there is a sense of time as repetitive, or circular—the myth of the eternal return. I am uncertain how objective is my feeling that the movement of these two ideas, one against the other, is another aspect of the new world picture;

though others feel with me. I seem to want to think these ideas motionless, and so hope to consider dispassionately the choice and sacrifice that holding exclusively to one or the other involves. But no ideas are motionless, except to the intellect. As in all other aspects of the new world picture, we are challenged by a contradictory multiplicity of situations, to which we can only respond by choosing and by sacrificing.

The difficulty, and indeed the inadequacy, of such an elaborate rationalization of our predicaments as I have attempted to make here is, I hope, plain enough. It is indeed like commanding everything to be motionless so that the intellect can make a dispassionate judgement. But few things in life outside the realms of mathematical science (so far as that still remains certain) are thus motionless before the intellect: and art is not one of them—or at any rate, only in a limited manner. There is always an aspect of art which throws the emphasis on measurement and relation, rather than on the sensuous. It is indeed possible so to exaggerate the idea of art as a once-for-all discovered system of relations that art can nearly disappear into mathematics. The tradition seems to come in the West from Pythagoras and through Plato. Some of the problems arising from it (viewed as a choice and a sacrifice) were lately discussed, in a perceptive article in *The Times Literary Supplement* concerning Mallarmé, not only in terms of poetry but by analogy with music and painting:

Since [such art's] true content is the perception of relations, it matters little in what order we perceive the things related: narrative sequences, temporal order and statement belong to the world of nature, time and chance. If things are truly in relationship, the relationship will emerge from every permutation of these things. Mallarmé intended to juggle with every possible combination of his elements of form as Bach juggled with incredibly varied arrangements of the elements of his theme in the Musical Offering. But in the most purely ingenious parts of the Musical Offering Bach's reversals and inversions of his theme were limited; he did not go in for purely mathematical permutations of notes.[8]

Such perceptive writing helps us to set the claims of abstract art into proportion. We choose purity, and we may sacrifice allure. We choose richness, and we may sacrifice form. Yet both these seemingly contradictory movements in art may spring from a response to the challenge of our time. The one may feel that only by setting the fundamental and unchanged purities of line and volume (to use sculptors' language) as an image before a debauched public can the creative artist be true to his function. The other may feel that only by enriching the sensibility in as many directions as possible ('Ripeness is all') can the starved soul of the technologist be given fresh nourishment to come alive again.

[8] *Mallarmé, The Man and the Dream*: (anonymous) review of Jacques Schérer, *Le Livre de Mallarmé*, in *Times Literary Supplement*, August 23, 1957. p. 503.

To sum up by reiterating one point: if our most real responsibilities are to inner values which are in opposition to the general run of our time, where do we get the strength to live by these values, as indeed we must, in all the societies that wish to make the expression of these values impossible? If, on the contrary, we live in a country where expression of these values is permitted, if discouraged, would it be peevish not to 'wear our tribulation like a rose'?

Chapter 28

'DREAMING ON THINGS TO COME . . .'

Not mine own fears, nor the prophetic soul
Of the wide world dreaming on things to come . . .
Shakespeare, Sonnet 107

At the end of a filmed interview in Paris in 1994, I was asked a final throw-away question: Do you think it possible for there to be another Tippett in the next millennium? My reply, perhaps rightly, was dismissive: one is enough! But then I began to think what indeed might be the future for a composer embarking on a career, as I had early in this century, with high aspirations and ideals and a determination to sustain them through thick and thin. Of course, I could not predict the course of world events in a century I might be just lucky enough to glimpse, though not to experience to any degree.

Young composers and performing musicians today are obviously starting out in circumstances quite dissimilar to my own. My generation had no radio, no discs, no television; communications and travel were infinitely slower; access to professional music-making limited. Composers now grow up with an ever more versatile array of technologies, adaptable to musical purposes and increasingly central to everyday living. Every parent is daunted by the speed and assurance with which their tiny children learn to use computers. In a more specialized context like that of music, a radical transformation is under way, such are the facilities for dreaming up, exploring, setting down, publishing, and reproducing new music. The interaction of cultures across the globe is prodigious and intricate. What guide-lines, thus, could one possibly hope to offer succeeding generations? Is all that one has struggled to accomplish over many decades anachronistic? It might well seem to many that the historical archetypes of symphony and concerto, of the standard orchestra and other genres, are exhausted. With what are they to be replaced? The composition of notional archetypes extending and replacing the old is even more of a leap in the dark.

Others have also faced this challenge, and set down their thoughts about the kind of musical future they think might lie ahead. A notable example is

Pierre Boulez, whose voluminous writings offer a quite comprehensive guide to the issues that have to be faced. Boulez's formidably ratiocinative approach to these issues commands respect, and has won him many admirers. Boulez has a vision of history. It has a direct, undeviating trajectory. Moreover, it is identified with his own intellectual and artistic evolution. He chooses carefully his own antecedents. He is aware of the obstacles to continuing along a directly evolutionary path: the nature of existing musical institutions, of concerts and of concert-halls as presently conceived, of programme building, of the restrictions imposed by musical instruments in satisfying the imaginative demands of composers—and so on. Boulez has greatly enlivened the musical scene with his conducting, his programme-planning, and so on. His consummate solution, as he sees it, to the problems he as a composer has faced has been the creation of a Bauhaus-style research centre—IRCAM. It is not for me to judge the products of that utopian institution; on the contrary, how wonderful that a society somewhere has assigned such value, allotted such immense financial resources, to the fulfilment of an artistic dream.

But there are, it seems to me, certain underlying drawbacks within the Boulez prescription. Chief amongst them, Boulez assumes a centripetal thrust within our musical culture, rather than a centrifugal one. All roads lead, if not to Boulez, at least to IRCAM. There I part company. Some roads lead away from IRCAM, and quite decisively so. And the question that then demands attention is: what is the basis for an alternative to IRCAM—a medium for plurality and diversity?

My temperament draws me thus back to the theatre—to what Peter Brook encapsulates as 'the empty space'.[1] A composer dreaming on things to come is probably best occupied thinking how to fill that empty space, and can certainly derive stimulus, as I have, from Brook's example and ideas. To begin with, the danger to the music of the future lies not with prescriptive dogma or centralization by Boulez or anyone else, but rather with commerce. What Brook calls 'The Deadly Theatre',[2] subordinating artistic innovation to a network of legal and financial transactions, is more prevalent than ever before. The musical theatre tradition, so gloriously vital from Gershwin right up to Sondheim, has tended of late to become an excuse simply for investment in the technology of the spectacular. Dramatic and musical contents are reduced to an anodyne level, but the lighting, special effects, and so on are amazing. What remains, in artistic terms, is an empty shell. The marketing methods of rock music, as applied to art music, have also been immensely beneficial, but they too have their dangers. In my time I have seen an abundance of trends and fashions, schools and coteries, come and go. But those of today seem to acquire incredible commercial backing, even they also evaporate equally quickly. Composers may be more tempted than ever before to surrender to the falsity of commercial hyperbole. And who can blame them in a period of

---

[1] Peter Brook, *The Empty Space* (London, 1968).   [2] Title of ibid., ch. 1.

nasty, selfish monetarism? They want to survive. Composers certainly have higher material expectations than when I started out.

On the other hand, a wonderful realm of creativity beckons. The extension of the realm of notional archetypes is made possible just by starting with an awareness of established theatrical genres—what Brook calls 'The Rough Theatre', 'The Holy Theatre', and 'The Immediate Theatre'.[2] These are not tightly defined exclusion zones, let alone a final, exhaustive list. One of their excitements lies in their potential for intermixture and development through new genres of presentation. New concert music inevitably follows as an off-shoot of this, just as new genres of concert will follow, too. In this way, as much room is available for the quasi-scientific approach, such as that of Boulez, as might be allowed for the quasi-primal or the improvisatory.

I dream, therefore, not of the Tippett of the future, but of the successors to the holy theatre of Harrison Birtwistle's *The Mask of Orpheus*, the rough theatre of Mark-Anthony Turnage's *Greek*, the video-documentary theatre of Steve Reich. . . . The list can go on and on, and I have only hinted at where it might begin. My dream is indeed that there will be a new plurality of theatrical genres beyond my immediate apprehension.

In the present day, architecture has been perhaps the most obvious point of fusion between artistic and technological innovation, and, as such, constantly at the crossroads of intellectual revolution. If this leads us to expect of its most successful practitioners an ultimate visionary proteanism, it is rarely so. To take but two examples, the polarity between Norman Foster and Richard Rodgers, the one commercially well focused, the other dreaming less immediately realizable projects, is acute.

In musical theatre, such a fusion, such a visionary proteanism, are both relevant. The dreams are never cheap, but they seem likely to be the foundation of renewal across the spectrum of creative music-making. It is not the Tippett of the next millennium that matters, but metamorphoses, fresh reincarnations galore.

[3] Titles of ibid., chs. 2–4.

Appendix

The sources of the essays in this volume are given below. The following abbreviations have been used:

MAQ: Michael Tippett, *Moving into Aquarius* (London, 1959; rev. edn. with additional material, 1974). All references are to the rev. edn.

MAG: *Music of the Angels: Essays and Sketchbooks of Michael Tippett*, selected and edited by Meirion Bowen (London, 1980).

PART I

Chapter 1: as originally published in MAQ, 14–18.

Chapter 2: as originally published in MAG, 17–27.

Chapter 3: as originally published in MAG, 37–43.

PART II

Chapter 4: the first section as originally published in 'Moving into Aquarius', in MAQ, 35–42; the second as originally published in 'Arnold Schonberg' [sic], in MAQ, 28–34; the third as originally published in 'Air from Another Planet', in MAQ, 43–9; the fourth as originally published as the second part of 'Schoenberg', in MAG, 100–8. The first three sections began as talks broadcast on the BBC Third Programme in Jan. 1952, altogether forming a radio obituary for Schoenberg; the fourth was a revised version of an article in the *Listener*, 74 (29 July 1965).

Chapter 5: as originally published in MAG, 85–96. It began as a radio talk on the BBC Third Programme in 1947, serving as an introduction to a broadcast performance of *Les Noces* by Morley College forces, conducted by Walter Goehr.

Chapter 6: based on material drawn from a variety of talks broadcast on BBC radio in the 1940s, along with the article 'Purcell and the English Language', contributed to the programme book of the Art Council of Great Britain's 'Eight Concerts of Henry Purcell's Music' at the Festival of Britain, 1951. Also published in MAG, 67–76.

Chapter 7: as originally published in MAG, 77–84; the second section began as a tribute to Britten in the *Observer*, 17 Nov. 1963, the third as an obituary in the *Listener*, 16 Dec. 1976.

Chapter 8 is new.

Chapter 9: an expanded version of an article published in the *Listener*, 60 (13 Nov. 1958), 800.

Chapter 10: originally a book review for *Quarto*, no. 3 (Feb. 1980), 7; repr. in Meirion Bowen, *Michael Tippett* (London, 1981), 161–6.

Chapter 11: published in MAG, 113–16, now slightly revised; originally an article for the *Listener*, 81 (5 June 1969), 804–5.

PART III

Chapter 12: The first section of this chapter (pp. 89–95) is adapted from Tippett's contribution to Robert S. Hines (ed.), *The Orchestral Composer's Point of View* (Norman, Okla., 1973); the rest has been written afresh, though a small amount has been adapted from *Prefaces to Verses for a Symphony* (MAQ, 157–9).

Chapter 13: as originally published in MAG, 117–26. It is an extended version of an essay first published in Hines (ed.), *Composer's Point of View*, 111–22.

Chapter 14: as originally published in MAG, 127–87.

Chapter 15: originally sections (i), (ii), and (iv) of 'The Nameless Hero', in MAG, 188–97.

Chapter 16: The first section originally appeared in MAQ, 67–84; the second in MAQ, 50–66.

Chapter 17: Some of this chapter appeared in 'Love in Opera', in MAG, 210–21, and 'Dov's Journey', the second part of 'A Private Mayflower', in MAG, 236–8; but the latter sections are new.

Chapter 18 is new.

Chapter 19: The introductory section is new; the second section, originally entitled 'Music of the Angels', appears as originally published in MAG, 60–6; the final section is a new version of the composer's preface to the score of *The Vision of St Augustine*.

Chapter 20: The first section was originally the transcript of a BBC World Service broadcast, published in MAG, 49–55; the second appeared first as *Personliches Bekenntnis*, in MAQ, 117–21, an edited transcript of a broadcast talk for the BBC German Service *c*.1957–8; the third was originally the Postscript (1979) added to the first when it was published in MAG.

Chapter 21: an expanded version of 'The Mask of Time: Work in Progress', in E. S. Shaffer (ed.), *Comparative Criticism: A Yearbook* (Cambridge, 1982), 19–30.

PART IV

Both chapters (22 and 23) are new.

PART V

Chapter 24: as originally published in MAQ, 94–100. It first appeared as the transcript of a BBC Home Service broadcast, published in the *Listener*, 52 (4 Nov. 1954), 757–8.

Chapter 25: a rewritten version of 'Contracting-in to Abundance', MAQ, 43–9. It originated as a pamphlet, *Abundance of Creation: An Artist's Vision of Creative Peace* (London, 1944).

Chapter 26: as originally published in MAQ, 122–8.

Chapter 27: as originally published in MAQ, 130–44.

Chapter 28 is new.

Readers wishing to investigate Tippett's writings in more detail may like to consult Gordon Theil, *Michael Tippett: A Bio-Bibliography* (New York; Westport, Conn.; and London: Greenwood Press, 1989).

Index

Adelphi Theatre, 67
African Music, 14
Akhmatova, Anna, 80–2, 234; *Poem without a Hero* 233; *Requiem* 233
Albee, Edward, *Who's Afraid of Virginia Woolf?*, 221
Aldeburgh Festival, 7
Algarotti, 203
Allen, (Sir) Hugh, 23
Altenberg, Peter, 32
Ambrose, Bishop, 234
Ansermet, Ernest, 56
Apostolic Constitutions, 233
athletics, 288–9
Auden, W. H., 49, 199; *Anthem for St Cecelia's Day*, 299 n.; *The Ascent of F6*, 201; *The Orators*, 68
Augustine, St, 226–36, 252; *Confessions* 228, 229 n., 234
Aurelius, Marcus, 201

Bach, J. S., 91, 138, 239; *Art of Fugue, The*, 77; *St Matthew Passion*, 13; *Well-Tempered Clavier*, 76–7
Balzac, Honoré de, *Séraphita*, 38, 243
Bardi, Count, 188
Barleycorn, John, 229
Barrault, Jean-Louis, 209–10, 296
Bartók, Béla, 27, 28, 31, 73, 84, 91, 279; Concerto for Orchestra, 90
Baudelaire, Charles, 33
Bauhaus, 193
BBC, 196, 209
Beethoven, 92, 94, 193, 194; *Missa Solemnis*, 245; Ninth Symphony, 13, 98, 100, 278; *Pastoral Symphony*, 108; String Quartet in F minor, 92; Triple Concerto, 101
Becker, John, 85
Bellini, Vincenzo, 45
Berg, Alban, 31, 32, 33, 199; *Lyric Suite*, 29; *Wozzeck*, 207

Bergmann, Walter, 16
Bergson, Henri, 10 n.
Berliner Ensemble, 209
Bernstein, Leonard, 89, 90
Birtwistle, Harrison, *The Mask of Orpheus*, 309
Bizet, 269
Black power, 84
Blake, William, 98, 283, 296; *Illustrations of the Book of Job*, 170
Blauer Reiter, Der, 33
Bliss, (Sir) Arthur, *The Olympians*, 200
blues, 96, 223
Boosey & Hawkes Ltd., 67
Boulanger, Nadia, 94
Boult, (Sir) Adrian, 73
Bowen, Meirion, 267, 310
Brace, Harcourt, 109
Brahms, 33; Double Concerto, 101
Brancusi, 106
Bream, Julian, 267
Brecht, Bertolt, 189, 209, 210; *Leben des Galilei*, 299
Brezhnev, 82
Bridge, Frank, 68
Britten, Benjamin, 57, 66–72; *A Boy was Born*, 66; *Billy Budd*, 191; Canticles, 69; *Death in Venice*, 71; *Hymn to St Cecilia*, 67; *Owen Wingrave*, 72; *Peter Grimes*, 67, 69; *Spring Symphony*, 69; *The Turn of the Screw*, 71; *War Requiem*, 71
Bronowski, Jacob, *The Ascent of Man*, 247, 251
Brook, Peter, *The Empty Space*, 308–9
Brosa Quartet, 66
Bruno, Giordano, 25
Bunyan, John, *The Pilgrim's Progress*, 179
Burkhardt, Jacob, 195, 284–5
Busoni, Ferruccio, 31
Butler, Samuel, viii
Butterworth, George, *A Shropshire Lad*, 74
Byrd, William, 57

Cafe Griensteidl, 32
Campbell, Joseph, 229 n.
Carter, Elliott, 84
Cary, Joyce, 278
Cawley, A. C., 230 n.
Cézanne, 18
Chambers, G. B., 229 n., 231 n.
Chekhov, Anton, *The Cherry Orchard*, 221
chess, 288
Chicago Symphony Orchestra, 107
Chinese music, 14
Churchill, (Sir) Winston, 74
Citizen Kane, 204
Claudel, Paul, *Christophe Colombe*, 209, 296
Cocteau, Jean, 49
Columbus, 296
Confucius, 18, 282–3, 285, 294–5
Congress of Soviet Composers, 82
Connelly, Marcus C., *Green Pastures*, 132
Constable, John, 261
Cooper, Emile, 50 n.
Copland, Aaron, 83
Corbusier, Le, 193
Covent Garden, Royal Opera House, 217–8
Cranko, John, 268
Cross, Joan, 67
Crossley, Paul, 267
Cubism, 27, 28

Dada, 39
Dal, *Dictionary of Russian Phrases*, 50
Dante, 238, 252; *Divina Commedia* (*Divine Comedy*), 192, 235
Darwin, Charles, viii, 11, 25; *The Descent of Man*, 245
Darwin, Francis, 11 n.
Davies, Peter Maxwell, *Mirror of Whitening Light*, 253
Davis, Colin, 100, 104
Debussy, *Ibéria*, 104; *La Mer*, 108
Delius, *A Mass of Life*, 245
Deller, Alfred, 66
Diaghilev, 47, 48, 51, 56
Dickinson, Emily, 85
Dillard, Annie, 249–50, 252
Dowland, John, 57, 60–1, 222, 229
Doyle Carte, 170
Drury Lane Theatre, London, 50 n.
Dryden, John, 60

Easter Rebellion, 182
Ehrenzweig, Anton, 14 n.

Eidlitz, Walter, *Der Berg in der Wuste* (*The Mountain in the Wilderness*), 41
Einstein, Albert, 290–1, 294
Eiseley, Loren, 245–7
Elgar, 48; *Falstaff*, 100; Introduction and Allegro, 92
Eliot, George, 195
Eliot, T. S., 39, 109–11, 113–6, 193; *The Cocktail Party*, 201, 205; *East Coker*, 285; *The Elder Statesman*, 100; *The Family Reunion*, 110, 196–8, 199, 200, 290; *Gerontion*, 174; *The Humanism of Irving Babbitt*, 237, 299; *Murder in the Cathedral*, 182; *Poetry and Drama*, 299; *What is a Classic?*, 298–99; *The Waste Land*, 251
Ellington, Duke, 206
Emerson, Ralph Waldo, 83
English Opera Group, 70
Eranos Yearbooks, ix, 228
Euripides, 19, 188; *The Bacchae*, 19, 188, 195, 197, 251, 280; *Hecuba*, 213; *Hippolytus*, 19, 189–91; *The Trojan Women*, 213
Expressionism, 46, 220
Ezekiel, Book of, 232

Faber & Faber Ltd., 110
Feiffer, Jules, 12
Forster, E. M., *A Passage to India*, 298–9
Forsyth, Cecil, *Orchestration*, 92
Frazer, J. G., *The Golden Bough*, 107; *Folklore in the Old Testament*, 195
Freud, Sigmund, 26, 27, 238, 291
Froehe-Kapteyn, Olga, 228
Fry, Christopher, 199; *A Sleep of Prisoners*, 201
Fussell, Paul, 74–5

Galileo, 296, 299–300
gamelan music, 104
Gandhi, 184
Gaugin, 245
George, Stefan, 33
Gershwin, George, 33, 83; *Porgy and Bess*, 113
Gibbons, Orlando, 57, 60; *Fantasias for strings*, 101, 261–2; *Sing unto the Lord*, 58–9
Gilbert & Sullivan, 170
Gluck, 189, 199
Goehr, Walter, 310
Goethe, J. W. von, viii, 96, 185, 193; *Faust*, 114, 242, 245; *Iphigenia auf Tauris*, 194; *Magische Netz*, 223; *Wilhelm Meister*, 226
Goldmann, Lucien, 209
Goodfriend, James, 83

Greek theatre, 190, 207, 211
Green Pastures, 37, 112, 132
Gumilyov, 80

Hackforth, R., 8 n.
Halley's Comet, 247
Hammerstein, Reinhold, 233 n.
Hancock Shaker Village, 242
Handel, G. F., 57, 62, 64, 90; *Concerti grossi*,
   90, 92; *Messiah*, 60, 65, 92, 111, 114, 126,
   134, 182
Harrison, Jane, 195
Harty, Hamilton, 72
Havel, Vaclav, 220
Hawker, Karl, 95
Haydn, 251, 280; *The Creation*, 245
Hebrews, (Epistle to the), 232
Hemingway, S. B., 230
Heraclitus, 247
Higginson, Thomas, 85 n.
Hildegard of Bingen, 233
Hindemith, Paul, 31, 69, 84; *Ludus Tonalis*,
   76–8; *Unterweisung im Tonsatz (The Craft of
   Musical Composition)*, 77–8
Hines, Robert S., 311
Hitler, 80, 182
Hoffmann, E. T. A., 38; *Der Goldene Topf*, 203
Hölderlin, 240, 287
Holmes, Richard, 252
Holst, Gustav, 57, 73–5, 236; *Egdon Heath*,
   74–5; *Hymn of Jesus*, 73, 74, 75; *Ode to
   Death*, 73; *The Perfect Fool*, 74; *The Planets*,
   73–5; *St Paul's Suite*, 73
Homer, 195; *Iliad*, 216, 219
Horvath, Odön von, *Ein Kind unserer Zeit*, 134
Housman, A. E., 74

Ibsen, *A Doll's House*, 277
I-Ching, 299
Indian Music, 13
Indonesian music, 13
IRCAM, 208
Isaiah, Book of, 233
Ives, Charles, 83–5; *Concord Sonata*, 85; *The
   Fourth of July*, 85; Fourth Symphony, 236;
   General William Booth Enters Heaven, 85; *The
   Unanswered Question*, 85; *Three Harvest Home
   Chorales*, 85; *Three Places in New England*, 83

James, Henry, 71
James, William, 19
jazz, 13, 29, 183, 304
Jefferson, 96, 98

John of Patmos, 232
Johnson, Hall (Choir), 112
Johnson, James Weldon, 133
Johnson, (Dr) Samuel, 239
Joyce, James, 18, 28–9, 49; *Finnegan's Wake*,
   29; *Ulysses*, 28
Jung, Carl Gustav, viii, ix, 32, 112, 168,
   238–41, 286, 292

Kaganovich, 80
Kandinsky, 33, 40
Kennedy, J. F., 184
King, Martin Luther, 99, 184
Kirjeievsky, Peter, 50
Kokoschka, Oskar, 33, 48, 294
Kolisch, Rudolf, 32, 38
Kosygin, 82
Kraus, Karl, 31, 32

Lake Nemi, 107
Lamarck, viii
Langer, Susanne K., *Feeling and Form*, 9 n.;
   Problems of Art, 100 n.
Lawrence, D. H., 11, 296; *Lady Chatterley's
   Lover*, 79
Leibniz, 254, 290
Lemare Concerts, 66
Lewis, C. Day, 12 n.
Lindsay Quartet, 267
Lindsay, Vachel, 85
Listener, The, 20, 310–12
Lloyd, Roderick, 67
London Sinfonietta, 91, 95
London Symphony Orchestra, 89
Loos, Adolf, 31, 32
Louvre, The, 18
Lutheran Passions, 111–2, 114, 182
Lutosławksi, 89

McArthur, Margaret, 67
Mahler, Gustav, 3, 32, 89; Eighth
   Symphony, 245; *Das Lied von der Erde*, 96
Mallarmé, 18, 33, 305
Malraux, 304
Man and the Masses (Ernst Toller), 195
Mandelstaum, Osip, 81
Mann, Thomas, 32, 72; *Das Gesetz (The Law)*,
   32, 37, 28; *Dr Faustus*, 37
Marlowe, Christopher, 57, 59
Marowitz, Charles, 17
Marx Brothers, 5
Marxism, 7

Maude, Evelyn, 250
Meck, Galina von, 81
Mellers, Wilfrid, 83
Mendelssohn, Felix, 57
Menotti, *The Telephone*, 277
Mercouri, Melina, 220
Mercury Theatre, London, 67
Messiaen, Olivier, 33, 93
Meyerhold, 80
Michelangelo, 3
Migne, J. P., 231 n.
Milhaud, Darius, 209
Mitchell Christian Singers, 112
Modlen, Graham, 107–8
Mondrian, 21
Monteverdi, 67
Morelli, 16
Morley College, 67
Morley, Frank, 109
Morley, Oliver, 109
Mozart, 3; *Don Giovanni*, 199–200, 205;
    Die Zauberflöte (The Magic Flute), 202,
    205–6; Sinfonia Concertante (K.364),
    101
Mussorgsky, *Boris Godunov*, 215
My Fair Lady, 62
Mystery plays, 230

National Gallery, 18
Neumann, Erich, 287 n.
Newton, viii, 290
New York Metropolitan Opera, 269
Nicholson, Ben, 21
Nietzsche, 20, 195, 240–1, 245
Nijinsky, 56
Nijinska, 56
Norman, Jessye, 160

Occam, 20
Old Vic Theatre, 222
Olympians, The, 200
Ormandy, Eugene, 83
Owen, Wilfred, 115; *The Seed*, 118, 122;
    Strange Meeting, 160

pacifism, 282–286
Paderewski, 220
Pasternak, Boris, *Dr Zhivago*, 224–5
Pater, Walter, *The Renaissance*, 10
Pavlov, 283
Payne, Robert, 217 n.
Pears, Peter, 66–7, 70

Perotin, 4, 91
Phaedrus, 7, 8, 289–90
Picasso, 17, 18, 28, 75, 291
Pirie, Gordon, 291
Plato, 7, 8, 289, 305
Poussin, 17, 18
Probst, F., 233 n.
Puccini, 199, 204; *La Boheme*, 200
Purcell, Henry, 57–65, 66, 67; *Dido and
    Aeneas*, 62–3, 70; *The Fairy Queen*, 62;
    Fantasy No. 4 for Strings, 64; *Music for a
    While*, 61; *My beloved spake*, 59–60, 66;
    Nymphs and Shepherds, 60; *Ode to St Cecilia
    (1692)*, 61, 65, 66
Purcell Society, The, 57
Puritanism, 283
Pythagoras, 305

Quispel, Gilles, 228

Rachmaninov, 51
Racine, 196, 209, 212, 286 n.; *Esther*, 192;
    Phèdre, 191
Racz, Aladar, 53
Ramuz, C. F., 52
Reagan, Ronald, 220, 284
Reich, Steve, 307
Reith Lectures, 16
Renault, Mary, *The Mask of Apollo*, 255
Rennert, Gunther, 211
Revelation of St John, The, 232
Rilke, *Sonnets to Orpheus*, 254, 296
Rimsky-Korsakov, 93
Rosa Quartet, 67
Royal College of Art, 16
Royal College of Music, 16
Royal Philharmonic Society, 74
Rudkin, David, 42

Sadler's Wells Theatre, 67
St Augustine, 208–236
St Hilary, 231
St John, Gospel according to, 35
St Luke, Gospel according to, 232
St Paul, 111, 182, 232; *Epistle to the
    Philippians*, 236
St Paul's School, 74
Sargent, (Sir) Malcolm, 73
Sargent–Courtauld Concerts, 73
Sassoon, Siegfried, 74; *Everybody Sang*, 255
Scarlatti, Domenico, 90
Schafer, Murray, 68

Schiller, 96, 186, 199; *Ode to Joy*, 98;
  Wallenstein's Lager, 185; *William Tell*, 185
Schliemann, 216
Schnabel, Artur, 109
Schoenberg, Arnold, 18, 25–46, 68, 84, 91;
  *Das Buch der hängenden Garten (The Book of the
  Hanging Gardens)*, 33; Chamber Symphony
  No. 1, 95; *Die Jakobsleiter (Jacob's Ladder)*,
  30, 32; *Moses and Aaron*, 34–46; String
  Trio, 39
Shakespeare, 4, 57, 212; *Hamlet*, 211;
  Macbeth, 218; *A Midsummer Night's Dream*,
  199; *Measure for Measure*, 221; *The Tempest*,
  221–2, 272; Sonnets, 107, 307; *Troilus and
  Cressida*, 213
Shaw, Bernard, viii–ix, 48, 194, 195, 200;
  Back to Methuselah, viii, 195, 225; *Getting
  Married*, 201; *Heartbreak House*, 26, 198,
  221; *St Joan*, 194–5, 199; *The Second Mrs
  Tanqueray*, 200; *Three Plays for Puritans*,
  198
Shelley, 220; *The Triumph of Life*, 252
Shepherds' Plays, The, 230; *The Chester
  Shepherds's Play*, 230
Shostakovich, Dmitri, 69, 78–82; Fifth
  Symphony, 90; Eleventh Symphony, 81–2
Sibelius, Fifth Symphony, 90; Seventh
  Symphony, 100
Sidney, (Sir) Philip, 57
Sitwells, The, 110
Socrates, 289
Solti, (Sir) Georg, 107, 260
Solzhenitsyn, Alexander, 82; *The First Circle*,
  222–3
Sondheim, Stephen, 308
Song of Solomon, The, 59
Sophocles, 19; *Oedipus Rex*, 239
Spencer, Edmund, 57
Stein, Erwin, 40 n., 41 n., 43 n.
Stein, H. von, 185
Sternfeld, Frederick, W., 229 n.
Stevens, Wallace, *Metaphor as Degeneration*,
  249
Strauss, Richard, 33; *Die Frau ohne
  Schatten*, 208; *Ein Heldenleben*, 100; *Salome*,
  48
Strauss, Walter A., 243 n.
Stravinsky, Igor, 17, 18, 31, 40, 51, 68, 69,
  91, 93; *Chroniques de ma vie (Chronicle of My
  Life)*, 50 n., 56 n.; Concerto for piano and
  wind, 91; *Firebird Suite*, 75; *L'Histoire du
  soldat (The Soldier's Tale)*, 21, 59, 91; *Mavra*,
  91; Octet, 51, 91; *Le Rossignol (The
  Nightingale)*, 50, 91; *Les Noces*, 47–56, 91;
  Petrushka, 29, 51; *Poétique musicale*, 10 n., 45,
  49; *Ragtime*, 29; *The Rake's Progress*, 39, 40,
  45, 51; *Le Sacre du printemps (The Rite of
  Spring)*, 29, 49, 50, 51, 52, 90; Symphonies
  of Wind Instruments, 91
Strindberg, 21
Strunk, Oliver, 243 n.
Sukharov, 50
Swayne, Giles, *Cry*, 75
Sweden, King of, 110
Swedenborg, 32, 38

Tallis, Thomas, 30, 57; *Spem in Alium*, 75
Tanglewood Music Festival, 242
Thody, Philip, 209 n.
Thoreau, 83
Tillett, Michael, 267
Time and Tide, 170
Times, The, 73
Times Literary Supplement, The, 17, 305
Tippett, Michael, *The Blue Guitar*, 267;
  Boyhood's End, 67; *Byzantium*, 104–6;
  A Child of Our Time, 67, 110–84, 210, 244,
  265–6; Concerto for Double String
  Orchestra, 92; Concerto for Orchestra,
  93–5, 106, 265; *Divertimento on Sellinger's
  Round*, 261–2; *Fantasia Concertante on a
  Theme of Corelli*, 106, 264–5; *The Ice Break*,
  225–6, 271–3; *King Priam*, 209–19, 269,
  270–1; *The Knot Garden*, 220–4, 267, 269,
  271–2; *The Mask of Time*, 245–55; *The
  Midsummer Marriage*, 63, 93, 95, 104,
  185–208, 210–11, 217, 219, 265, 268,
  269–71; *New Year*, 104, 226–7, 260, 273–4;
  Piano Concerto, 101; Piano Sonata No. 1,
  104; Piano Sonata No. 2, 93, 265; Piano
  Sonata Nos. 3–4, 267; *The Rose Lake*, 104,
  107–8; *Songs for Ariel*, 221–2; *Songs for Dov*,
  224–5, 267; String Quartet No. 1, 67,
  266; String Quartet No. 2, 64, 262; String
  Quartet No. 3, 266–7; String Quartet
  No. 4, 101–2; String Quartet No. 5, 267;
  Suite for the Birthday of Prince Charles, 280–1;
  Symphony No. 1, 92–3; Symphony No. 2,
  93, 262–3; Symphony No. 3, 96–100, 262;
  Symphony No. 4, 100–1, 260–1, 263;
  Triple Concerto, 101–6; *The Vision of St
  Augustine*, 228–36, 251, 267
Tolstoy, Aleksei, *Aelita*, 260
Tolstoy, Leo, 18

Turnage, Mark-Anthony, *Greek*, 309
Turner, 107

Underhill, Evelyn, 170; *Mysticism*, 237
Unknown Soldier, The 178

Vaughan Williams, Ralph, 57; *Fantasia on a
  Theme of Thomas Tallis*, 66, 92; *Hugh the
  Drover*, 72; *Pastoral Symphony*, 74; *The
  Pilgrim's Progress*, 208
Verdi, 454, 189, 199, 204; *Don Carlos*, 204–5;
  Otello, 215
Vidal, Gore, 220
Virgil, 252
Vivaldi, 90
Volkov, Solomon, 82

Wagner, Richard, 18, 33, 45, 189;
  Götterdämmerung, 77; *Die Meistersinger*, 69,
  77; *Oper und Drama*, 199; *Parsifal*, 204; *Das
  Rheingold*, 186, 205; *Der Ring des Nibelungen
  (The Ring)*, 13, 40, 205; *Tristan und Isolde*,
  45, 69, 204, 215; *Die Walküre*, 186
Wakefield Prima Pastorum, 230 n.
Wanamaker, Sam, 210, 218

Warren, Sister, 217
Weber, *Der Freischütz*, 119
Webern, Anton, 84
Webster, David, 210, 218
Weelkes, Thomas, 60
Weill, Kurt, 113
Westminster Abbey, 58, 178
White, Eric Walter, 50, 91
Wilde, Oscar, *Salome*, 48
Wilhelm, Helmut, 254, 283 n., 285 n.
Wilhelm, Richard, 254
Willey, Basil, 283
Wind, Edgar, *Art and Anarchy*, 16–21

Yeats, W. B., 110, 188, 197, 245, 252, 254,
  281, 302, 304; *Byzantium*, 106–7; *The Death
  of Cuchulain*, 186–7; *The Gyres*, 301; *High
  Talk*, 248; *Sailing to Byzantium*, 106; *Two
  Songs for a Play, I*, 180

Zatopek, Emile, 291
Zemlinsky, Alexander von, 32
Zhdanov, 81
Zoschenko, 81